Thank you so [much for]
coming to change minds
and lives at Fort Hare !!.

Lots of appreciation !

♡ Rianna Oelofsen

P.S. See you soon!

Maverick

LAUREN BEUKES

Extraordinary women from South Africa's past

Oshun

Published by Oshun Books
an imprint of Struik Publishers
(a division of New Holland Publishing (South Africa) (Pty) Ltd)
PO Box 1144, Cape Town, 8000
New Holland Publishing is a member of Johnnic Communications Ltd
First published 2004
1 3 5 7 9 10 8 6 4 2

Publishing manager: Michelle Matthews
Editor: Cecilia Barfield
Cover design: Dale Halvorsen
Text design and typesetting: Hirt & Carter
Production manager: Valerie Kömmer

Set in 12 pt on 16 pt Adobe Caslon Pro
Reproduction by Hirt & Carter (Cape) (Pty) Ltd
Printed and bound by Paarl Print, Oosterland Street, Paarl, South Africa

ISBN 1 77007 050 8

www.imagesofafrica.co.za
IMAGES OF AFRICA
PHOTO LIBRARY

For Alec, Wendy and Peter

Contents

The Upfront Bit

This is not a history book. If you're looking for the kind of dense and weighty tome crammed with dates, facts and socio-political-economic analyses and lessons to be learned so you can say, 'I saw that coming!' when people in the present cock up in exactly the same way they did in the past, I'm afraid to say this isn't it.

It's also not an academic treatise, a feminist manifesto or even a conventional collection of biographies of women who left huge indelible marks on the pages of South African history although, admittedly, it might have little bits of all that stuff scattered about. And there are some dates. Couldn't get away from the dates.

It might help to think of this book not as a book, but as a cocktail party. And not the staid variety where some tiresome bore in a stuffed shirt with a stuffed Vienna on a pointy stick corners you and blabs endlessly about socio-political-economic analyses. Not with the likes of Brenda Fassie, Helen Joseph, Ingrid Jonker, Dolly Rathebe and Bessie Head in the house.

Naturally, you may have some questions about the guest list. Like why all the attendees happen to be women (just don't tell James Barry). Or just how we came up with this bizarre and rambunctious mix where politicos and pop stars share a table with prostitutes and poets, artists and writers, a space traveller and one furry feline. Or why there are some very big names glaringly absent from the buffet table.

Here are the answers:
The single sex proviso was decided not out of any vindictiveness towards the boys (who have been generally well represented and done the book circuit to death already), but simply because there hasn't been an all-women bash quite like this before. And it's good to innovate.

The guest list was devised over months of sleuthing into the potential candidates' backgrounds, picking and choosing the most fascinating stories, so that the final selection would ensure there was never a dry and awkward lull in the conversation.

It would have been lovely to make this a comprehensive guide to South Africa's most memorable and momentous women, but the venue just wasn't big enough to accommodate everyone. Instead, it's a sample smattering of just some of the most riveting and rollicking life stories that have already wound to a close.

You may have noticed that all the guests, sadly, are dead, with the sole exception of stripper Glenda Kemp, but then, at her age, she's not going to be picking up the career that made her notorious in the '70s. But it's still unfortunate to have had to leave out dazzling dames and heroes like Gugu Dlamini, Cissie Gool, Mantathisi, Frances Ames, Modjadji, Dr. Kesaveloo Naidoo, Angela of Bengal, Groot Catrijn, Lady Anne Barnard, Sussana Smit and Charlotte Maxeke, among a whole bunch of others too numerous to mention.

Among those still alive, the likes of Winnie Madikizela-Mandela, Helen Suzman, Nadine Gordimer, Mamphela Ramphele, Miriam Makeba, Patricia de Lille, Evita Bezuidenhout and Antjie Krog, while all certainly mavericks, were too busy to come and play. And while they're still running around out there, still doing big things and changing the world, we felt it was too early to close the chapter on them.

So, sit back, relax and charge your cocktail shaker. You're set to meet some captivating real-life characters who defied convention and damn the consequences. (You might want to make that a double.)

Acknowledgements

This book would not have been possible were it not for the devoted biographers who meticulously unpicked the telling details and then stitched them back together into full-length candid and compelling life stories.

I'm especially grateful for the brilliant work done by Gillian Stead Eilersen, Lawrence Green, Bongani Madondo, VC Malherbe, Mona Berman, Isobel Rae, Andrew Whaley, Petrovna Metelerkamp, JB Peires and Gillian Slovo, as well as documentary makers such as Chris Austin, Chris du Plessis and Zola Maseko, and not forgetting those who wrote their own life stories – Elizabeth Klarer, Helen Joseph, Ruth First and Sarah Raal. If you're looking for the gory details in minutely researched detail, these writers are all well worth checking out.

Special thanks also to everyone who gave of their time, pointed me in the right direction and willingly shared intimate memories, including in no particular order: Glenda Kemp, Memory Ngoyi, Smilo Duru, David and Maureen Klarer, André Brink, Patrick Cullinan, Abigail Khubeka, Ilse Fischer, Craig MacKenzie, Jurgen and Claudia Schadeberg, Sandy Smith, Rob Allingham, Johan Wolfaardt, Christopher Peter, Valerie McCarthy, Di Guess, Anne Forbes, Deep Throat at the SAAF, Gabriel Athiros, Vivian Bickford-Smith, Meg Samuelson, SD Fourie, Gail Smith, Hoeda Salaam, Freddy Ogterop, Dirk de Villiers, Jonathan Ancer and Jane Ayers among others.

Also instrumental were the fabulous resources of the Bailey's African History Archives, The South African Heritage Resource Agency, the University of Cape Town's African Studies library, the National Library, the Simonstown Museum, the Cape Film Library and back issues of *Drum*, *Marie Claire*, *The Star*, *The Sunday Times*, *City Press*, *The Sowetan*, *The Weekly Mail* and *The Mail & Guardian*.

A shout out to my über-perfectionist editor, Cecilia Barfield, dominatrix whip-cracker Ceridwen Morris, researcher Sukeena Palekar and Oshun publisher Michelle Matthews who got me into this fix in the first place. I'm in total awe of my friend Dale Halvorsen who designed the exquisitely quirky cover and spent months raiding weird little flea markets to dig up intriguing objects that cunningly tie in to the stories.

I'm indebted to my friends and family, and my fiancé Matthew Brown, who put up with me and my endless anecdotes of weird and wonderful women dropped into conversation at the slightest opening.

And finally, thanks to my very able research assistant Sarah Peer, who snooped out contacts, compiled and referenced information, returned my library books on time and generally kept me sane throughout.

Pure Poison

Daisy de Melker

Daisy de Melker was not overly concerned when she went on trial in 1932 for fatally poisoning two plumber husbands and one slacker son who had failed to become a plumber or much of anything at all.

In fact, the murderess with the slight lisp confessed her delight to her lawyer, Harry Morris, at all the people who had come to see her. Daisy would greet the crowds with the elegant wave of a 'cinema star' and was seen taking copious notes in court, which she planned to develop into a 'Hollywood scenario' after she was acquitted. She had no doubt that she would be.

The public was enthralled. They would queue for hours to get a look in on the trial and some were prepared to pay as much as 25 shillings from savvy scalpers to secure a primo seat in the galleries that were crammed to capacity.

That a woman could perform such vile and heinous deeds was shocking enough – but what a woman! Author Sarah Millin, who later wrote a rather dull novel about Daisy called *Three Men Die*, described her in another book, *The Night is Long*, as 'really ugly', although she was of the opinion that this was as much to blame on Daisy's appalling fashion-sense as any physical limitations.

'She was small, thin, with tousled grey hair, claw-like fingers, a faded skin, large spectacles, a mouth like a fish and a cleft palate,' Millin wrote. 'She made no attempt to look beautiful. Her lips were not reddened, nor her cheeks painted. She wore, every day for six weeks, the same black dress with the same lace front. After a time, I looked at the stale lace front with nausea.'

But despite her dowdy looks and her general sullenness in court, which included hissing 'Liar!' at witnesses she felt to be twisting the truth like a *koeksuster*, Daisy could be surprisingly charismatic. Morris described her as being very sociable, bright and chatty with 'enormous vitality'. He also said she had a strong sense of humour and related how she was gaily amused when he recommended absent-mindedly that she take arsenic, meaning aspirin, to combat the effects of a bad night's sleep.

There were also rumours that she was a demon in bed. In his memoirs, Morris described her as 'over-sexed', although whether these types of sordid details came out in the course of the trial or whether they were the result of conjecture by people such as Sarah Millin, is not entirely clear.

Millin was appalled that everyone who came into contact with Daisy seemed to quite like her. She was even more horrified by the unstinting devotion of her surviving husband, former Springbok rugby player, Sidney de Melker.

She wrote, 'I thought of all the meritorious, agreeable women who, in their lives, had never found a man to love them and I asked myself why this ugly, cruel, avaricious, death-dealing woman had so easily engaged the interest of men.'

For a time, it appeared as though Daisy's confidence (and Sid's faith in her) was justified. Her lawyer was a quicksilver-tongued charmer with a reputation for genius. Morris excelled at compelling arguments, counterbalancing evocative emotional appeals with taut reasoning and thorough research that would catch unwary expert witnesses off guard.

As for the details of the case, there was no doubt that her 20-year old son, Rhodes Cowle, had died from a fatal dose of arsenic in his coffee, rather than a relapse of cerebral malaria as Daisy claimed. And the exhumed bodies of her unfortunate previous husbands revealed faint traces of strychnine still lodged in their vertebrae, coloured a soft pink from the dye chemists used to mark the poison at the time. It was evident that someone had taken out Daisy's nearest and dearest, but there wasn't sufficient proof to damn *her* for the crimes.

Even her feeble turn on the stand, contradicting herself and trailing off mid-sentence, her lisp lapsing into an ugly whine, wasn't enough to do her in. But just when it looked as though she might get off, she was undone by an imaginary cat and a keen-eyed pharmacist.

Daisy Louise Hancorn-Smith was born in Seven Fountains near Grahamstown in 1886, into a family almost as crowded as the courtroom would be 46 years later, as one of 11 children. At around ten or 12, Daisy moved to Bulawayo, in the then Rhodesia, to live with her father and two of her brothers. Reportedly, her brothers would dispose of 'vermin', such as lion and jackals, sometimes using strychnine, which was readily available in Rhodesia. It may well have given Daisy some ideas in taking care of her own unwanted pests.

Three years later she moved to Cape Town to attend the Good Hope Seminary, where she stood out as a popular and intelligent pupil. At 17, she returned to Bulawayo, but frustrated by the lack of opportunity, went to study at the Berea Nursing Home in Durban, where she undoubtedly would have learned about medicines and drugs, and perhaps made a passing acquaintance with poisons. Unfortunately, she couldn't have studied this latter too thoroughly or she would have learned that while arsenic and strychnine are effective and sneaky tools for dishing out death because the symptoms mimic real illnesses, they have the distinct disadvantage of hanging about far too long in the corpse afterwards.

On her holidays from nursing school, Daisy visited her family in Rhodesia and on one trip, around 1904, she met a handsome young civil servant, Bert Fuller. They saw each other repeatedly over the next few years, although Daisy seemed to want to keep the relationship a secret until she finished her studies. When she started work in Johannesburg in 1907, the couple announced their engagement, but barely a month before they were due to be married in March 1908, she received word that Bert was desperately ill. She raced to Bulawayo Hospital to be with him and was at his bedside when he died, apparently of blackwater fever. She inherited £95. The windfall may well have planted a nasty little seed in her subconscious.

Daisy didn't waste too much time in mourning. Within several months, she'd met another man, a 36-year old Johannesburg plumber by the name of William Alfred Cowle. She married him a year to the day of Fuller's death.

The Cowles had five children – or at least they tried to. Four of them died; the twins in infancy, supposedly premature and fragile, the second, Rhodes Cecil, born in 1911, survived until just before his 21st birthday in 1932 when Daisy had finally had enough, the third lasted four years before he died of convulsions and liver trouble and the fifth was struck down by convulsions and bowel problems – or so Daisy claimed. It's said that she really wanted a girl.

Nothing particularly eventful happened for the next ten years, Rhodes was reportedly showered with love by his parents, who were known to be a devoted couple, and presumably, the little family was happy. Then in 1922, Daisy took out an insurance policy on Rhodes' life for £100, to mature when he reached 21, possibly inspired by the deaths of all her previous little ones, although why she did it then was the question. It was one no-one thought to ask and Daisy paid the monthly installments herself for the next ten years.

Her husband, who she affectionately called 'Alf', was a reliable and robust sort and didn't miss a day of work in the six months prior to his death. However, he did suffer from bouts of constipation, so it wasn't entirely unusual for him to drink the dose of Epsom salts Daisy prepared for him on the fateful morning of 11 January, 1923.

Before he could even make it out the front door, he doubled up in pain and Daisy raised the alarm, calling her neighbours and phoning the doctor for help. It was to become a tried and tested routine for her.

The doctor was not impressed and dismissed Alf's ails as 'hysteria', prescribed some bromide and took off. To the neighbours' horror, Alf's condition worsened. He was in terrible agony, his face had turned purple, he was foaming at the mouth and he'd scream if anyone tried to touch him, his body alternately going rigid or arching backwards. Daisy called in another medical expert and when Dr Pakes arrived to find the man having a seizure, he rushed home for a stomach pump and chloroform. By the time he arrived, a message came in to say that Mr. Cowle was dead.

Back on the scene, Daisy showed Dr Pakes the bottle of salts. It seemed as risky a move as summoning two doctors and her neighbours to bear witness to her husband's death in the first place. But Daisy was a canny operator. If she hadn't played the part of a concerned wife, the gossip might have raised more questions than any medical examination. As for the salts, it was more likely that she would have put the poison in the glass and washed it out, rather than the bottle.

Of all the doctors who attended to Daisy's suffering loved ones over the years, Dr Pakes was the only one to suspect poisoning, although he didn't imagine for a second that it was intentional. Still, he told Daisy that he couldn't issue a death certificate until the police had analysed the bottle of salts for strychnine. Conveniently, she 'forgot' and the doctor performing the autopsy diagnosed cerebral bleeding and kidney disease. Pakes, assuming that the police had given it the all clear, saw no reason to question the findings.

William 'Alf' Cowle was buried in Brixton cemetery. Daisy told her neighbours he'd died of bleeding and 'complications', but implied that he'd died of heart failure to her sister who came down from Kimberley to visit her. She inherited £1 245, plus another £533 paid out by his pension and the house. She'd done well out of Cowle's death, but to supplement her income, she took a job working as a porter at the Johannesburg Children's Hospital.

A more respectable three years passed before Daisy got hitched again, at 40, this time to Robert Sproat, who was also a plumber, but quite well off, with assorted shares and savings to the tune of £4 000 on top of his salary of £350 a year. They settled down in 1926 in the house Daisy had inherited from her last hubby and all seemed well until Daisy discovered an obstacle to her future happiness. It seemed that Bob's will left everything to his mother in England and he wasn't in any rush to change it. Daisy thought he needed a little persuasion.

One pleasant Sunday morning in October 1927, Bob suddenly became very ill after drinking a beer. He collapsed, suffering terrible stomach cramps and convulsions and couldn't bear to be touched. Again the neighbours were summoned, together with Dr Pakes and another physician, Dr Mallinick, who diagnosed a ruptured gastric ulcer, then high blood pressure and hardening of the arteries before he finally settled on cerebral haemorrhage. Bob spent the rest of the day writhing in agony in bed and at one point, possibly convinced he was about to die, asked a close friend attending to him, to tell his brother, William, that 'Daisy must get everything, lock, stock and barrel'.

The brother in question hopped a goods train from Pretoria in his hurry to get to Bob's bedside, arriving on the Monday afternoon to find him still wracked with pain and strapped down to the bed. Over tea, Daisy tried to persuade William that he needed to convince Bob to sign a new will right away. William was reluctant, but Daisy whipped out a ready-made will she just happened to have on hand. William and a neighbour propped Bob up in bed while he scrawled his name on the piece of paper and a builder next door acted as witness. Later that evening, Bob turned the corner and made a full recovery. But his reprieve was to last only a month.

On 6 November, 1927, a frantic Daisy once again called in her neighbours and Dr Mallinick, who arrived to find Bob apparently on his last gasp, collapsed in a settee, bleeding at the brain. Within minutes he was dead. Dr Mallinick attributed it to a nasty and convoluted case of lead poisoning, resulting in hardening of the arteries that lead to a clot in the brain, which had, in turn, caused the cerebral haemorrhaging.

But William Sproat was not so easily satisfied, particularly as he'd recently received a letter from his brother proclaiming his fine return to health. He tried to insist on a post mortem. Daisy replied, 'Oh, not that. It will cost £7,' and managed to secure a death certificate without going through all the fuss and bother of an autopsy.

The following evening, when friends arrived at the house to console her, the widow was already cheerily preoccupied with wrapping up the estate. William was hurt and shocked by her behaviour when his brother wasn't yet even in the ground. Daisy barely noticed. She inherited £4 174 and was paid out £566 from the Municipal Provident Fund.

But then Daisy made a mistake. She wrote a letter to Bob's mother in England, claiming that the funeral costs, together with all the cups of tea she had to serve to the flocks of well-meaning visitors, had devoured the couple's savings. She pleaded for money to take Rhodes to Europe on the trip his late stepfather had promised him.

Jane Sproat was a little taken aback. She'd just received another missive from William saying Daisy had inherited well. She forwarded the correspondence to him and William confronted Daisy. When she tried to deny it, he pulled out the letter and told her to leave his family alone and that he never wanted to see her again. 'I have lost all faith in you,' he said, but also remarked to his wife, 'There is more behind this than I know.'

In the meantime, Rhodes had grown up to be a spoilt yob, who seemed more attached to his mother's purse than Daisy herself. At 17, he had zero ambition and outside of football and motorcycles, no real talents or interests.

After his stepfather's death, Daisy took him on a tour of Europe and bought him his first motorbike for £65, which she shipped to South Africa. But then Rhodes demanded a car. Daisy bought one for £395. A year later, he wanted to trade-up and Daisy went along, shelling out another £300. Then he decided his current bike wasn't powerful enough. Daisy purchased a faster, sleeker one. He took up music. Daisy bought him a pianola and continued to pay for his clothes, his records and his living expenses – a necessity considering he couldn't hold a job.

He trained as a plumber, but hated it so much he quit. He bumbled around through several other jobs without ever finding one that suited him for longer than a few weeks. Eventually, Daisy landed him a position working on the railways in Swaziland, but still paid out of her pocket for his spending money. When she went up to visit him for his 19th birthday, she just happened to take a will form along for him to sign, which would make her the beneficiary of his assets.

In 1931, she married Sidney de Melker, the rugby player who had toured triumphantly with the Springboks in 1906, and moved into a little house in Germiston with him and his daughter, Eileen. By then, Rhodes was bored out of his mind with the quiet rural life in Swaziland and had, besides, contracted malaria. He returned to Johannesburg, and continued to bugger around and leech off his mother.

While Rhodes could be very charming in public, he was a menace at home. The mother-son dynamic was several screws short of a full toolkit. Daisy appeared to dote on her son. She indulged his every absurd desire and nursed him to health when he came back with malaria, but then had no compunction about killing him when his demands became too much.

Rhodes would lark about with the lads, refuse to get out of bed to go to work and would fly into violent rages, assaulting Daisy on several occasions and had half-heartedly attempted suicide on a couple more, ramming his head into a wall. It was also becoming painfully obvious that he intended to sponge off her for the rest of her life. Despite all this, while he was still in Swaziland, he wrote a letter to a friend, possibly inspired by homesickness, which indicated how much he thought of his mother, that she was his best friend and that he knew and appreciated everything she had done for him.

But perhaps he also had an inkling of what she'd done to her former husbands. He boasted to his friends about his inheritance and his plans to buy a new car, as if he expected a whole lot more than £100 on his 21st birthday. In letters to her sister, Daisy seemed to have despaired of him. 'He really makes me very worried and ill ... his one ambition seems to be how nasty he can be towards me ... I feel happy that none of your boys will ever say or do to you what my boy has done or said to me.' She might well have been referring to the verbal and physical assaults or his wanton ravaging of her bank balance, but perhaps she was afraid he intended to blackmail her.

On Wednesday, 2 March, Rhodes left for work with the sandwiches and flask of coffee that his mother usually prepared for him. During his tea break, he shared a capful of caffeine with a co-worker, James Webster, and drank the rest himself. Two hours later, he had a burning pain in his stomach and felt 'lame'. In spite of this, he went off to play rugby as usual after work, but by the time he returned home, he was feeling very *naar* indeed.

Rhodes suspected it was a relapse of malaria and took to bed, while Daisy fell back on her usual practice of phoning the neighbours and summoning a doctor. The doctor diagnosed a vicious bout of 'flu, but said there was no cause to worry.

Across town, Webster was experiencing exactly the same symptoms, but he blamed his stomach-ache on the overload of bananas he'd eaten at lunch time and by the following morning, he was dandy.

The next day Rhodes was alive, but not well. Apparently, Daisy had misjudged the dose. She was quick to remedy the situation. On Friday afternoon, she coaxed Rhodes back to bed and took the night vigil beside him. By Saturday morning, he was crying and convulsing, foaming at the mouth and turning purple from lack of air.

The doctor was called again, but he was in surgery and another arrived instead and tried, in vain, to save Rhodes with artificial respiration and various injections. Daisy was howling and weeping, the very picture of a devastated mother.

There was some contention about his last words. A neighbour claimed he said he was 'finished' with his mother, while Daisy claimed he pointed to the dressing table and started to make what sounded, expediently, like a suicide confession.

The autopsy revealed the classic symptoms of arsenic poisoning, including an enlarged spleen and an inflamed stomach, but the doctor had never had to deal with arsenic and was thrown off by Rhodes' history of malaria. The death certificate was signed and stamped with no mention of anything untoward. Rhodes was buried and Daisy claimed the insurance policies right away without wasting time on the arduousness of prolonged grieving. She'd already shed her tears.

But someone else had been keeping track of the series of unfortunate events that befell Daisy's men. William Sproat reported his suspicions to the police and, based on the uncanny similarities of the deaths, they decided to dig up the bodies, which were conveniently buried beside each other.

A week later, to Daisy's consternation, she was arrested. But when the police searched her house, there was no sign of poison. The prosecution had only circumstantial evidence to link her to the crime. It wasn't enough for a conviction and they had to face the real possibility that Daisy might get away with it. The police desperately scoured the poison registries of pharmacies, but without any luck – until a local newspaper printed her photograph.

As the most hyped trial of the time, Daisy was headline material, but for several weeks, none of the papers could find a photograph of her. Then *The Star* scooped a studio photograph that someone supplied and published it with much fanfare. Daisy, still on a high from all the attention and fully expecting to be acquitted, was annoyed. 'I'm much better looking than that,' she complained to Morris, 'It's an awful picture. Let the papers come and take a better one of me.' But in Kenilworth, a pharmacist by the name of Spilkin picked up the same paper and recognised an old customer.

Daisy had made a phonecall to Spilkin on 25 February, claiming to need arsenic to kill a cat. When Spilkin offered to put down the animal for her, she claimed it was too far to travel with it. It certainly was a long way to go. Daisy had to walk a considerable distance and catch two trams to reach Kenilworth from Germiston, measures that seemed a tad excessive to kill a mangy moggy, when she could have just as easily purchased arsenic for the same purpose at her local pharmacy down the road.

When she came in to buy the poison, Spilkin recognised her as Mrs. Cowle, but she signed the poison register as Mrs. Sproat and gave her old address, explaining with a smile that she had remarried. He handed her the 60 grams of the white powder in a small cardboard box and didn't think any more of it until he saw the photograph in *The Star*.

The prosecution sprung Spilkin as a surprise witness. When she saw who it was that had been called to testify, Daisy's smugness dissolved into 'amazement, terror and fury'. Morris scrambled to undo the damage. Daisy claimed she'd been visiting a friend in the area and happened to pop by the pharmacy, that she'd tossed the cat in a dustbin and forgot to mention it to her family, and that she'd signed her old name by force of habit, even though she'd been de Melker for 13 months already. It was futile.

On 25 November, the courtroom crammed with people jostling to see (women spectators outnumbered men five to one), the judge launched into a three-hour verdict. Towards the end, when it became clear which way he was going, Daisy broke down. She was acquitted of the murders of her husbands, lacking sufficient evidence, but Justice Greenberg had no doubt that she had poisoned her son. She was sentenced to death by hanging.

When her estate was wrapped up, it was discovered that the hasty second will Robert Sproat had signed from his sickbed was out of order and the court ruled that the £4 000 had to be returned to Jane Sproat. But at the end, Daisy was broke. Her properties were mortgaged to the hilt. She had nothing to return.

The leftover arsenic was eventually found some time later, cunningly concealed in a wireless radio, probably for later use and probably intended for Sid, if the letter Daisy had written to her sister, claiming he had a heart condition (he didn't), was anything by which to judge.

She was also suspected of killing seven others, including her fiancé Bert Fuller and police officers from Bulawayo hung around during the trial, intending to arrest her the moment she stepped out of the courtroom if she was acquitted.

South Africa's first recorded female serial killer was hanged on 30 December 1932 in the Lock Street Gaol in East London. Daisy proclaimed her innocence to the end and Sidney, to Sarah Millin's disgust, laid white violets on her coffin.

You can visit the place Daisy choked her last; The Lock Street Gaol now functions as a shopping mall, but still boasts the original drop gallows, sandwiched between the boutiques and cafés and surf stores. Some of the shopkeepers have reported strange things happening at night, including screams and clanking and dimming lights, but as yet, no-one has complained of finding arsenic in their take-away coffee.

Venus on a Leash

Sara Bartmann

While the South African public were eager to sardine themselves into a courtroom to see a real, live murderess in 1932, London's citizens were even more rabidly keen, in 1810, to ogle the spectacle of a genuine Khoekhoe woman in the flesh – and Sara Bartmann's keeper was careful to ensure that there was always plenty of it on show.

Europeans had fostered an unhealthy obsession with the Khoekhoe ever since they first encountered them on forays into the *fynbos* in the 1600s – and most particularly with their genitals. Blame it on ugly sexual hang-ups (these were the predecessors to the prudish Victorians after all) and racist pseudo-science, but Europe couldn't get enough of the rumoured differences.

Generally, the early settler commandos who raided the Khoekhoe in retaliation for the Khoekhoe raiding their cattle weren't really into anthropology. They came for the slaughter and occasionally the kind of gruesome trophy more appropriate to serial killers, such as one group in 1739, which cut off the female victims' breasts and turned them into tobacco pouches, according to historian Nigel Penn.

Eventually, more scientific-minded men started tagging along on some of the less violent excursions, sketching the new peoples and taking notes. For a time, the explorers were convinced that the Khoekhoe men had only one testicle. Possibly bemused by all this fuss (when they weren't being hunted down and eradicated of course), it seems that some of the Khoekhoe played along. One laughable account apparently detailed a ceremony where the Khoekhoe would cut out a boy's testicle and replace it with a ball of sheep fat.

It was inevitable that the would-be naturalists' fixation would turn to the female of the species they'd ever so sensitively classified as 'Homo Monstrous'. Unlike the men, however, the Khoekhoe women did actually have some notable physical differences. They had ample posteriors and, to Europe's gleeful titillation and fascination, some of them also boasted elongated labia, known equally sensitively as the 'Hottentot Apron', which was apparently considered a sign of great beauty among the Khoekhoe.

Was it any wonder that Sara Bartmann (or Saartjie as she was called in her time by white society) was an instant hit in London?

The ad, which first appeared in the city's *Morning Post* on 20 September 1810, read:

'The Hottentot Venus — Just arrived (and may be seen between the hours of One and Five o'clock in the evening at No.225 Piccadilly) from the Banks of the River Gamtoos, on the Borders of Kaffraria, in the interior of South Africa, a most correct and perfect Specimen of that race of people.

From this extraordinary phenomenon of nature, the Public will have an opportunity of judging how far she exceeds any description given by historians of that tribe of the human species. She is habited in the dress of her country, with all the rude ornaments usually worn by those people. She has been seen by the principal Literati in this Metropolis, who were all greatly astonished as well as highly gratified with the sight of so wonderful a specimen of the human race.

She has been brought to this country at a considerable expence, by Hendric Cezar, and their stay will be but of short duration.'

Piccadilly was even then a hub bristling with all manner of dodgy entertainments, including regular freak shows. Hendric Cezar was confident his Venus would fit right in with the other 'specimens' on display in the area. But who was this Cezar guy and how did Sara Bartmann end up under his influence, dancing almost naked on the end of a rope?

Sara was born somewhere in the vicinity of the Gamtoos River in the Eastern Cape, approximately in 1789. She eventually made her way to Cape Town, probably in a bid for economic survival, not unlike many of her people at the time, or indeed, many of the people living in the rural Eastern Cape now. There is no record of what her original name was, but by the time she was living in Cape Town, she was called Saartjie.

The young woman, who was likely Quena (although the Griqua have also claimed her), found work as a servant on the farm of Peter Cezar just outside the city. And then, one fateful day, Peter's brother Hendric and a British physician by the name of Alexander Dunlop popped by with a little business proposition.

They convinced the 20-year-old that she could make her fortune if she accompanied them to England and displayed herself 'just as she was'. The scheming impresarios would have painted a compelling picture in technicolour of the fame and success and riches to be hers. Compared with her prospects in Cape Town, when some of her peers were forced to turn to prostitution to survive, it's hardly surprising that she agreed.

She apparently signed a contract (although the copy of it is rather suspiciously dated *after* her arrival in London in October) binding her to their service for five years. It specified that she would share in the profits and be paid 12 guineas a year on top of that. At the end of it, Hendric guaranteed to send her home at his expense.

Sara set off with the conniving duo in March 1810 and, after an arduous three months at sea, they arrived in Liverpool in June, where Dunlop and Cezar tried to pawn Sara and a giraffe skin off on the curator the natural history museum, William Bullock. Bullock apparently purchased the skin, but refused the young woman, not unreasonably considering slavery had been abolished in England four years prior. This abolition would eventually prove very troublesome for Cezar.

Dunlop panicked and insisted that Cezar buy him out. Still convinced that there was cash to be made from Sara's assets, Hendric did. He spent a few months getting his act together (there's no documentation of what he was up to during this time) and then launched his debutante into London society in September with the ad in the *Morning Post*.

The show was competitively priced to pack them in at two shillings a head and while the initial exhibitions occurred at 225 Piccadilly, Hendric expanded his mandate to include bars, galleries and private showings for the nobility and the 'noble' men of science.

Contrary to some accounts published recently, Sara was not paraded naked. Victorian society wouldn't have stood for *that* vulgar an atrocity, although being put on display attired in the 'dress of her country', was close as dammit.

Sara's little beaded apron skirt did prevent the more lascivious Londoners from getting a look at what they were really hoping to see (as in one impious French cartoon where a London lady is trying to peek up between her legs). Instead, the crowds had to be satisfied with gawking at Sara's bottom – for an extra fee, you could touch it – and her full, pendulous breasts.

Sara was an overnight sensation. Bawdy songs were written about the young woman who had become the hottest topic of dinner table conversation in town. Illustrations and satirical cartoons appeared in the papers, the more conscientious of which sent up the spectators (slavering men armed with telescopes to better take in her bottom) rather than the mostly naked girl in their midst.

But while many of the illustrations seem to show a proud savage nonplussed by all the attention, sometimes smoking her pipe, the journalistic accounts, such as the following one from *The Times*, told a different story:

'The exhibition took place on a stage raised about three feet from the floor, with a cage or enclosed place at the end of it – the Hottentot was produced like

a wild beast and ordered to move backwards and forwards and come out and go into her cage, more like a bear on a chain than a human being. When she refused for a moment to come out of her cage, the keeper let down the curtain, went behind and was seen to hold up his hand to her in a menacing posture. She then came forward at his call and was perfectly obedient.'

It wasn't long before letters of outrage started pouring in to the newspapers. Hendric Cezar had unwittingly touched a raw nerve so short a time after the abolition of slavery. A number of horrified spectators came out to publicly and loudly condemn the exhibitions, based on the blatant mistreatment of Sara, her obvious reluctance to participate and the gross debasement of the one-woman freak show. Sadly, it was probably as much a response to the lewdness of the show and the sexual rapacity it might inspire as the issues of Sara's rights as an indentured black woman.

Hendric replied to the accusations that he was exploiting her against her will with a letter of his own to the newspaper, claiming that he and Sara were mutual beneficiaries and that he treated her 'not only with humanity, but the greatest kindness and tenderness'. If his critics didn't believe him, he said they could ask her themselves, if, of course, 'any person who can make himself understood to her'. Conveniently, no-one took him up on this offer. He would have been confident that nobody would call his bluff when few people in England spoke Dutch let alone Khoekhoe.

However, Hendric's letter wasn't enough to satisfy the detractors, particularly a humanitarian group known as the African Institution, which worked to protect the rights of freed slaves. On 24 November, Hendric was the one reluctantly dragged to a showing – before the King's court of law.

Unfortunately, it seems he'd coached Sara well. Through a Dutch translator, she refuted that she was ill treated, despite the eye-witness accounts that Hendric threatened her with raised fists or bamboo sticks and forced her to perform even when she was sick or tired. She claimed, through the mediator, that she was happy in her circumstances, that she exhibited herself willingly and shared in the profits.

In light of this, the magistrate had no choice but to dismiss the case, although he warned Hendric that the law would move on him if 'any immodest or indecent exposure of this female stranger should take place'. Hendric probably thought the current form of the show fell under that description, because he and Sara disappeared from London a few days later.

Their whereabouts for the next few years remain a mystery. A baptism certificate for Sara cropped up in Manchester in 1811 and apparently she claimed at a later date that she had married a West Indian black man and bore two children during this time. What became of her husband and kids, if they existed, is unknown, but in 1814, Sara and Hendric boarded a ship for France, sending the Parisian papers into a frenzied hubbub with the news.

Hendric took Sara to the Parisian equivalent of Piccadilly, the gardens of the Palais Royale, where he sold her contract to an animal tamer named Réaux and vanished from her life.

Within days, Sara was reliving her London experience. Again an ad was placed in the paper, again the crowds crammed in to see her, and again the newspapers were full of stories and irreverent cartoons. Her appearance even inspired a vaudeville show called *The Hottentot Venus or the Hatred of Frenchwomen* in which a young widow impersonates 'the savage' Venus to win the heart of a noble who has sworn off his smarmy 'over-civilised' countrywomen. All ends well, except for the Venus, whose fate doesn't even feature in the one act comedy's denouement.

In real life, Sara seemed to be very unhappy. There are almost no records of her side of the story, but a journalist's report in *Journal des Dames et des Modes* on 12 February 1815, describing a private showing depicted a desperately wretched young woman. The original text isn't readily available, but Zola Maseko's documentary *The Life and Times of Sara Bartmann*, relays it as follows:

'Someone announces that a marvel was to come. The doors opened and you could see the Hottentot Venus approaching. At her sight all our ladies huddle and hide behind the curtain. This poor Venus notices and grows sullen. Her head leans on her chest, tears fall from her eyes ... She jumps, she sings

... someone gives her sweets to encourage her to do this or that trick in her manner. She is like any other woman, a little stubborn. Sometimes she sulks for nothing. She gets angry for nothing. Her mood changes though when you compliment her. Around her neck, she wears a tiny piece of turtle shell, she often holds it between her two hands, holds it to her lips and looks up to the sky. I was moved.'

The same journalist, the documentary says, interviewed Sara afterwards, based on the little French she had picked up. She allegedly said, 'My name is Sara. Very unhappy Sara who did not deserve her fate.' She told him that her father was head of the hunters and her mother organised the tribe's festivities. She was popular and set to be married, but the celebration fires gave them away to the commandos and a terrible battle broke out. She was separated from her family. Her next words seem a tad too poetic to be believable, 'Alas, I will not ever see again this sacred land,' before she lapses back into broken grammar. 'Poor Sara, your husband, your father, your family, everyone is lost.' She apparently made no mention of her West Indian husband in England.

Along with the public ogling, Sara also had to suffer being poked and prodded by the scientific fraternity. Georges Cuvier, the most eminent naturalist of the time who served under Napoleon, was especially taken with Sara, but strictly as a specimen. He first encountered her when his mentor and later rival, Etienne Geoffrey Saint-Hilaire, put her on show in the Jardin des Plantes, amongst the other exotic flora and fauna, for a group of painters and scientists including Georges Cuvier and Henri de Blainville.

Cuvier's notes express surprise at Sara's sharp memory and her ability to speak Dutch 'tolerably well' together with a little English and a few words in French too. But despite all this, he seemed determined to reduce her to an animal or a savage.

He described her movements as monkey-like, her habit of pursing her lips, equivalent to behaviour he'd observed in an orang-utan. He also wrote, 'Necklaces, belts of glass beads and other savage finery pleased her very much; but what flattered her taste more than anything else was brandy.'

When she miserably agreed to pose naked for them, the greatest minds of France tried to bribe her with brandy and then money to open her legs, but Sara refused, keeping her 'apron' hidden between clamped thighs. Henri De Blainville recorded in his journal later with a tinge of regret, that they caused her 'great sorrow'.

Cuvier would finally get his chance to delve between Sara's legs when she died from tuberculosis, penniless and alone and quite likely an alcoholic, at the age of 26 on 29 December 1815. There have been rumours that she died of syphilis, but considering that she wasn't prepared to open her legs for Cuvier's callipers, it's unlikely that she prostituted herself as some have intimated.

Cuvier certainly didn't mention any signs of syphilis when he performed the autopsy and he was calculatingly thorough in his dissection. He cut into her buttocks to confirm that they were really composed of subcutaneous fat like ordinary bottoms, sliced open her back to ascertain that her spine was not malformed and then cut out her vulva, her anus and her brain and pickled them separately in glass jars. He also made a plaster cast of her and donated all of these parts of what was once a woman together with her skeleton for display in the prestigious Musée de l'Homme.

But that wasn't the end of Sara's story or even of the barbaric and humiliating treatment of her people. There were other Khoekhoe dragged out for display in later years. In 1829, another 'Hottentot Venus' was the belle of the ball at a party thrown by the Duchess du Barry in Paris and in 1845, a little boy and a little girl performed 'some feats' at the Egyptian Hall in Piccadilly. The little girl danced, the boy demonstrated spear-throwing. In 1847, a family of four Khoekhoe was brought to England by a Liverpool merchant and one of the women gave birth on the ship en route, which only created more hype. The little group would sing and dance and demonstrate 'their manner of fighting and defence'. Some reports made a big deal of the fact that the women showed 'extreme affection towards the baby', while an accompanying lecture by one Dr. Robert Knox pointed out that the 'Bushmen' seemed to be the missing link between man and monkey. Included among the gawping guests were Napoleon Bonaparte, Prince Louis, the Duke of Wellington and Mrs. Charles Dickens.

In the meantime, Sara's remains were on view to the public in the Musée de l'Homme on and off until as late as 1985 when they were finally shelved in Case # 33, among other similar grisly human relics collected over the centuries. It would take almost 200 years for France to surrender her.

South Africa started campaigning for Sara Bartmann's return in 1994, but it was only on 6 March 2002 that she was finally brought home and only after the French voted in a law to allow it, which was carefully worded to prevent it being used in other cases by other outraged peoples.

Sara was buried in the Eastern Cape on Women's Day, 9 August 2002 on Vergaderingskop, just outside the village of Hankey in the Gamtoos River Valley. Buchu and other herbs were burned, a bow was snapped and stones were packed around her grave in keeping with Khoekhoe tradition. Winnie Mandela reportedly caused a fuss by arriving late.

The tragedy of Sara Bartmann is how little is known about who she was – even now. As the tormented mother symbol or contemporary artist's inspiration she's become, she's almost as much an intangible construct as she was when she was a performing specimen on stage.

The Fabulist

Helen Martins

Nieu Bethesda is the very archetype of a dreamily rustic Karoo *dorpie*, the kind of place city dwellers would rush to buy holiday homes if it weren't so damn far away. Set in an unusually verdant valley amidst the dusty scrublands of the Eastern Cape, the town comes complete with a white-washed church, dirt roads still traversed by the occasional donkey carts and unadorned Victorian homesteads that are big on overhanging *stoeps*. But as pretty as it is in that stark Karoo way, Nieu Bethesda never *really* had much going for it until a tiny wizened bird of an old lady with no baby toes turned her house into a hazardous palace of luminous colour and broken glass.

Helen Martins, or Miss Helen as she was known, was considered positively potty in her lifetime. While there may have been truth to the rumours at the end (when she became ever more reclusive and paranoid, fluttering around nude between the statuary) at the time she first conceptualised the Owl House with its bespangled interiors and menagerie of fantastical beasts, her mind was as sharp as the twinkling shards that coated her walls.

When she died a gruesome death in 1976, some of the residents wanted to have the place razed to the ground. Instead, her private paradise has become a National Monument. The property that once attracted sneers from two-faced neighbours (inspiring the double-headed owls mounted on the gates), now draws frantically clicking cliques of tourists and academics armed with art theory and guides to symbolism.

A hoard of mystifying things awaits the hordes who come to admire and analyse. Almost every surface (including much of the furniture) is coated with a menacing glitter of glass. Kitsch trinkets, gewgaws and lanterns are arranged on every horizontal plane, lining shelves and recessed alcoves or dangling off the outstretched arms of sculpted ladies holding candles. Giant gaudy grinning suns beam down from ceilings and windows. Mirrors cut in hearts and stars, moons and suns, and the silhouettes of enlarged hand-mirrors, open up unexpected perspectives on a slice of bright-striped ceiling, or glimpse of limber-grey figures in the Camel Yard outside, or endlessly refracting other reflections.

All art tells a story about its creator, even if some of the pages are missing, but Helen's work is complicated in that she had co-conspirators. She was always the visionary, but her fantasies were given concrete form over the 30 plus years of evolution by a series of untrained craftsmen: Jonas Adams, Piet van der Merwe and the finest of all, Koos Malgas, who worked with her for 12 years. In the end though, the place is the fable of her life and Helen claimed it and proclaimed it in wire words twisted on the fence, 'This is my world.'

As you'd expect, there are owls aplenty among the 520 sculptures crowded ramshackle in the Camel Yard, with eyes made from broken glass or concave hollows, perched serenely on the ground or with wings flared, but there are also Mona Lisas and mermaids, and sphinxes and beckoning bottle-skirted *meisies*.

The atmosphere outside is quietly riotous, a scramble of spirituality with chubby buddhas happily resting beside lithe worshippers arched backwards in graceful arabesques to face the sun in joyous prayer, while an eerily arrested procession of pilgrims head 'east' on their camels to renditions of both Mecca and Bethlehem. (In fact, they're going south, but when Helen realised this, she rearranged reality to suit her, sculpting a bilingual sign of wire on the southern fence that reads 'East/*Oos*'.)

Much of the Owl House and the Camel Yard is turned over to whimsy shaded with an unsettling air of melancholy. There are fascinating contradictions – she hated confronting her own reflection, for example, yet her house is overwhelmed by mirrors. And there also things stranger and darker that offer cryptic clues to the woman who directed the fashioning of a world more suited to her liking than the reality that so deeply disappointed her.

In the Camel Yard, a nymph with ruby nipples rides atop a winged mutant owl-camel and holds up her hands defensively to block out the light. Similarly intriguing is the outside room, 'The Lion's Den'. The room in which Helen's father lived was sealed up and the walls painted black, and is guarded by a mangy lion with bristling whiskers and no mane. More mysterious is the incongruously named 'Honeymoon Room', where a sun with 'jealous eyes' blazes in the window keeping watch over two single beds kept apart by a heavy wardrobe plonked between them.

But strangest of all is the only piece Helen made with her own hands. On the bare floorboards of the Green Room, a monstrous decapitated thing lies immobile – a stuffed 'bag body' of buckskin, from which creepily protrudes one human leg and one bony *bokkie* hoof. Helen always said if she bore children, they would have cloven hooves. This was the closest she came.

Her feelings may well have been inspired by her own childhood. She was born in the village in 1897 to Hester and Petrus or Piet Martins, the *laat lammetjie* in a flock of 10 children. Four of them had died and Helen, like the eccentric feminist Olive Schreiner, was burdened with being a replacement child, named for a deceased older sister.

She was nicknamed '*helletjie*' (little hell), by her father, Piet, who had a reputation in Nieu Bethesda as a slacker scoundrel of note. He was a cussed and wilfully difficult character. Caught in the act of grazing his goats on other farmers' lucerne while they were at church, he refused to go before the magistrate and had to be carted to court in a wheelbarrow.

On another occasion, visitors arrived to find him lying on the ground with an orange box on his head. When they tried to talk to him, he lifted the box, snapped, 'Can't you see I'm busy?' and replaced it firmly, refusing to acknowledge anyone thereafter.

He apparently carried around a whopping great Bible in which he would jot notes about his neighbours' sins next to verses he thought applied, causing all manner of trouble in the community, but most especially at home.

Once, he sabotaged a family holiday, by letting loose the carthorse so that they missed their train. He was also phobic about germs, blocking up keyholes so they couldn't filter in and refusing to eat bread if he caught anyone in the act of kneading the dough by hand, which was particularly warped considering there was no other way to do it. He was a damaged and maliciously damaging man, who turned fully malignant at approximately the same time that cancer started eating his bowels, some 30 years later, when Helen exiled him to the little room outside.

On the other hand, Helen adored her mother. However, worn out by 16 years of popping out children non-stop, Hester was to spend the first six months of Helen's life in hospital with heart trouble and even after she recovered, she remained pretty much an invalid for the rest of her days. Helen was also close to her sister Alida, whose postcards from distant and exotic places like Egypt would inspire Helen to try to recreate the scenes in her backyard.

At 17, Helen left school with a standard seven certificate (all that was required in 1914) and went on to a teaching college where she was praised as a 'born teacher' by one of the staff. She graduated in 1919 and taught for about two years in a little school in Wakkerstroom until the day she married a very sharp, very dapper and quite 'aggressive' young teacher, Johannes Pienaar, apparently an even match for Helen.

Her father did not approve. Perhaps it was Johannes' way with the ladies or that he was involved in theatrics or, worse, that he was an atheist! Or maybe Piet was just being his contrary self. But if Helen had paid heed to his advice, she may have saved herself some of the pain that was to follow.

The couple were married in January 1920 in a small ceremony in a private house rather than in church, which must have dismayed the staunchly Calvinist majority contingent of the village. She was 22 and he was 27.

Johannes was quite the cultural intelligentsia. He was president of an Afrikaans language organisation and head of a small theatre troupe that toured several cities performing some of the productions he wrote and in which he and his wife appeared. In around 1923, Helen was the star of a five act musical Johannes scripted called *Saul* with 25 cast members, but she kept running off stage, overcome with nausea from an unexpected and unwanted pregnancy.

Helen was reportedly frightened of having children, fearing that they would be born with horns and cloven hooves (although some claim she said 'black', which, unfortunately, would have been synonymous to 'mutant demon child' to many people at the time). Terrified by the prospect of babies, and possibly egged on by Johannes, she had one abortion and possibly another during the course of her marriage. At least one researcher has suggested that scribbles in her Bible suggest that she suffered pangs of doubt about her decision. In a letter to her sister, Annie, on the birth of her first child, she wrote, 'Nobody will know what goes on in my soul when life with its happenings flashes past my eyes so quickly – and both of you my sisters also now mothers – may God help me – I must stop now.'

The relationship seemed rocky almost from the beginning, not helped by Johannes' infidelities or Helen's repeated attempts to leave him. In 1921, Helen accepted a teaching post in Cullinan as 'Miss' Pienaar, miles away from Johannes' post in Volksrust. They apparently separated after about a year or two, but considering their appearances together in *Saul* in 1923, 1924 and 1925 and Helen's pregnancy, obviously something still simmered between them.

In the meantime, Johannes had become embroiled in left wing politics – and a new romantic affair with a young Miss Wimble, who taught at his school. One or the other or perhaps the combination was considered due cause for him to be fired from his teaching post.

In January 1926, he sued Helen for divorce, claiming that she'd deserted him. He departed for overseas shortly thereafter, leaving Helen with £6 a month in alimony over five years, which was offset by the sizeable debt of some £360 he left his brother-in-law, in whose house they had been staying. Decades later, after his death, his daughter from his second marriage came to the village to visit Helen and to see the house where her father grew up.

Very little is known of Helen's activities for several years after her divorce. She went to Muizenberg, Cape Town, where she worked either in a pharmacy or a restaurant, but somewhere between 1927 and 1929, she was called back to Nieu Bethesda to look after her ailing ageing parents. As the only singleton among her siblings, she was the obvious choice, although the next 16 years were to prove draining.

Piet was still a difficult bastard and illness only made him nastier. He tore up Helen's letters before she was able to read them and treated her and her mother despicably. It's a good indicator of how vile and abusive an old man he was that Helen and Hester finally took the drastic step of exiling him to the outside room.

Hester died of breast cancer in 1941 and Helen was so bereft, she slept in the room with her mother's coffin because she didn't want her to be alone. At the funeral, it was Hester's wish that Piet and Helen should be photographed together, but Piet refused to stand beside her. Helen refused to have anything more to do with her father and a social worker was forced to take care of washing him and his clothes.

She did, however, deign to administer his medicine, although when he died in 1945, she became convinced that it was due to an overdose she'd given him. In her tortured anxiety, she didn't eat for four days before she finally confessed to the doctor. To her relief, he convinced her that it was impossible to kill someone with an overdose of mere bromide.

After Piet's death, she bricked up the windows of the room, painted it black, coated it in glass and affixed the words 'The Lion's Den' to the exterior. No-one was allowed inside and she had Koos Malgas construct a fierce and scrawny lion to guard the door.

But while her father was still pickling in bitterness and cancer in the outside shed, Helen had found a measure of happiness, albeit tainted by secrecy. In 1939, Johannes Hattingh and his family moved to the village. He and Helen became close friends and then, in spite of his wife, much more.

Their relationship probably started in 1940 or 1941. They were both peculiar in their own ways. After 16 long years caring for her parents, Helen had been forced to give up any hope of making her own way in the world and was already more shy and reclusive than she'd been in her youth.

For his part, Johannes had been struck by lightning – twice – and it had turned him a little strange. He was a tall man and obviously an easy target for the bolts from above that hit him seven years apart: first when he was working on the roof, the second while walking in the veld. While Johannes miraculously survived both occasions, he didn't come away unscathed. After the second strike, his family said he underwent a personality change that was probably in line with brain damage. His memory was shot to the extent that he had to carry notebooks and make lists to remember things. He was prone to sudden mood swings and would fly into fierce rages with little provocation.

Before her father died, Helen had already started transforming her house on a whim. Lying sick in bed one night, she was struck with an idea, like a lightning flash, by how dull and grey everything looked in the moonlight. She was reported to have said, 'There was very little brightness in my childhood. As soon as I was able to I began to express the brightness around me.' And so she commenced on a systematic process of redecorating that would carry on for the better part of 30 years.

Johannes was involved from the beginning, supervising structural changes and supplying advice on practicalities such as how best to construct a statue from cement – a medium not designed for fine sculptural work – by first creating a wire framework. He made many of the mirrors and more importantly, likely provided Helen with enthusiastic encouragement.

He also lent her his moral support when she was arrested for making and selling wine to the coloured community and testified on her behalf, to his wife and daughters' outrage and humiliation. Helen's short-lived shebeen stirred up quite a scandal in the community, although it did have the benefit of bringing in gifts of food from her neighbours, who assumed the only reason she could have done such a dreadful thing was because she was short of cash.

Their assumptions weren't far off. Helen's father had left her with a pittance of some £55 and by the time she got into full swing on her house, she was living on bread and black tea, spending all her pension money on cement and labour and ordering prints of the Mona Lisa and mirrors cut to her specifications. She bought bottles from the local children, insisting that they be unbroken so as not to cut their hands – although her own were lacerated to bits.

Grinding the glass was the only work she did herself. Initially, she crushed it between two flat stones before sorting it meticulously into grades and colours that were stored in jars in her pantry together with her preserves. Then she hit on the idea of using heavy-duty coffee mills, but after grinding six or seven of the things *stukkend*, she resorted to using stones again.

The glass wasn't only a hazard to her; the men who applied it to the walls also suffered cuts and sometimes the agony of glass dust in their eyes, which Helen would help them wash out, although she admonished that there was nothing to fear, showering a handful over her head like confetti.

She took her inspiration from dreams and the exotic postcards and pictures friends sent her of foreign lands, or prints of paintings by artists such as Blake and the poetry of the *Rubáiyát*, or nude photographs she and her sisters had innocently experimented with in their youth, as well as a profusion of ordinary household items. The sphinxes in the yard, for example, were designed from the illustration on the Lion matchbox cover, while the suns that adorned her house were based on the anthropomorphised face on the Sunbeam floor polish tin.

She filled the house with candles and lamps, turning coloured brandy snifters upside down to use as lampshades and when she lit them all, the place was transformed into a 'dream palace', a 'fairy palace'. While it was designed to be admired from the inside and Helen did everything she could to make her home seem welcoming to guests, with a profusion of toiletries scattered around and, bizarrely, little piles of money, like pirate treasure to create an illusion of wealth, she only rarely had anyone over.

Helen used to sleep in a different place every night to be able to fully experience the effect of her amazing house. The one room she never slept in, however, was the Honeymoon Room where the red sun with green eyes glared in from the window. When she was asked about the incongruity of the single beds kept separated by the wardrobe, she said, 'Ah! But love is always kept apart!'

Strictly, that wasn't true. In 1947, to placate his wife, Johannes moved his family back to Peddie, but would stay over in Nieu Bethesda, in the house with Helen for two weeks at a time. Helen had even adapted a bed in the Green Room to cater to his height, extending it with a small table. Their affair was made trickier by Johannes' failing eyesight, so when letters from Helen arrived, his wife was the one who opened and read them.

In 1954, Helen inexplicably married a widower pensioner, Johannes Machiel Niemand, who, at 67, was ten years her senior. After the wedding in the Graaff-Reinet magistrate's court, Helen went back to her house and he to his and it's unlikely the marriage was ever consummated. It was all over within six weeks ostensibly because Helen claimed she didn't want to be a 'Niemand' (a nobody). It is likely that Helen was trying to force Johannes' hand to divorce his wife. The ploy didn't work and instead Helen was the one to annul her marriage.

In the meantime, the house was progressing splendidly and strangely. Helen had filled her yard with live birds as well as stone ones, hemmed in by nets and fences. She employed a succession of three labourers from the coloured community, none of whom had ever sculpted anything more sophisticated than a brick wall before. The first was

Jonas Adams, then Piet van der Merwe and finally Koos Malgas, who was far and away the most talented of the three and spent the longest time with Helen.

It was he who sculpted the various renditions of the Mona Lisa in the garden, the beckoning *meisies* who showed visitors the way and the glass beehive interpretation of Mecca, cheekily made from empty booze bottles. He didn't always understand everything 'Miss Helen' commissioned him to make, such as the giraffe heads (although Helen was to explain that their bodies were underground, so they could reach the short bushes that grew around them), but she paid him well – between R50 and R130 a week – depending on how well she liked his work.

Her house was drawing regular visitors and not only from the local children who came to sell her bottles or alternately throw stones on her roof. The house's fame had spread and although the first interview with Helen was only to appear in the early '70s, people turned up at her door on hearsay. Often she was delighted, but she could also be very shy, despite her propensity for wandering around her yard in the nude, and sometimes she refused to answer the door. Once, when she discovered that she'd turned away the renowned firebrand artist and critic, Walter Battis, she was greatly upset, perhaps hoping for recognition from a 'real' artist.

Her increasingly reclusive behaviour was made worse by the mutilation of her feet. She'd suffered terribly from bunions, but somewhere in the late '50s or early '60s, when she went to have them removed, the surgeon misunderstood and cut off her baby toes instead. Helen was unable to wear shoes after that and mostly went around barefoot or in 'slops', even in the icy Karoo winters. She was so humiliated by the appearance of her feet, that she'd avoid going out except when absolutely necessary. If she was on the way to collect her pension and she chanced upon someone in the street, she would crouch down over her sadly deformed little feet so that her skirts concealed them.

Helen knew that prevailing opinion held that she was loopy, but she said, 'Here in my loneliness, I am happy.' She must have reconsidered when she heard in February 1963 the devastating news that Johannes had died, via a curt telegram from his wife that said simply, '*Mnr. Hattingh oorlede*' (Mr. Hattingh deceased). His failing sight had been a symptom of cancer behind his eye and when the pain became too terrible, he returned to Peddie to be nursed by his family. The last time Helen saw the man she described as the great love of her life was October 1962. The single beds in the Honeymoon Room would forever remain separate.

In 1968, she was dealt another blow with the death of her sister, Alida, and then in 1972, a friendly neighbour died too. In the early '70s, she befriended two young women from Cape Town, Jill Wenman and Francie Lund, who provided her with a link to the outside world apart from the post office, and in whom she could confide her terror of abandonment. Although she worked with Koos daily and they seem to have been very fond of each other, he was the only person she came into regular contact with and he wasn't always able to give her everything she needed.

For a while, Helen had been struggling to do up her buttons because of crippling arthritis in her hands. She'd been forced to rely on Koos to help her dress, and although she handled the situation with her typical wry humour, commissioning Koos to make a statue in the Corner of Debauchery of a Cock Man with a gut protruding so far he can no longer do up his fly, she was distressed about what people would say. Jill solved the problem, buying elasticated tracksuit pants that Helen could pull on herself.

But Koos was the one who was there when she committed suicide.

Apart from her painful hands and feet, Helen also suffered from failing eyesight. She became increasingly paranoid, suspecting the neighbour who left her food of trying to poison her and even harbouring dark thoughts about Koos. She wrote a letter to her sister Annie, confiding her fears of being alone and asking her to come stay. After she died, Annie's response, agreeing to come, was found unopened in her home.

She was terribly depressed. When Jill helped her write up her will during her last visit, she told her, 'Dying isn't the problem. Living is the problem. That is why we must live our lives passionately and to the full. My agony would be to "live dying" without being able to work.'

One cold winter Friday, Helen tried to dispatch Koos unusually early to run her errands, saying off hand that once he was done, he could go home. When Koos protested that he hadn't yet put in a full day's work and there were still things he wanted to do, Helen confessed to him that she no longer wanted to live. 'If I had a gun, Koos, I'd want you to shoot me dead.' He objected strongly, 'Miss Helen must not say such things!'

Despite his concerns, Helen persuaded him to collect her insurance and buy bread, but on his way he stopped in at the police station. The officers on duty didn't take him seriously. They'd heard from the sisters at the clinic that Miss Helen often complained about how she didn't want to live anymore and made a cursory promise to have a look in after lunch.

Koos returned to the house, defying Helen's instructions, only to find a neighbour waiting on the stoep. She demanded to know where he'd been, adding, 'Your madam has done a terrible thing!' In the kitchen, the *dominee* and his wife and the local nursing sister were clustered around Helen, who was sunken into the couch, looking pale and terrified and unable to speak as blood seeped from her mouth. On the table was a bottle of caustic soda, the highly corrosive alkaline that she used to clean the floors. And a teaspoon. Despite all attempts to save her, it took three days for her to die in agony in hospital.

Helen left explicit instructions in her will that she should be carried out the back of the house, because she believed the villagers so clumsy that if they took her out the front, they would scrape her precious glass off the walls. She wanted to be cremated and for her ashes to be mixed with ground glass and applied to the plumage of her favourite cement owl, Oswald. But her will was unwitnessed and therefore invalid.

Her remains were not painted on Oswald. But despite some minor ransacking of the house by family members, her heart's wish was fulfilled when the house and the grounds were declared a National

Monument in 1986. Koos left the village, but returned in 1991 to restore and preserve the world he and Miss Helen had shaped together, until his retirement in 1996. He maintained an interest in the restoration until his death in 2000.

Amongst the ecstatic worshippers and imagined beasts, Helen populated her yard with several people she knew. There are representations of two village men, Oupa Frans and Oom Piet Meyer with his walking stick and his dog and Koos' two young daughters, holding hands and rushing east, which Helen always maintained was a depiction of her, pulling Jill around the garden. And there are more obtuse references too, the fierce maneless lion and the drunkard slumped in the Corner of Debauchery near her father's room, the jealous sun of the Honeymoon Room and the bag body with its cloven hoof, that Helen treated quite irreverently as a doorstop.

But there is only one figure on the property expressly designed to represent her. It is of a slender little woman adorned in blue mosaic, her legs folded beneath her and ending in delicate little feet that are missing the baby toes, one hand stretched to the sky with a hint of the enigmatic Mona Lisa smile of the true believer.

The Curious Case of the Cross-dressing Doctor

Dr James Barry

British army doctor, James Barry was a genius surgeon, but an ornery bastard. He cost himself more than one big-league job thanks to his habit of penning scathing letters to high-ups who dared to disagree with him on medical policy issues, and even raised the ire of Florence Nightingale (who was a bit of a contrary character herself) when he called her 'an interfering old maid'.

James was especially quick to take umbrage if anyone made a snide comment about his feminine voice or slight build. He would call for a duel at the drop of a glove and apparently one of his favourite and oft-used quotes was, 'I would very much like to cut off your ears!' He was pernickety about such slights to his manhood and earned the nickname *kapok dokter* (or cotton wool doctor) for the get-up he wore tramping around 19th century Cape Town, which consisted of elevated shoes, a tremendous cocked hat, a coat allegedly bulked up with towels and cotton wool, and a hulking great sword.

While James was a master swordsman as well as a rapier wit, most of his challenges to detractors were merely grandstanding and he only carried one duel through to its stand off – with pistols rather than swords. Interestingly, for once, the duel wasn't at his instigation. When James made a disparaging remark about the 'nice Dutch filly' the Cape Governor, Lord Charles Somerset, was consulting in his office, Captain Josias Cloete called him out on it when he demanded, 'Retract your vile expression, you infernal little cad!' They paced off in opposite directions on the southern terrace of the estate, turned and fired. Luckily both missed. However, the incident added a benzine lamp's worth of fuel to the already rampant flames of rumour that James was having an affair with Lord Somerset.

It was after he died on 25 July 1865 at around 70, that it was revealed that the good doctor had good cause to be sensitive about his masculinity being called into question. The truth about James Barry, which many claimed afterwards to have suspected all along, came out when he, or rather, she was prepared for burial.

Before he passed away, he had specifically requested that no post mortem should be performed and Dr. McKinnon, who signed the death certificate for James (as a male) respected his old friend's wishes, but he slipped up when he allowed a charwoman to perform the gory task of embalming the corpse. The outraged lady claimed that James not only had the body of 'a perfect female', but also bore stretch marks that she claimed were clearly the scars of someone who had 'had a child when very young'.

Unfortunately, we have to take her word for it and considering that she demanded a little gold from McKinnon to keep it a secret, her motives are a tad suspect. McKinnon brushed her off, saying it was no secret of his and his own opinion was that Dr. Barry was a hermaphrodite. By the time the press got hold of the story in mid-August, it was too late to have the body exhumed, but the number of eye witness accounts that started appearing claiming to have stumbled upon James' little secret long ago, stoked the mythos.

The dodgy testament of the charwoman notwithstanding, there is little doubt that James was a woman. James was slight and effeminate, barely five foot tall and the portrait of her at the Alphen Hotel in

Cape Town, shows her pale face and high cheekbones that she kept suspiciously smooth, even when beards were all the rage in the mid 1800s, and a head of sandy curls that was later dyed red.

At the time she was born in London, around 1795 (she was never clear about the particulars of her age), hermaphrodites were seen as a sign of God's wrath and the birth was 'concealed' – a repellent euphemism for drowning the baby or bashing its brains out. It's extremely unlikely James would have survived beyond infancy if she'd been intersex.

As for her own pregnancy, that is rather dubious. James was something of a prodigy. She qualified as a doctor at Edinburgh University, she claimed at 13, already living as a boy, and launched right into a long and frenetically active career that was very much in the public eye. It would have been very difficult to pass off a belly swelling with child on her slender frame as a beer *boep*, particularly as James was a teetotaller who only drank goat's milk and was a devout vegetarian. If she did have a child, it was cunningly carried out and there are no records of what may have become of it.

The one person who might have been able to shed light on the mystery was her black manservant, John, but he was dispatched back to Jamaica with haste after her death, apparently after making a remark about the clean padding towels he had to prepare for her every morning to disguise her figure.

After she died, several books appeared claiming to have known all along, although as most of them were published after the truth was uncovered, the veracity of the writers' memories is questionable. A case in point was the memoir of a Mrs Fenton, published in 1901, who apparently recorded an encounter in her journal with a nurse in Mauritius in 1829 who said she'd walked in on James in her bedroom and seen all. The nurse maintained that James had flown into a 'most violent passion' and thereafter refused to make house calls in any home where she was employed.

A Colonel Rogers who had shared a cabin with James en route to Barbados recalled that she had chased him out every morning so she could get dressed and in 1881 he published a fictional account about

James called *A Modern Sphinx*. In the book, he includes the apparently true testimony of the assistant surgeon, Dr. O'Connor who tended James when she was deathly ill with yellow fever in Trinidad. Fearing James was dying, O'Connor and a friend entered her bedroom unannounced, and discovered the same thing the nosy nurse had some 25 years before. James woke up and blinking through her fever implored the pair to swear to keep her secret as long as she lived.

Of course, people had their suspicions, although equally, others were totally oblivious. At Edinburgh University, her best friend, John Jobson declared that he never suspected for a moment, although he had noticed that she seemed 'timid of walking alone' through the rougher parts of town. He was also disappointed that his attempts to teach her to box failed because of her habit of keeping her arms over her chest to protect it.

There was only one contemporary account, put out by Count Las Cases, a French nobleman who wrote a memoir of his time in exile with Napoleon. When he met James in Cape Town in 1817, he wrote, 'The grave Doctor who was presented to me, was a boy of 18, with the form, the manners and the voice of a woman.' James' story inspired several books based on her story, although initially, in keeping with the romantic mores of the 19th century, fictional accounts such as *The Journal of Dr James Barry* penned in 1932 by Olga Racster and Jessica Grove, typically portrayed her as a hysterical girl who joined the army for the love of a surgeon and only escaped undetected because of the protection of a mysterious friend in authority.

In fact, James was anything but. She was able to maintain her cover through the sheer force of her rather formidable personality. She was a fiercely ambitious and dedicated doctor with a nasty temper who refused to compromise on her principles even when it hurt her prospects. And it often did. On that point, the fictions got it right because Lord Charles Somerset often had to step in to keep James out of trouble – and boy, did she get herself into trouble.

We still don't have a clue as to who James was really. Some historians have said that her real name was Miranda Stuart, but it's possible that they got muddled with General Francisco de Miranda, one of two men (the other was the Earl of Buchan) to whom James dedicated her doctoral thesis. General Miranda was the would-be liberator of Venezuela, one-time lover of Catherine the Great and James' mentor. He also happened to have the finest private library in London, which he allowed James the privilege of using. How he knew James is a little murky, but it seems she may have been the niece of an artist by the name of James Barry R.A., whose works General Miranda admired and who shared some of James' qualities – he was also short, sharp and snappy.

It's perhaps a little convenient that James apparently only made contact with General Miranda after her supposed artist-uncle namesake died in 1806. Might she have been trading on the name, confident that he wasn't around anymore to dispute it? There are some tantalising hints that General Miranda, who was an open-minded gentleman about women's rights (then unheard of), was in on the secret to some extent.

In 1810, in a rather prosaic letter to him detailing her plans to go to university, thanking him for the use of his library and extending the regards of his 'aunt', Mrs Bulkeley, James included an intriguing p.s.: 'As Lord B_ nor anyone here knows anything about Mrs Bulkeley's Daughter, I trust, my dear General that neither you or the Doctor will mention in any of your correspondence anything about my Cousin's care for me.' It's not entirely improbable that James was the daughter in question, posing as an imaginary cousin named for a possible uncle, although there's no proof either way.

James continued her friendship with General Miranda through university and was supposed to follow him to Caracas as soon as she'd obtained her degree, but he was captured by the Spanish in 1812 and died four years later.

If James had been the simpering sentimental girl the novelists imagined, she would never have made it through Edinburgh's medical school, at the time one of the best in the world. Some of its practices, however, were considered dodgy, including dissecting corpses for the very unpopular gruesome practicals, for which James was one of only a handful of students at the time to enrol. These were so controversial, that the lecture theatres had secret entrances and while universities retained their own corpse procurer (read: grave robber), these men would not have been on the official payroll.

In fact, after James left, Edinburgh endured a major scandal when it was discovered that two gentlemen in the university's employ, by the name of Burke and Hare, had decided stealing corpses from cemeteries was too much hassle and instead started creating their own. It was probably much appreciated that the cadavers they delivered were so fresh, but the murderous pair were eventually caught out. Burke turned state witness but Hare was hanged in 1828 and ended up on the dissection table himself. The university still has a grisly relic in its collection – a wallet made from his skin.

James qualified as an MD in 1812, the first woman in Britain to do so, although only she knew it at the time. She enrolled in the army medical services almost immediately, somehow bypassing the mandatory physical examination. She was first stationed at Plymouth, where the chief medical officer objected to her youthful appearance, and then Chelsea before she sailed off in 1816 for the Cape of Good Hope with a letter of introduction from the Earl of Buchan to Lord Charles Somerset.

James fast became a favourite in the Somerset household. She was appointed official physician after just six months and accompanied the governor, who was then a handsome widower of 49, and his two daughters on a tour of the colony in 1817. At the high society functions she attended, she was noted for her stylish dress sense and for her habit of flirting with the prettiest girls. While there were rumours initially that she was courting one of Somerset's daughters, her girlish appearance together with her devotion to the man and his haste to constantly bail her out of trouble, skewed the speculation in another direction entirely.

But what were these dilemmas from which she needed rescuing? James was a very competent doctor and in fact performed the first-ever successful caesarean in the Cape (and one of the first in the world) where both mother and child survived. Usually the procedure was reserved for hopeless cases where the mother was already dead and it had only been performed once before in Zurich in 1818. Even James' lecturer at medical school, who had taught her the procedure, had not been successful in his two attempts and her accomplishment would leave its mark on history in more ways than one.

James refused payment, asking only that the grateful mother name the child for 'him', which she did. The baby boy was called James Barry Munnik and when he grew up, his child, also named for him, would become godfather to General James Barry Munnik Hertzog, who became Prime Minister of South Africa in 1924.

James was promoted to Colonial Medical Inspector, which gave her carte blanche over all things medical in the city, the same way the Fiscal, who was to become her sworn enemy, managed all the judicial processes. At first, this worked swimmingly. James was able to put into practice many of her theories about proper nutrition and hygiene and although some of her ideas seemed bizarre, for instance, advising patients to bathe in wine, the antiseptic properties of the grape extract actually worked pretty darn well (and has since become a popular spa treatment). She also introduced a regulations board for the pharmaceutical industry, noting how people were being poisoned by drugs dispensed willy-nilly by unlicensed apothecaries. This caused her some trouble when she refused to examine a man who had learned the business from his father, but hadn't been through medical school. Put under pressure, James dug in her heels, Somerset intervened and handed over the matter to a committee who eventually voted to grant the man a licence to continue running the business he'd been working at for 26 years already.

James never learned the subtle art of politics and was an unrepentant social reformer and stirrer throughout her career. She stated her mind outright, with little thought for the consequences, and mightily pissed off, among several other high-ups, the manager of the leper colony with her suggestions for more humane treatment and the Fiscal when she criticised the deplorable conditions of the local gaol, the Tronk.

Somerset regularly had to step in to soothe ruffled feathers, but James blundered on regardless.

The most disastrous incident of her Cape Town career occurred in 1825, when Somerset was facing a political crisis. His governance had been called into question and he was facing a hearing in England. James chose this moment to get involved in the Tronk again over the matter of a prisoner who was supposedly mad. She examined the man, declared that he was not insane, provided he was kept off wine, and loudly condemned the fact that he'd been beaten by the warders. The Fiscal was furious, not least by the James' antagonistic tone, although, in her defence, she'd written the letter as a confidential report for the Chief Secretary of the Cape, Richard Plasket, who passed it on to the Fiscal with the demand that this 'apparently disgraceful' business be investigated at once.

The Fiscal wasted no time sending a messenger with summons for James to appear before the Court of Justice to explain herself. She ripped up the summons and fell back on her favourite bit of belligerence, threatening to cut off the Fiscal's ears! A second summons was sent, this time carrying a threat of its own – if she didn't appear, she would be imprisoned. Grudgingly, James did take her place in the box, but refused to take an oath or answer any of the questions put to her, maintaining that her correspondence had been confidential and that if such reports were to be shared, it set a dangerous precedent for the government.

A salvo of heated letters flew back and forth between James and Richard Plasket, tempers flared, harsh words were uttered and by the end of it, James found herself out of a job through some conniving politicking, despite her impeccable reputation as a surgeon and Somerset's best attempts to help her.

As to why Somerset was so willing to stick his neck out for James repeatedly, there was much conjecture. Apart from the duel with Josias Cloete over the snarky remark James made, which some interpreted as jealousy, there was also a little ditty doing the rounds, inspired by an incident when James famously arrived at the Dutch Reformed Church only to promptly turn around when she saw the governor's pew was empty.

It went:

'With courteous devotion inspired
Barry came to the temple of prayer,
But quickly turned round and retired,
When he found that his lord was not there!'

The real scandal only erupted after the episode of the billsheet in 1824, by which time both the good doctor and the not-so-good governor had made plenty of enemies.

In the days before newspapers, it was common practice for unofficial notices and advertisements to be stuck up on lampposts and walls and, at first glance, the placard that was *plakked* on the Hout Street bridge didn't seem out of the ordinary. On closer reading however, the merchant Captain Findlay who was on his way to check out the shipping schedules, discovered to his shock and outrage that the words inscribed thereon described a most deviant relationship between the Cape Governor and his physician.

By the time he returned, the ad had mysteriously disappeared, but the good honour of the governor had been impugned and reports of the ad had already caused a 'great sensation' in the city. A reward of 5 000 rix-dollars was offered for any information on the guilty party and an additional 1 000 for the defamatory paper itself. James indignantly added another 1 000 to the reward in her personal capacity and the merchants of Cape Town, apparently disgusted by the whole debacle, upped it by a further 1 500. It all came to nought and neither the billsheet nor the culprit were ever discovered.

Even after they had both left the Cape in 1827 – Somerset to retire in England, having managed to evade any disciplinary action for his governance, and James to take up a position as army staff surgeon in Mauritius – they remained close. The only time James ever disappeared without requesting leave of absence was when she heard that Somerset had taken ill in August 1829. She sailed for England immediately, although when she was questioned on this extraordinary behaviour, she claimed, off-hand, 'I have come home to have my hair cut.' She attended her old friend until his death in February 1831.

Although she would have normally been court-martialled for her actions, Somerset still had influence from the grave and thanks to his highly placed brother, Lord Fitzroy Somerset, who later became Lord Raglan, she escaped without a mark on her record and went on to become staff surgeon in Jamaica.

It is possible that James and Charles Somerset were involved in a romantic tryst, but while it makes for a juicy tale, some historians maintain it would have been highly unlikely. James' only companions throughout her life were a succession of little dogs all called Psyche and a series of black manservants. It seems improbable that she would have risked everything she'd accomplished for mere love and Somerset did, after all, remarry someone else. At the same time, if James *had* been involved in a torrid love affair, she would have been as circumspect about it as she was about her gender.

After Somerset died, James went on to a distinguished career as staff surgeon in various military outposts. She arrived in Jamaica just in time for the bloody riots of the 1831 Christmas Rebellion, in which 400 of the 50 000 black slaves who rose up lost their lives in the fighting, but only a handful of whites. It was the only time James had to serve on active duty and she had to deal with the wounded as well as the scores of British troops who died from tropical fevers.

In 1836, she received a promotion as principal medical office of the island of St Helena, where she quickly inspired animosity from the local officers with her vocal disapproval of the mismanagement of the hospitals, the bottleneck on fresh supplies and the number of women, forced to turn to prostitution, who were suffering from venereal diseases.

Stymied by the tangle of island bureaucracy, she went over the heads of the local authorities and appealed directly to Secretary of State at the war office. It was an unheard of thing to do and she was dragged before a court-martial for it. She was acquitted, but landed in trouble again a year later for some other offence, not recorded, and this time was found guilty and shipped back to London under arrest and in disgrace.

She was let off lightly with a slap on the wrist and a demotion and now in her 40s, set off for Barbados in 1838, where, miraculously, she managed to maintain an amicable relationship with the authorities, perhaps having mellowed with age. In 1845, in Trinidad she caught yellow fever, coming close to death and exposure. She was granted leave to recover for a year in England and went on to serve as principal medical officer in Malta and then Corfu.

When war in the Crimea broke out in 1854, she immediately volunteered, but was told that there was no space for someone of her high rank. She persuaded Lord Raglan to send his wounded to Corfu and she treated 500 men, of whom '400 returned fit for active service, having been restored to health in an unusually short period'. It was during this time that she clashed swords with Florence Nightingale. Although they had much in common, it's possible that James was annoyed that Florence claimed full credit for having been the first to consider the diet and living conditions of the troops when James had been advocating the same for the last 30 years.

She spent a brief two years in Canada, where she wasted no time implementing reforms, and 1859 returned to London only to be forced to retire by three junior officers who took one look at the cantankerous and frail 65 year old and declared her unfit for service. James was most put out and even more so when her hints that she'd like to retire, if she absolutely had to, with some indication of the Queen's favour, such as, oh, say a knighthood, passed unnoticed.

She spent her retirement quietly in London, making occasional trips to the countryside and spending winters abroad, and remarkably managed to avoid antagonising anyone else until the scandal of her death in 1865.

James survived all kinds of intrigues, diseases, a court martial and various enmities from petty-minded officials. She was a skilled surgeon and a principled reformer, but perhaps her greatest achievement was that of concealing her secret until the very end.

The Ontvlugting

Ingrid Jonker

℘oetry is a perilous profession. More than any other genus of writer, those who work with carefully cantilevered quatrains or frolicksome free verse are in the habit of hacking open their ribcages to expose their hearts to the world – raw and bloody and all too easily wounded. It's no wonder suicide is endemic to the genre.

When Ingrid Jonker's body was found washed up on the beach of Three Anchor Bay on 19 July 1965, with the finest of tiny shells collected in the dark curls of her hair and the hollows of her ears, it came as a shock, but not a surprise. She had been planning her escape for years.

At 31, she was one of the finest poets of her generation, loved by two of the giants of the literati scene of the Sestigers, André Brink and Jack Cope, and lusted after by many more for her childlike, impetuous vitality that was so at odds with the morbid proclivities that scarred her personality like the fine white lines marked on the inside of her wrists. It was precisely the tension that strung her taut between the contradictory impulses of life and death that made her poetry so achingly vulnerable and her company so beguiling.

Ingrid was always fascinated by the sea – and obsessed with drowning. Although able to 'swim like a fish', as a child she nearly drowned twice, and she and her sister Anna were witness to two watery deaths when living in the Strand: a young playmate who was crushed against the rocks in a tangle of kelp and two fishermen washed ashore after a storm.

Apart from her accidental near-deaths as a child and self-inflicted close-calls in adulthood, Ingrid barely made it into the world at all. According to Ingrid, her mother, Beatrice, considered aborting her when her father, the hard-drinking intellectual National Party MP and newspaper owner, Abraham Jonker, in a moment of jealous rage, accused his wife of carrying a child that was not his. Beatrice left him the same night and moved in with her parents together with her two-year-old daughter, Anna.

She gave birth to Ingrid two months later on 19 September 1933, but Abraham never accepted the girl child as his own, even though they both had the same 'broken' look in their eyes. Ingrid's *ouma* nicknamed her *'hartseerkind'* or heartache-child. She was to spend most of her life trying to win her father's love, or even his approval, and when that failed, she tried to replace him, indulging in a series of tragically doomed love affairs with older men.

When Ingrid's *oupa* died in 1938, the family was left destitute and drifted between the fishing villages of the Strand and Gordon's Bay, just outside of Cape Town. But while the children delighted in running wild, roaming the beaches and visiting the fisherfolk, Beatrice was unravelling, pining for the husband she still loved. One day, the family found her sitting in the window, calling for Abraham in a plaintive looped echo. She had a history of nervous breakdowns, even before the divorce, and over the next few years she sporadically returned to Valkenberg.

In 1942, during one of her stints in the psychiatric hospital, Beatrice was dealt another blow – she was diagnosed with cancer. She never came home again, but over the next two years her daughters made the long trek along the railway lines to visit her in the clinic, picking wildflowers along the way and crawling into her hospital bed with her, yet never quite knowing what was wrong.

When she died in 1944, Anna and Ingrid, now 12 and 10, were sent to live with their father. Abraham was a total stranger to them and their stepmother, the Afrikaans author Suzanne Jacomina (Lulu) Brewis, was more interested in her new baby, Koos, than the feral cuckoo fledgelings deposited at her door. Compared to Abraham's cold and *verkrampte* home, the days of poverty and wandering the beaches at will, were to take on the sepia sheen of a paradise lost in Ingrid's memory.

Ingrid found refuge from the chilly atmosphere at home in words. She'd started writing at six and her *ouma*, a lay preacher, had woven her verses into the informal sermons she gave in the coloured fishing villages. Despite Abraham's history as a high-profile writer and editor, he never encouraged her, so Ingrid sought out her sister's critiques instead, ambushing her in the most unlikely places, barging in on her in the bath, for example, to get her opinion on a new work in progress.

Several of her poems were printed in school magazines and in 1949, encouraged by her teachers at Wynberg Girls' High School, she submitted a volume of poems, *Na Die Somer* (*After the Summer*) for publication. It was rejected, but she earned the avid support of renowned poet and critic, DJ Opperman and by 16 she was corresponding regularly with various literary luminaries.

She matriculated at 18 and in 1952, moved into her own accommodation in the city and landed a job as a typist and proofreader.

Just before her 23rd birthday in June 1956, Ingrid published *Ontvlugting* (*Escape*), a collection of poems mostly written while still in her teens. The title number was her favourite, about an unbalanced girl who flees to the safety of her childhood where she can right the mistakes that have set her off kilter.

The publicity surrounding the book brought her into a close-knit circle of creatives, including Jan Rabie and his wife Marjorie Wallace, the poets Breyten Breytenbach and Uys Krige, and English writer Jack Cope, who would become Ingrid's lover. The intellectual and influential group of friends, which in due course also included André Brink, Adam Small, Richard Rive, Kenny Parker, Erik Laubscher, was later tagged the *Sestigers*.

Ingrid dedicated the collection to her father, but Abraham rebuffed her. He was quoted in *Die Burger* saying that he hoped there was something worthwhile between the covers and fully expected her to have shamed him.

Ingrid was to try again when her second anthology, *Rook en Oker* (*Smoke and Ochre*) was released much later in 1963, but when she contacted her father to arrange to give him a copy in person, he wrote her a letter to say she could see him at home, but not in public. He didn't want to be seen with her in the open after their very public falling out over the controversial new censorship bill he was heading up as National Party MP, that she and the *Sestigers* vehemently opposed. The spat spilled into the press and when Abraham dismissed his critics as a bunch of 'nobodies' in print, Ingrid's retort that the assertion was 'ridiculous,' was also published, to Abraham's mortification. Thereafter he refused to have anything to with her, even declining to help her with medical bills.

In 1958, at 25, she married Pieter Venter, a writer 15 years her senior who had been married twice before. Eleven months later, Ingrid's most fervent dream came true when she gave birth to a cherished baby girl, Simone. Pieter was transferred to Johannesburg in 1959, uprooting Ingrid from her scathingly smart circle of friends and her beloved ocean. She struggled to adapt to the city and her narrow-minded in-laws who threw her out of their house one night on discovering that she had coloured friends.

Just three months after arriving in Johannesburg, the marriage fell apart. In an unpublished novel, based on his life with Ingrid, Pieter claimed she'd come to him one day to tell him she'd made a terrible mistake. She wasn't designed for marriage. She needed to be free. The real story was messier.

A young actor, Pietro Nolte, had been staying with the couple. Although Jack Cope described the man as a 'moffie', Pieter became convinced that he and Ingrid were having an affair. The drama that unfolded put the play Pietro was rehearsing to shame with screaming arguments complete with a carving knife waved about threateningly.

It was only resolved with the intervention of the 19-year-old Breyten Breytenbach, who was backpacking around the country and lent Ingrid the money she needed to leave the whole ugly *gemors*. behind. She fled on a train, leaving her daughter behind and without taking even a change of clothes. She arrived in Cape Town full of 'gin, remorse and doubt' to stay with Jan Rabie and Marjorie Wallace.

Pieter penned poems in a vain attempt to impress her and win her back, despite the nastiness he'd recorded in his novel, that once acquainted with Ingrid, no man of relative intelligence would want to marry her. Eventually, she did return to him and they moved from Emmarentia to Hillbrow. Ingrid felt, 'the slum suits my heart better. One sees the life here, although only from the balcony.' But it was not to last. By 1960 it was evident that their relationship was never going to work and Ingrid packed up her things and her daughter for the last time and moved back to Cape Town.

She resumed her typing and proofreading, but wrote poetry whenever she could, jotting notes on scraps of paper or the back of cigarette boxes on the bus – and her career as a poet was gaining momentum.

Almost immediately Ingrid became embroiled with Jack Cope, who was considerably older than her, with two children of his own and a reputation for icy intellectualism. He warned her, 'You can't rely on me because I'm absolutely at the extreme of my capability. I'm trying to bring up two children and educate them … and I'm just like an old broken reed.' Ingrid retorted with a poem, *Die Lied van die Gebreekte Riete* (The Song of the Broken Reeds). Jack held it up as evidence that she was a true poet. 'Look how her imagination works, it's absolutely brilliant … She saw the whole humanity of it immediately.'

In 1961, she fell pregnant and Jack coerced her into having a backstreet abortion as he already had two children. Perhaps he felt that Ingrid was too unstable to be good mother material. She fell into such a dark depression that she had to be hospitalised twice. Tormented about terminating the pregnancy, considering her mother had faced the same choice about her, she wrote a poem, *Korreltjie Sand* (Small Grain of Sand) about her ambivalence, and presented it to her psychiatrist at Valkenberg.

In 1963, she became involved with André Brink, to the relief of her friends, delighted that she was finally involved with someone her age rather than the replacement father figures for whom she typically fell. André met her for the first time in April at a gathering at Jan Rabie's house and was immediately struck both by her electric presence and the fact that she was barefoot when everyone else was quite properly dressed. It was hardly the done thing, but she had particularly beautiful feet. He found her irresistible. She was involved in a heated debate with Jack at the time and André had no idea they were involved. They ended up cloistered together in her apartment for the remainder of the weekend.

He describes her as passionate and provocative but says she could also be utterly sweet and charming and adorable. She attracted bold and brilliant friends and had the effect of magnetising any room in a swirling orbit around her. While Ingrid was never a classic beauty, men couldn't stay away from her, partly because she was so comfortable in her body. She loved her physicality, swimming and climbing the mountain as well as drinking and smoking incessantly.

But she could also be volatile. Once when she and André were discussing Prime Minister Verwoerd, she asked, 'Do you really hate him?' When he replied that of course he did, she countered, 'Then go get a gun and shoot him. Tonight.' And she was totally serious.

Already there were signs that she was on the edge. She'd mentioned suicide often before to her friends and on that first weekend, she showed André the scars on her wrist that marked her previous attempts. After he left her, to return to his wife in Grahamstown, a disproportionate part of their correspondence was spent pleading with her not to kill herself.

One night, after wearying hours and hours of fighting that had dragged on until the early morning, Ingrid threatened to kill herself. Exhausted and fractious, and having heard it all before, André snapped that she should do something about it then. She disappeared into the night only to turn up half an hour later escorted by a strange and shaken man. She'd thrown herself in front of his car and he'd only just managed to hit the brakes in time.

In keeping with her mercurial nature, she was fine after that. The couple had a quiet night, drank some wine and after André went to bed, preparing to leave for Grahamstown at five the next morning, she sat on the balcony and penned one of her most tender and beautiful poems, *Plant vir My 'n Boom, André*.

All her relationships were tempestuous, but her affairs with Jack and André were especially chaotic and she pinballed maddeningly between them over the next two years. 'You could never be sure of anything,' André said. 'It was heaven and hell all the time.'

'She felt she was challenging life. She wanted to live a poem – and not the sweetie-sweetie kind. She was a living contradiction, divided by these complex impulses of life and death, which was very appealing and utterly appalling at the same time. It was very perturbing that she was always trying to prove something.'

Ingrid's writing was steadily gaining her a considerable reputation. Although most of her free-flowing poetry riffed off love and loneliness, playing with rhythm and imagery soaked in sensual surrealism, it was one of her few political poems that gained national attention. Inspired by the pass demonstrations and the brutal suppression of the unrest, she wrote *Die Kind Wat Doodgeskiet Is Deur Soldate By Nyanga* (The Child Who Was Shot Dead by Soldiers At Nyanga) in 1960 to commemorate a mother and baby killed at a roadblock. She was surprised when people described it as political and would have been even more so that – almost 30 years after her death – Nelson Mandela would read it at his inaugural address at the opening of parliament.

She published a play, *Seun Van My Hart* (Son of My Heart) as well as a short story, *Die Bok* (The Goat). In 1963, almost eight years after *Ontvlugting*, Ingrid finally felt ready to release her second anthology, *Rook en Oker*.

This marked the beginning of a darker and more mature stage in her work. The critics recognised it and in 1964 she was awarded the prestigious *Afrikaanse Pers-Boekhandel Prys* for the best Afrikaans book of the year. It was the critical acclaim and acceptance she'd always desperately craved.

But if the honour wasn't enough to reconcile her relationship with her father, who fobbed her off once again when she invited him to the prize-giving, the R2 000 cash prize did provide an opportunity for her to fulfil one of her most cosseted dreams – to travel. The money was more than enough for her to take in London, Paris and Amsterdam and then spend a month travelling around Spain with André. The experience was to prove a disaster.

Ingrid sent Simone to stay with Pieter and his new wife, Topsi, and booked passage on one of the Union Castle Line passenger ships that ran between Cape Town and Southhampton. On board, she met and utterly charmed writer Laurens van der Post. He seemed happy to shift into protective father figure mode and warned her that men were only out to sleep with her, although some of her friends have speculated that he was among them. He wrote later, 'Most of the men she met fell in love with her and thought of nothing else but going to bed with her. They succeeded in seducing a soul that was always full of love and eager to give with all of herself, as she did in poetry.'

Ingrid encountered just the sort of man he'd warned her about almost immediately in the form of Jack Cope's writer friend, David Lytton, who spent a day showing her around Stratford. When she uncharacteristically rebuffed his advances, he allegedly snapped, 'Now you've missed your chance with one of the lords of life.' Two years later he published an account of their day trip, which painted her as volatile and morbid, and totally unprepared for the realities of travelling on her own through Europe. Laurens had feared much the same thing and offered her a job in Berlin working for him as his secretary, but Ingrid was determined to stick to her plan.

In Amsterdam, she made contact with some of her favourite writers, but they were preoccupied with their own work and lives, and didn't have time to see her as often as she wanted. She was desperately lonely and wrote André a letter about how she felt as though she had lost touch with her body because her room lacked a mirror, but at the same time gave Jack an ultimatum to marry her or she'd go to Paris with André. She was still in the throes of her stormy love triangle.

Her spirits suffered even more when Jack sent her two bitter backhanded letters, the one bitching about a recently published poem she'd dedicated to André, the other advising her to pay no heed to the fact that 'people are beginning to say you are overrated, that you don't do better than *Rook en Oker* and that you have a swelled head'.

Ingrid was to refer to her waiting period in Amsterdam and then London again as a 'waking nightmare', but it was nothing compared to the 'bloodbath of Barcelona' to come.

André arrived in Amsterdam on 20 June, but while Ingrid wanted to celebrate by living it up and going to the finest restaurants and bars, André was on a tight budget (and feeling guilty about his wife). They started bickering almost immediately over banalities. They flew to Paris for the weekend and then to Barcelona, where André was on contract with a publisher to write a travel book and tied in to negotiating translation rights deals in return for R300 spending money – enough to pay for the trip. Ingrid was furious about his work obligations and that the trip was not the 'honeymoon' she had anticipated. The fighting continued.

She had sent word to Laurens in London that she was unhappy, but stranded in Spain without money. He sent her £50 and a green cashmere jersey on condition she come to London. Instead, she and André resolved that she should return to Paris to spend time with Breyten and Yolande, and when André wrapped up his trip, they could reunite. But in the taxi on the way to the airport, Ingrid refused to go. Just before her flight was called, she broke down and blacked out, collapsing in the middle of the airport. André called a doctor who said she was in no fit state to travel, so they returned to the hotel. In their room, she lost it completely, screaming at the top of her voice and running into walls, to André's consternation. The next morning, she was almost unnaturally calm and subdued, and he managed to bundle her onto the plane without further upset.

In Paris, she checked herself in to the St Anne's psychiatric hospital, with a picture of André clasped to her breast and flew back to Cape Town in early July, only three and a half months after she'd set off. She arrived at the airport wearing a nightgown André had bought her in Paris and the green cashmere jersey from Laurens.

Back in the city, she tried to reinstate her romance with Jack, but he was unmoved. In a letter to a friend, Ingrid described the situation, 'I've landed in a perfect mess. I made a terrible mistake to come back to SA – Jack says he doesn't believe in me after Paris anymore and he is just friendly. Well, I suppose he's justified. But I cannot go on living in this emotional slaughterhouse and will have to leave again for Paris and try to be serious …' To Laurens, she wrote, 'I know there are other things in life apart from love, but one has to have a basis to go out from. Without it, my whole wretched past lifts its dreadful head, and looks at me with that sad and wasted look which paralyses me with terror.'

She didn't hear from André for several months, but after he arrived back in Cape Town in December, they picked up the relationship, although as before, André was only able to come down intermittently from Grahamstown. Once more, it was an on-again, off-again affair.

Like her ex-husband Pieter, André was inspired to write a book based on his relationship with Ingrid. *Orgie* was an audaciously progressive novel, as much for its format, which was tilted 90 degrees, to a landscape presentation – most unusual for books in those days – as its two interlinked narratives unfolding in a conversation in facing columns; his voice and hers', with different fonts marking past and present. Ingrid contributed a great deal to the book, critiquing, writing and breaking up stanzas so that it read more like poetry. Jack Cope even made an uncomplimentary appearance, as the poet 'x'.

By early 1965, Ingrid was in a bad way: she was going overboard on the booze and her medication. In early January, she was admitted to Valkenberg after yet another breakdown. She put an ultimatum to André to choose between his wife and child or her, Simone and his baby that she claimed to be carrying. There was never any evidence of a child, so it was either a false alarm or she had made it up out of desperation.

Orgie was published in March, but by then André had had enough and when he met a new woman in Pretoria – providing a way out of his marriage and his affair with Ingrid – he broke it off with Ingrid for the last time. She was enraged, he said, but also relieved. She'd been as much looking for a way out as he had. But in her diary on 28 April, she wrote, 'Here begins the end, André.'

Never one for strict monogamy, Ingrid was by then already involved with a 28-year-old Flemish artist, Herman van Nazareth, who Jack disparagingly referred to as her 'little boy'.

On 24 May, she broke her leg, apparently during an illegal protest march; when in the chaos of fleeing the police, she fell and someone stood on her, although she also gave two other versions of how it happened. It drove her nuts to be incapacitated. She was always active, as if she needed the reassurance of her physicality to confirm that she was actually there.

On 28 June, she wrote Jack a suicide note, with the intention of sending Simone in a taxi to deliver it to the Clifton bungalow he shared with Uys.

In it, she listed all the people she loved, including her friends and their almost baby, 'the little chicken we buried in heaven', expressed her devastation that their relationship could not work because of her failings, implored him not to carry any guilt over her death and chillingly laid out her plans in detail to stage what would look like an accidental drowning. 'Don't worry about my being physically tormented when I'm out at sea, once there I've got some capsules, just enough to make me fairly unconscious – I shall die like a beast, I've always been a physical coward.' Over the page was a short scribble. 'One may think this is heartless, defiant, or all the rest, but to me it is really no more heartless than a person dying from stomach cancer – I've got it in the soul now. That's all.'

She never sent it.

In July it all came tumbling down. At the beginning of the month, Herman left Cape Town to backpack around the country. Ingrid had lost her job and was desperate for money. Although she was due to start work at *Die Burger* on the 19th, in the meantime, she was unable to pay her phone bill or her rent. Her broken leg was driving her to distraction, she'd tried, unsuccessfully, to contact her dead mother through a medium and finally she received word that André was engaged to be married.

Her friends were aware that she was in depression, but no-one realised how dark. When she asked her father if he wanted to take her on holiday, he reportedly told her, 'I'll buy you a one way ticket to Valkenberg.' Instead, a friend, Bonnie, came to visit her for a weekend in her flat at Bonne Esperance in Sea Point.

On Sunday, the 18th, Ingrid had a blow-up with Jack. She wanted to go to Johannesburg to start over and asked for money to buy a train ticket. He refused. It was the final nail in her coffin.

That evening she was restless and, after Simone was asleep, Bonnie took her out for a drink, but when they returned well after one in the morning, Ingrid slipped out barefoot into the night. When Bonnie followed her, she turned on her with eyes black as 'wet coal'. They sat and talked for a while on the promenade, but on returning to the flat, Ingrid told her she was going to commit suicide. She fled back to the beachfront, followed by Bonnie dragging Simone in tow. The trio ended up at the police station, where Ingrid was already well known. The officer usually in charge was an old confidante who would drive her around to help her calm down when she was feeling lonely or suicidal. But he wasn't on duty that night.

Bonnie decided to take Simone to Jack and Uys so she could concentrate on looking after Ingrid, but when she returned to the police station, Ingrid was gone. The officer at the desk reported that they'd dropped her off at the flat, but of course, by the time Bonnie got there, there was no sign of her. She spent the rest of the night wandering the promenade, calling for her. The last time she stopped in at the police station, she was greeted with grim news. 'We've found your friend. You must come identify her.'

Simone was sent to live with her father and his new wife. Pieter Venter told her the shocking truth of her mother's death immediately. Simone was devastated but not surprised. She said she knew something was going to happen – to either Ingrid or her.

Others took it less well. When André heard the news, he was so shocked and grief-stricken he went blind for several hours. He floundered for some time after that, starting several books only to abandon them again later. Jack got outrageously drunk, threw himself on her grave, sobbing, and had to be forcibly escorted from the stilted funeral, which was a divided affair between the conservative family, headed up by Abraham, who had also been drinking all day, and Ingrid's bohemian friends.

Although Jack pulled himself out of his alcohol haze to begin feverishly translating Ingrid's work into English, Abraham drank himself to death within six months, and on his deathbed called feebly for his daughter in the same manner his lost ex-wife had once called for him.

Ingrid's friends held a second funeral, more in keeping with her free spirit, an informal gathering around her grave where they read poetry. In remembrance of her they published a collection of writings called *In Memoriam* and set up the Ingrid Jonker Poetry Prize, now considered the most prestigious in the country. Posthumously, in 2004, she was awarded the Order of Ikhamanga for her contribution to literature and the struggle, which was accepted by her daughter, Simone.

Ingrid never found the love and reassurance she hungered for – and as one of her friends said, no mortal would have been capable of giving it to her.

When Nelson Mandela invoked her at his first presidential address on 9 May 1994, he described her as a woman 'who transcended a particular experience and became a South African, an African and a citizen of the world ... In the midst of despair, she celebrated hope. Confronted with death, she asserted the beauty of life ... To her and others like her, we owe a debt to life itself.'

Unfortunately, there is a bleak footnote to Ingrid's legacy. Her collection of letters, which had been kept in the trust of the English Literary Museum in Grahamstown, were loaned to her sister Anna for the purposes of writing a book about Ingrid. When she suffered a heart attack and died a few years ago, the letters were left in the care of her son, Anthony Biaros.

He hawked the collection – without Simone's knowledge or permission – for R50 000 to Holland's poet laureate, Gerrit Komrij, who had long been a fan of Ingrid's work and had translated her poetry into Dutch. When Simone discovered what her cousin had done, she laid a charge of theft against him at the Fish Hoek Police Station, whose jurisdiction, unfortunately, does not extend to Portugal, where Gerrit Komrij now resides. Ingrid's extensive and deeply intimate correspondence has still not been recovered.

Lady in Red

Ruth First

When Tilly First finally got to see her radical writer daughter in prison in 1963, she was taken aback by her appearance. As she was ushered out of the cell, the visit over, Tilly whispered, 'Are you cracking up?' It was the first time she had seen Ruth without lipstick.

Ruth First was known as the stylish revolutionary. Even during the Treason Trial of 1956, she had surprised her fellow inmates, including Helen Joseph, by packing silk panties and cosmetics when they had brought with them only the tattiest of bare essentials. While on the run from the Special Branch, she refused point-blank the suggestion that she disguise herself as a dowdy little old lady and wore a striking red wig instead. Ruth loved Italian shoes, expensive perfumes, beautiful clothes and gourmet cuisine. But that's not to say she ever put fashion before the cause.

Ruth was born into both style and communism in 1925. Her parents, Matilda (Tilly to her friends) and Julius were, respectively, Lithuanian and Latvian Jewish immigrants who had toiled their way up to a good life in their newly adopted country. They were also instrumental in launching the Communist Party of South Africa and in 1923 Julius was elected chairman.

At a young age, Ruth picked up *stompies* of socialism from her parents' conversations with their left wing radical friends and became actively involved when she and her little brother Ronnie (who remained resolutely apolitical throughout his life) started tagging along with Tilly and Julius to the Communist Party's Sunday night meetings on the steps of Jo'burg City Hall.

In 1941, Ruth matriculated from Jeppe Girls High School and went on to study at Wits, where she became involved in various student societies, including the Young Communists League, and hung out with handsome provocateurs like Nelson Mandela (a snappy dresser himself), Ahmed Kathrada and a charismatic law student by the name of Ismail Meer. Ismail's slatternly flat on Market Street was a hotbed for student activists, who came to indulge in Indian curries and heated political discussions. To their parents' mutual dismay, Ruth and Ismail became an item.

While Tilly was delighted that Ruth was involved in such a radical circle, she wasn't that keen on Ismail, although it's not clear whether it was because he was Indian or because he wasn't Jewish or because she simply didn't like him. Despite her mother's reservations and the eyebrows they raised in public as a mixed-race couple even before the Immorality Act was declared in 1950, the love affair lasted four years.

Ruth graduated in 1945 and went to work for the welfare department, with the idea of researching the rapidly growing urban black population. Instead, she was assigned the mind-numbing task of working on Johannesburg's 50th Jubilee. When the mine workers' strike broke out, she quit her job without notice and reported to strike headquarters the next day to offer her services.

After the strike was crushed, Ruth joined the leftist weekly newspaper, the *Guardian*. It was the first in a string of papers that were banned by the apartheid government one after the other, only to re-emerge with the same staff and same ideals, but under a new name. When the *Guardian* was banned in 1952, it was resurrected within weeks as the

Clarion. She went on to work for the *People's World*, *Advance* and *New Age* as a journalist and editor, and eventually took over the helm of the incendiary monthly *Fighting Talk* from Lionel 'Rusty' Bernstein.

Ruth focused on social and labour journalism, writing up to 15 stories a week on poverty in the townships, gang violence and the bus boycotts. Her thorough, probing reporting balanced some of the rabidly dogmatic pro-communist pieces in the leftist papers for which she wrote and her investigative journalism was pioneering. She felt she could do much more than play an impartial and impassive camera and she took an active role in her stories to not only expose injustice, but also bring about change.

So, when she covered the women's anti-pass campaign and the march of 20 000 women on the Union Buildings in 1956, led by Lilian Ngoyi and Helen Joseph, she wasn't merely recording the events, she was raising awareness of the struggle, building heroes and educating people on more effective campaigns.

Among her most important work was the reporting she did over 17 years on the brutal farm labour scandals. In 1947, at just 22, following up on a 'cryptic little paragraph' in a rival newspaper, she and a churchman, Michael Scott, uncovered horrific abuses on a Bethal farm. Black labourers were bound with chains, beaten with sjamboks and forced to sleep naked and chained together in a cramped and filthy room. While her gender and complexion ruled out going gonzo undercover as *Drum*'s star reporter Henry Nxumalo did in 1952, her exposé caused a public uproar, not least from the 1 500 farmers and townsfolk who threatened to lynch the reporter and the priest for their 'unfounded allegations' when the pair returned to Bethal. They barely escaped, only to go straight on to meet with a group of black workers, who told them that far from blowing this out of proportion, Ruth had only touched on the edge of the foetid rottenness in the community. The labourers scrounged together enough money to pay the way for six representatives to return to Johannesburg with them to state their case.

The government responded with only a superficial investigation and the mainstream media were content to let it go at that. But Ruth dug deeper. She discovered that the government was rounding up illegal black immigrants and presenting them with the choice of volunteering for slave labour on potato farms or being deported. Then pass offenders were targeted. They were bust in police raids and told their infraction would mean months or even years in jail. Or they could work on a farm. The ugly truth was that the worst punishment a pass offence held at that time was a fine of a few pounds.

Ruth and the *Guardian*, together with a former labourer-turned-firebrand, Gert Sibande, led a campaign against the brutal conditions and later a legal assault on the farm owners. Little changed and the abuses dragged on for years.

In 1959, a gaunt man in filthy rags walked off the street into Ruth's offices at *New Age*. He'd come to her because of her reputation. There were new abuses and this time, labourers were being beaten to death on the farm of a man called Potgieter. He'd only just managed to escape after nine months of trying. He didn't come to complain, but to beg for help for a friend too weak to get away. Ruth set off at once, with her friends Wolfie Kodesh and Joe Gcabi, an ex-boxer she'd trained as a journalist. They dropped Joe off just outside the farm and while they waited for him in the car, Wolfie noticed a scrabble of raised dirt mounds by the side of the road.

Joe assumed a cringing stance and, cap in hand, went to ask the farmer if he could deliver a message to one of the labourers. The farmer nodded curtly, but minutes later, Joe was running down the road, hotly pursued by a *bakkie* and three *baas boys* on bicycles with sjamboks. The farmer's son had become suspicious. Joe dived into the car and they roared away, but not before Wolfie had another good look at those mounds and recognised them for what they were – shallow graves. Ruth wrote up the story immediately.

The ANC, using *New Age* as its mouthpiece, demanded a judicial enquiry and called for a national boycott on potatoes. It was the first time such an economic tactic had been used in South Africa and it was dazzlingly successful, spreading from the city centres to the most rural of communities. For three months potatoes piled up in shops and markets across the country, forcing the government to initiate a commission of enquiry. However, the most the Farmer's Union and the Bantu Affairs Department would concede was that the scandals were 'isolated incidences' and that there had been a 'technical fault' with the allocation of labour.

In her personal life, Ruth had become involved with another law student in 1948, a magnetic young socialist known as Joe Slovo. His real name was Yossel Mashel Slovo and although the 22-year old was slightly podgy, he was a charmer and a reveller, and with his brown curly hair and square-framed glasses, utterly adored by women.

Joe had been in love with Ruth for years. While he'd initially dismissed the beauty with her dark curls and immaculate make-up as the kind of intellectual who only liked to gab about making a difference, he was soon disabused of the assumption. When Ismail and Ruth split up, he was waiting.

The couple weren't an obvious match. Outside of their shared commitment to communism and changing the world, they were very different people. Joe was a genial raconteur with an easy, earthy sense of humour, while Ruth was focused, intense and, despite her fierce intelligence, desperately insecure, a trait she disguised with a veneer of arrogance. Their lifetime romance would prove to be tumultuous, marked by long separations, imprisonments, infidelities, ideological differences and wounding arguments, but for all their differences and the sharp cruelties, there was also a sense of fierce love, commitment and support – they buttressed each other against the world.

By 1949 they were living together and Ruth was pregnant with the first of three girls born in quick succession over the next four years: Shawn, Gillian and Robyn. That same year, the couple decided they'd flouted convention long enough and tied the knot at the magistrate's court with a simple signing of the registry. Ruth kept her last name and they celebrated with a raucous garden party at Tilly and Julius' house in Kensington, attended by every high profile dissident in town.

Ruth's parents bought them a house and a Citroën. Joe started practising law and Ruth, ever ambitious, took up motherhood and her career in journalism simultaneously. The '50s were idyllic years for the couple, fired up on activism and carried by a sense of optimism that the state's overthrow was imminent.

They travelled extensively together and apart. Ruth went to Prague, Dubrovnik and Moscow, attending youth conferences or reporting on communist states. In 1954, she spent four months in China, leaving her new two-month-old baby, Robyn, in the care of Tilly.

But the newly instated Nationalist Party government was cracking down, and Ruth and Joe were soon to feel the effects personally. In 1950, the Communist Party was banned. Undeterred, Ruth and Joe and their fellow subversives started up the Communist Party again in 1953, only this time underground and based on a cell structure to ensure secrecy, so that most members didn't know who their fellows were.

The first banning orders were just coming into effect and Ruth and Joe together with Nelson Mandela, Water Sisulu and hundreds of other activists were barred from attending public gatherings or meeting with more than two people at a time or joining any other anti-apartheid groups.

The Special Branch of the South African Police (known as Grey Shoes for their bad dress sense that identified them immediately to the discerning eye) started raiding activists' houses and offices for inflammatory literature and to ensure that no-one violated their banning orders. Once, they rocked up at Ruth's workplace at *New Age*, but she wasn't in yet. When she eventually *did* come clipping through the doors in her high heels and saw the pair of plainclothes cops waiting for her, she used a decoy to escape, nonchalantly asking a cub reporter, 'Is Miss First here?' Luckily the junior journalist caught on and when she replied in the negative, Ruth turned on her stilettos and clipped out again. She would not always be so lucky.

On 5 December 1956, *The Star* ran a photograph of the three Slovo daughters gathered around the breakfast table eating Rice Krispies. It was newsworthy, because, as six-year old Shawn explained, 'Mummy's gone to prison to look after the black people.' During the night, the government had rounded up and imprisoned 156 dissidents and 'troublemakers' involved in the Congress movement, including Ruth and Joe. They were to be tried for treason.

The trial, which dragged on for four years, was an untidy affair (documented by Helen Joseph in her book *If This Be Treason*) with bungled evidence and incomprehensible arguments from the prosecution that only proved the pettiness of the fascist state. Eventually everyone was acquitted.

In 1958, after charges were dismissed against all but 30 of the accused, Ruth and Joe threw a bash at their home to celebrate, only to make the headlines when the Special Branch descended, having heard that there was scandalous interracial fraternising going on and blacks being served liquor. By the time the police burst in, the assembled revellers had managed to ditch all the alcohol and the party picked up again with soft drinks after they left.

But Ruth and Joe were not off the hook just yet. When the State of Emergency was declared in 1960 after the Sharpeville Massacre, Joe was picked up in a mass arrest that scooped up 20 000 people. Ruth, for some reason, wasn't on the list, but she didn't wait around. Donning a bright red wig, she took the girls to Swaziland, followed soon after by her parents, where they hid out for six months, together with other activist families.

When the furore died down, the children and their grandparents returned to their home. Ruth went into hiding in Johannesburg, already planning the reformation of the opposition. She ended up staying with architect Donald Turgel and his wife, then one of the many secret safe houses dotted about, although in some cases the owners who rented out a room or let a friend of a friend crash on the couch were ignorant of just who they were hosting. In the beginning, Donald was under the impression that Ruth was Ruth Gordon, a friend of his wife's. When she eventually dropped her guard, she let him in completely and the two embarked on a four-year-long affair.

On this particular account, Joe was hardly innocent either. He was renowned as a flirt and once when a potential conquest reacted with surprise when he kissed her on the mouth during a party, he told her,

'You've got the wrong idea about communism. It isn't about making everyone miserable; it's about making everyone happy.' It was only after his death in 1995 that his daughter Gillian discovered he had an illegitimate son he had never acknowledged.

Joe was released six months after his arrest, but it was becoming painfully clear that the ANC's policy of passive resistance was not working. In 1961, Nelson and Joe made the difficult decision to set up a paramilitary wing of the ANC and the Communist Party, citing the old African saying '*sebatana ha se bokwe ka diatla*' ('the attacks of the wild beast cannot be averted with bare hands'). It became Umkhonto We Sizwe and while a select group were sent to China for training, Joe led the first wave of sabotage. He was interrupted trying to set a home-made bomb that was intended to burn down the Drill Hall, used for preliminary hearings at the Treason Trial, and was forced to abandon the attempt.

In the meantime, Ruth found that she was being silenced, as surely as if she had hands choking her throat. The Congress of Democrats, of which she was an executive member, was banned in 1962, as were both the papers she edited, *Fighting Talk* and *New Age*. The latter resurfaced almost immediately as *Spark*, but this time the government had outmanoeuvred her – all the staff, including Ruth, were banned from writing or even setting foot in the door of a newspaper's offices. *Spark* soon folded.

In 1960, she had spent time in Windhoek researching a book on South West Africa, then still under South Africa's dictatorial mandate. Over the next few years, she completed her incisive history and in 1963, violating her banning order, had it published overseas by Penguin. The government retaliated by slapping her with another banning order, forbidding her from leaving Johannesburg. Still, she carried on, writing pamphlets for the movement, involving herself in the pirate station Radio Freedom, broadcast from a mobile transmitter and studying to become a librarian, in an attempt to get around her banning, although she found the work of cataloguing a poor replacement for the highs of investigative journalism and fomenting revolution.

Joe, who was being painted by the press as the very embodiment of the *Rooi Gevaar* or Red Peril, was being watched by the Special Branch and his every move reported in the papers. He left one day on a 'short trip' and skedaddled over the border to oversee the training of MK recruits and to wheedle arms and ammunition from neighbouring countries sympathetic to the cause, fully intending to return. But something momentous happened that would prevent this, and would cripple the struggle for years to come.

On 11 July 1963, an innocuous baker's van followed by another innocuous dry cleaner's van rolled through the gates of an equally innocuous Rivonia farm. In reality, the vans were bristling with Special Branch cops and the Lilliesleaf Farm was the nerve centre of the resistance movement. Ironically, the night before the point had been raised about how dangerous it was for all the resistance leaders to be together in one place. Now it was too late. The van doors flew open and 40 cops swooped on the property, taking 14 activists into custody and confiscating damning evidence that included maps of potential sabotage sites, provocative pamphlets and bomb ingredients.

They came for Ruth one month later. Special Branch cornered her in the corridor of Wits University and escorted her home to watch them search for evidence that would implicate her as a co-conspirator in the Rivonia farm debacle. Tilly orbited outside, peeking anxiously through the windows as the police turned the house upside down. Ruth had long since destroyed anything incriminating, but while the police failed to find the secret drawer built into her desk, they did find a long-forgotten back issue of *Fighting Talk*. Possession of the banned publication could cost her a year in jail. Ruth was furious with herself for the oversight. Just before they took her away, Julius arrived home with the three girls and seeing what was going on, Shawn fled to the garden so Ruth wouldn't see her cry.

Although her friends, including Nelson Mandela, Walter Sisulu and Govan Mbeki were to be dragged before the judges in the Rivonia Trial facing 222 counts of sabotage and charges of organising an armed uprising in October, Ruth was detained under the controversial 90-day clause that allowed the government to keep dissidents for three months without charging them. It's been speculated that she wasn't put on trial because the government feared the public reaction if a white woman appeared in the dock facing a possible death sentence. Perhaps they didn't have enough evidence to nail her or maybe they were hoping she would turn state's witness. Whatever the reason, Ruth was to endure a hellish time of solitary confinement that nearly broke her.

Her cell was dark and claustrophobic, barely larger than her bed. She wrote that it reminded her of the inside of 'a steel trunk'. She was denied any reading material except for the Bible and the obscene graffiti scratched into the walls. Worst of all, she had little human contact with anyone except her interrogators and the wardresses, although Joe sent her carefully self-censored letters of support and encouragement. Very occasionally she was allowed visitors.

She remained fastidious throughout. She was allowed to keep her make-up and she meticulously applied it every day, put on her earrings and brushed out her thick curls, that she usually had straightened once a week at the hairdresser. When she held onto the bars to look out her little window, she did so using a tissue to avoid dirtying her hands. She was 38 and afraid she was losing her looks.

She was moved to Pretoria Central Prison just before the Rivonia Trial commenced. She was sick with loneliness, succumbing to ennui and frustration. To prevent the onset of insanity, she plucked out the hairs on her legs one by one with her tiny pair of tweezers, made and re-made her bed, repeatedly packed her suitcase, folded her clothes, wiped down the walls, unstitched the seams of her pillow case and sewed them back up, over and over. After her unbearable isolation and the interrogation tactics designed to break her down, could she really be blamed for responding to a gesture of kindness whatever the source?

Ruth had refused to co-operate from the first. But towards the end of the year, four days before her 90 days were up, a finical 34-year old lieutenant entered the scene. A former fraud squad officer, Johannes Jakobus Viktor told Ruth he was very reluctantly 'on loan' to the Special Branch. He did everything right to set her at ease, playing good cop to the evil bastards who yelled at her in the interrogation room. He said he'd known Joe, had actually saved him once, from a gang of stiletto-wielding prostitutes who were chasing him down the court corridors after a case where he'd represented a rival madam. Viktor had shown him another way out. Ruth was too smart to fall for his show of sympathy, yet too vulnerable not to. He wanted her cooperation. She wanted an ally.

In the unflinchingly personal book she wrote about her time in prison, *117 Days* Ruth recorded, 'Between Viktor and me there was an atmosphere of bristling animosity. He was provocative; I was waspish. And felt all the better for it.' For his part, Viktor declared that he had fallen in love with the beautiful red and encouraged the later (false) rumours that he was the one procuring her special privileges such as the gift of a crossword book.

Her daughters were allowed to visit her days before her release, but Tilly also brought news that an imprisoned comrade who knew her was spilling his guts. It could mean that Ruth would be charged. She was on tenterhooks and when one of her interrogators called her to a room and told her that she was to be released, she didn't believe him and shouted at him that he was being unnecessarily cruel by raising her hopes. 'Don't bluff me ... Don't make a farce out of this thing.' Eventually he convinced her and in spite of herself, Ruth could feel the giddy elation building. The wardress helped her pack her suitcase and a smiling sergeant behind the desk filled out her release papers.

Outside, she was five steps away from the phone booth, coin already in hand, to call Tilly to tell her to come and pick her up, when two policemen intercepted her and grimly served her with another 90-day sentence. They escorted her back into the charge office where the no-longer-jovial sergeant put a new set of papers in order.

Back in her cell she sat for hours, shaking with sobs as she unleashed the self-pity that she had kept tightly locked in during her humiliation outside. And then she made two horrible mistakes. She went on hunger strike in protest and, in her debilitated state, decided to give a statement to find out what they knew. It was better than sitting around waiting, she reasoned and she thought she could outwit her captors.

After the first terrifying session surrounded by cops gagging for information, willing her to slip up, she realised the extent of her blunder. She revealed only names they already knew of people who were outside the country, but she knew she couldn't endure another session. The next day she started eating, but refused to accompany Viktor back to the interrogation room. He said her mother was there to see her and unable to resist, Ruth went to see Tilly. It was on this occasion that she neglected to put on her make-up. When Tilly whispered on her way out, 'Are you cracking up?' Ruth nodded. Her mother added, 'We're depending on you.'

It was too much for Ruth. Deprived of everything she loved and suffering the effects of months of seclusion that were eroding her sharp mind and her ability to concentrate, she became convinced that she had already committed a hideous betrayal in saying as much as she had. She tortured herself over the razor-edged flirtation with Viktor and terrified that her friends would condemn her as a traitor (she always worried too much about what other people thought), she wrote a suicide note in the back of the crossword book she had been allowed. She apologised for her cowardice, expressed her love for her family and then swallowed every sleeping pill her doctor had brought her on a recent visit.

She woke up hours later. Still alive. Ruth wept hysterically for days, but when she finally emerged from the jag, she had recovered a sense of calm. She refused to resume her statement and spent the rest of her days in confinement quietly. On the 117th day of her confinement, she was released, this time for real. Ruth had no idea why they were letting her go, but she wrote that she had the terrible feeling that the Special Branch were not done with her. That they would come for her again. Eighteen years later, they did.

Ruth immediately started making plans to join Joe in exile in England. She knew he could never return under the existing regime and her banning orders, which remained valid, made it impossible for her to continue her work in South Africa. But she still felt as though she was giving up.

She tried her luck by applying for a passport that would allow her back into the country at a later date, but was refused and she was forced to apply for a one-way exit permit instead. Even this took months to come through, despite Prime Minister Vorster's claims that he was quite happy to be rid of people like her.

She was still restricted to Johannesburg and she spent the Christmas of 1964 alone. The children were holidaying with friends in Cape Town and most of her intimates were either in exile or banned themselves and forbidden from contacting her. Finally, her exit permit came through in March 1965 and together with the children and her mother Tilly, Ruth moved to London and was reunited with Joe.

The family had trouble adjusting to the city and on the first night in their new house a sharp crack and a splintered window convinced them that assassins were trying to kill them. It turned out to be two teenagers messing around with an air rifle .

Ruth didn't have a job and the British papers pegged her as a 'Marxist' and refused to use her, claiming she was incapable of objectivity. She became involved in anti-apartheid politics instead, holding talks and seminars and took to writing her account of her time in prison, *117 Days*. It was her most personal and painful work and, as she had feared, when it was released, some of her so-called friends vilified her for cracking under pressure even though the information she had revealed was worthless. The book was later made into a movie, bizarrely re-named *90 Days* with Ruth playing herself.

Joe travelled a great deal, spending time in Angola, Zambia and Moçambique for his work in coordinating the armed insurrection. Ruth and Joe were beginning to fight over ideology – Joe was a hardline Marxist who thought the Soviet regime could do no wrong, while Ruth was outraged by the USSR's invasion of Czechoslovakia and believed that Communist China was a better model for the new world.

Ruth was also travelling and writing and in 1973, landed a job lecturing at Durham University on the sociology of underdevelopment. In the late '60s, she researched and edited several activists' books, including Nelson Mandela's *No Easy Walk to Freedom*, Govan Mbeki's

The Peasant's Revolt and was deported from Kenya for working on Oginga Odinga's *Not Yet Uhuru*.

In the '70s, she published *The Barrel of A Gun* on military coups in Africa, *Libya: The Elusive Revolution*, *The Mozambican Miner: A Study in the Export of Labour* and in 1980 co-wrote a biography of proto-feminist Olive Schreiner with a British academic, Anne Scott.

In 1976, she moved to Moçambique with Joe, leaving her now grown children behind to take up the post of professor and research director at the Centre for African Studies at the Eduardo Mondlane University in Maputo.

Joe was still blowing stuff up, coordinating sabotage attacks from his base in Maputo, such as the spectacular destruction of a state-of-the-art coal-to-oil conversion plant and nearby refinery just outside of Johannesburg in 1980. He was jumpy in those years, always checking the undercarriage of his car before driving it and carrying a pistol, strapped to his ankle. He had good cause to be skittish. In the '80s, Ruth's journalist friend, Joe Gqabi, was gunned down outside his house in the then Rhodesia, another two ANC activists died in a car bomb in Swaziland in front of their children and the organisation's headquarters in London were firebombed. But no-one could have predicted that it would be Ruth they targeted next.

Moçambique mellowed Ruth. The primitive conditions meant that she was no longer able to indulge her taste for high fashion or immaculate grooming. She took to wearing simple cotton dresses and letting her hair dry naturally in a frizzy semi-afro. She used her expensive Italian shoes to beat off the hordes of cockroaches that assailed her kitchen.

Her success in the Centre also made her feel less competitive with Joe. She was doing good work and getting kudos for it. Under her guidance, the Centre became known for its serious and innovative research, undertaking work specifically commissioned by African governments looking for answers to social or development problems, rather than getting bogged down in academia simply for the sake of it. Of course, some of what she did could have been seen as a danger to the apartheid regime, such as her research into how Moçambique could pull itself out of its economic dependence on South Africa, but it wasn't as though she was actively involved in the struggle or even still a member of the Communist Party. But she was still Joe's wife.

Unbeknown to the ANC, most of the mail for Southern Africa was routed through Johannesburg's Jan Smuts airport and sorted in a huge chamber nicknamed the 'bomb room'. Missives to listed persons were often intercepted and when a parcel from a UN agency addressed to Ruth First landed in their laps, Special Branch leapt at the opportunity. They unsealed the manila envelope using kettles specially modified for the purpose, wired it with explosives and sent it on its way.

On 17 August 17 1982, Ruth was in her office with three friends and colleagues, Pallo Jordan, Aquino da Braganza and Bridget O'Laughlin, waiting to have a farewell drink with a colleague. When Ruth went to collect her post from her cubbyhole, Aquino teased her good-naturedly, 'You always get mail.' Ruth shot back, 'That's because I, unlike you, always write letters.' As she tore open the unassuming brown envelope with its hand-written address, it ripped the office apart. The force of the blast blew out the window and brought the industrial air conditioning unit crashing to the floor. Pallo, Aquino and Bridget sustained burns and injuries and burst eardrums. Ruth was collapsed over the desk. Weeping, Bridget called frantically for an ambulance, forgetting in her trauma that Maputo had none.

When Joe received a frantic phone call, he rushed to the scene, arriving just as Ruth's three companions were being shuttled to the hospital in a commandeered jeep. He shoved his way through the shocked crowd, but when he saw Ruth's feet in the tan high-heel shoes (her favourites) sticking out from the ruins of the room, he stopped abruptly. The stillness and the angle of her legs told him everything he needed to know. In the aftermath, they would have to scrape her remains from the walls.

In the Truth Commission hearing held 17 years later in South Africa, apartheid spy and mastermind Craig Williamson denied that Ruth was the intended target, even though the envelope was clearly addressed to her and she would never have opened Joe's mail. To the horror and outrage of Ruth's friends and family, he was granted political amnesty. Later, her daughter, Gillian Slovo, confronted Craig Williamson while she was researching her autobiographical book on growing up with Ruth and Joe as parents. He told her it was just business as usual in the strategy of 'terrorising the terrorist' and 'almost luck of the draw'. He expressed no remorse, but confided it was Special Branch that had started the rumours blaming Joe for Ruth's assassination.

Writer Ronald Segal described Ruth's death as 'the final act of censorship'. She was buried in Maputo beside 19 black men, all MK soldiers. Statesmen and ambassadors from some 34 countries attended the funeral.

Joe returned to South Africa in 1990 to join the peace talks and remarried. In 1994 he became Housing Minister in the new ANC government, but only a year later died of cancer. Shawn wrote a screenplay about her mother's life, *A World Apart*, Gillian wrote her autobiography *Every Secret Thing* and based two novels broadly on her family's experiences, *Ties of Blood* and *Red Dust*, recently released as a film. After seeing Craig Williamson lie about her mother's death before the Truth Commission, she abandoned South Africa for good and now lives in London.

Commemorating Ruth's life at the time of her funeral, Joe wrote, 'She was a lady of style and elegance, both in wit and vanity. She was a comrade whose intolerance of hypocrisy, inefficiency and humbug won her the respect even of those who were discomforted by the razor-sharpness of her thrusts. She was a friend and companion with a rich, albeit private passion ... Why did they do it? Why was she who had nothing to do with the planning or implementation of armed activities, chosen as the target of their killing machine? The answer is crystal-clear. Her boundless energy and intellectual productivity in opposition to racist savagery posed a threat to them which was no less sharp than a whole arsenal of weapons.'

It's All Dolly

Dolly Rathebe

1940s Sophiatown – or Kofifi as it was known to its inhabitants – and the scene was kicking. Dubbed the 'Chicago of South Africa', the community was a ganglion for gangsters, firebrands, intellectuals, poets and politicians, musicians, bohemians, journalists, shebeen queens and ordinary wage slaves come to find work in the big bright city of Johannesburg, a scant seven kilometres away.

It was coloured by its populace, a riotous mélange of class, colour and education, and the American movies people flocked to see at the swanky cinema, the Odin, that informed both the fashion and the lifestyle. People would resort to mail order catalogues or friends overseas to get their hands on the coveted 'can't-gets', such as stylish brogues, zoot suits and hats that cost a week's salary.

Local gangs like the Americans, the Gestapo and the Spoilers were impressed not only by the sharp style of movie stars, but also by the trademark gestures of the cinematic hoodlums played by the likes of Humphrey Bogart, and would take to imitating their calling cards, for instance crunching down on a green apple after a fight. And there were many fights. Kofifi was a *rof* place, averaging two murders a week and a score more woundings in the metallic flashes of knife fights that broke out with the same speed and regularity as the police raids on the illegal shebeens frequented by white and black alike.

Sophiatown was the incubator for an emerging school of fired-up young writers that included Can Themba, Henry Nxumalo and Lewis Nkosi, who wielded words like the spitting Gatling guns of the gangsters on screen at the Odin. And it was a hotbed of the emerging struggle, where a young Nelson Mandela took on all contenders in the boxing ring 45 years before he finally KO'd the apartheid regime, while activists such as Lilian Ngoyi stirred hearts and crowds with provocative speeches.

Kofifi was also the place where a new brand of music was germinating to suit the urbane tastes of the emerging urban black population – and at the head of it all was one sultry swinging singer by the name of Dolly Rathebe, who at 19 was to become Africa's first black film star and a newly formed *Drum* magazine's favourite cover girl. Dolly was the face of the new African jazz movement and her role on screen and stage and pin-up posters would pave the way for others like Miriam Makeba and Dorothy Masuka.

Her name is still popular ikasi slang slung around today, meaning 'swell' or 'great' or 'everything's fine', as in: 'How's it going?' 'Dolly, man. Dolly Rathebe.'

Actually, Dolly Rathebe wasn't even her real name. The girl who would become the most famous and vivid chanteuse of Sophiatown's jazz scene was born Josephine Malatsi in Randfontein in 1928. She never liked her name and when she started singing, in the grand tradition of the glamorous showbiz metamorphosis, she took on a new one, nicked from a childhood friend, Eileen Dolly Rathebe.

Before she was Dolly, Josephine was a raucous tomboy who grew up in Sophiatown and revelled in playing pranks on her classmates, climbing trees and jitterbugging with her friends on the Makouvlei waste dump nearby, belting out radio hits in that smoky voice of hers. Without any formal training other than the staid and regimented school choir, Dolly took to singing at wakes, weddings and any social occasion that lent itself to a girl bursting into song.

She left school in 1943 with a standard five certificate, then regarded as an acceptable school-leaving qualification, at least for black girls, and took to the Sophiatown stage, winning over the hardline audiences who regularly booed acts off stage. That old New York maxim about how if you can make it here, you can make it anywhere could well have been written for Sof'town. There was nothing soft about it.

In the rollicking series *Drum* magazine ran on Dolly in 1957, hothead intellectual Can Themba described her as the woman who revitalised the scene with her shimmering voice and her voluptuous shimmy, using the stage like a boxer does the ring. 'She went before the audience and treated them to live, wriggling flesh and she purred to them in a shaggy, hairy, deep, sultry mezzo,' stirring up strange desires and 'dreams of torrid love and wanton abandon'.

She was inspired by Lena Horne, the darling of America's 1940s film classics *Stormy Weather* and *Cabin in the Sky*, Ella Fitzgerald, Dakota Staton, Ethel Waters and Sarah Vaughan and most significantly, the local 'Empress of the Blues', Emily Kwenane.

After making her debut in Sophiatown, she moved on to become the favourite of the white nightclubs of Johannesburg, although being a black songstress in those times came with its own brand of trouble. One night, returning from a show with the Manhattan Brothers, the troupe was stopped by the Flying Squad demanding to see their passes. When they were unable to produce them, they were locked up for the night.

She also had to be wary of the gangs. Ever since she was 15, she had been a gangster's moll, although not always willingly. As Can Themba writes, 'You must know one thing. When a girl hits the top with the general public, to certain brands of Africans, she becomes the 'fair prize' for the man who can throw the muscle – or swing the knife or squeeze the trigger.' One of her first boyfriends, a 'clever' (or sharp) Sophiatown *ou* called Hasie, beat her into loving him, not unlike her father, who abused her physically for years before he died. Hasie was to meet a violent end, stabbed to death in a drunken brawl in Alexandra, but like the 'nightingale' Miriam Makeba, Dolly went on to have a long association with the most notorious gang in Sophiatown – the Americans.

It was common practice for the gangs to kidnap beautiful women for a few nights of pleasure-taking, oft-times willing but just as often not. One night, Dolly came out of a gig to find a car waiting for her. Initially relieved to be spared the hassle of public transport, she became suspicious when a guy she didn't recognise in the back claimed he knew her from school days. She yanked open the door and made a break for it.

Despite her rising musical stardom, Dolly always said her life only really took off in 1949. It was the year her parents died in quick succession, leaving her an orphan, but it was also the year that she was discovered at a picnic by talent scout, Sam Alcock. He dispatched her to a movie audition at the Bantobang Social Centre, but she looked so ragged in her swing skirt and takkies that the pianist had to be convinced, reluctantly, to play for her. Dolly sang 'Salt Lake City Blues' by Kevin In The Sky like nobody's business, blowing away any concerns about her scruffy dress. The director Don Swanson was ecstatic and so was Dolly – winning the part meant she could afford a new pair of shoes.

Jim Comes To Jo'burg was the first film about black South Africa. Naturally, Dolly played the nightclub singer, swathed in a glittering dress and crooning the words of a ballad that summed up all the turmoil of the eponymous Jim when confronted with the turmoil of the big city – *'Jo'burg City, the Golden City / What did I come here for? / Oh, Jo'burg City, the Golden City / I'm far away from my home.'* In the film one of the characters says, 'when she sings, she sings like the low humming of a slow moving river.'

For the most part, the film disconcerted white audiences, while black audiences crammed into theatres to see, for the first time, a movie that reflected their lives. Dolly was a sensation and at the premiere she was met by crowds shouting, *'Mayibuye iAfrika!'*, meaning 'let it return', 'let us reclaim our culture.'

Ironically, while Dolly was already an icon in the black community, the object of desire of every man and the envy of every woman, it was to be an act of repression by the apartheid government that would make her famous among white South Africans. It was shortly after *Drum* was founded in 1951 that the black title 'discovered' the 19-year old songstress and film star, and commissioned its white German photographer, Jurgen Schadeberg, to photograph her for the cover.

Jurgen remembers that they already attracted odd looks from the white folks when he photographed her at Zoo Lake, but he didn't pay it any mind and they moved on to their next location, a small and easily accessible mine dump near Suburban Street as a stand-in for the beach. He started shooting Dolly in her bikini and then a sundress when suddenly a fervour of cops stormed up the 30-metre slopes of fine sand that swallowed their boots, breathless and losing their caps in the excitement of catching a white man and a black woman surely up to no good.

The cops were rough, pushing them around and insisting that Dolly lift her dress to reveal what she wore underneath, urging 'Higher! Higher!' before they hustled the pair away to the station to charge them with contravening the Immorality Act. Unable to prove anything, the charges were eventually dropped, but not before the station commander delivered a stern lecture to Jurgen, as a supposedly witless foreigner, of the perils of hanging out with 'these people'.

The photographer was livid when he got back to *Drum*'s office, then shared by the *Sunday Times* and *The Sunday Express*, and described to his colleagues the Gestapo actions of the South African Police. By the following Sunday it was splashed across the headlines of the papers and Dolly became a household name.

She never let the fame go to her head. Doll was always the epitome of the impetuous street-smart Sophiatown girl, albeit one now with a touch more grace and style as befitted a movie star. Her success wasn't a fluke. She went on to star in *The Magic Garden* a misadventure of comic misunderstandings when a thief buries stolen money in the garden of a desperately poor family. The cash passes through several hands before landing in the paws of actor Victor Qwayi who uses it to pay lobola for Dolly's character. She also had a bit part in the first film version of *Cry, The Beloved Country* and the film's star, Sidney Poitier, took her hit number – and all-time favourite song – 'Sindi' back to the States. (Coincidentally the tune was recorded at the same time by American jazzman Johnny Hodges as 'Something To Put Your Foot To'.)

Her music career was on fire (and perhaps not uncoincidentally, the swanky Ritz hotel happened to burn down the night she performed there with The Ink Spots). She performed at Selbourne Hall in Johannesburg and toured the country in the 1950s with Alf Herbert's Jazz Train, and when the canny promoter started his *African Jazz and Variety* revue in 1954, Dolly was the main attraction, requiring guards backstage to protect her from ardent fans. While the show originally showcased African music, promoting black musicians such as Hugh Masekela and Miriam Makeba, by 1956 it had turned into burlesque.

But while Dolly was out there killing her audiences across the colour bar, her personal life was messier than her immaculately groomed stage appearance suggested. She didn't have a home of her own and slept at friends' houses or in shebeens after a night of heavy drinking. She was a huge party girl and for a while, she *klapped* the bottle as did many Sophiatown residents, including Can Themba who eventually drank himself to death. The parties were notorious, frequented by white bohemians, black intellectuals and ordinary people who drank, talked and jived in someone's run-down backroom, where, if you were lucky, you might find a broken-down piano.

Dolly could be a bit *rof* herself and after a night out on the town, sometimes got into drunken brawls with other women, who were apparently either envious of her success or jealous because they thought she was after their men. Dolly gave as good as she sang and while Can Themba claimed her nickname 'Katz' was inspired by the tsotsitaal *'rats'* (meaning quick on the uptake), her son, Smilo Duru, says it was because she was known to use her nails like claws. One fight turned nasty and Dolly was hospitalised after a stabbing that just missed her spine. As to whether she *was* out to snare other women's guys, Dolly reportedly always loved boys and her relationships were tempestuous and often short-lived. Or as Can Themba wrote, 'Her love affairs of this period were like wisps of smoke. One moment thick and meaningful, the next moment gone and forgotten.' Her boyfriend at the time, Mboy, an Americans hoodlum, is credited with adding 'Dolly' to the lexicon of tsotsitaal, that remix of African languages, Afrikaans and slang that was spoken at the time. Although they never married, in 1952 Dolly gave birth to Mboy's daughter, Zola.

By the mid-1950s, one by one the Americans were being arrested for their daring raids on goods trains and shipped off to the Fort gaol. There were rumours that the Spoilers were gunning for Dolly, intending to kidnap her; in the face of all this, she sent her daughter to live with Mboy's parents and moved in with an aunt in Orlando, Soweto.

She was just in time. In 1955, despite mass protests, Sophiatown was unceremoniously dismantled: people were forcibly removed to Meadowlands in trucks with all their possessions, while the bulldozers tore down their houses. Any fledgling hopes of tolerance and equality that had been so much a way of life in the community that no-one thought to comment on it, disappeared.

In Soweto, Dolly met Welcome Duru, a boxing promoter who was also the leader of a small-time band, the Basin Blues Combo. Because Dolly had been involved with all the major gangsters, but none had yet produced a ring, Welcome figured the way to win her was to marry her as fast as possible. He promptly shelled out lobola to her remaining family and whisked her off to the Eastern Cape (although it's also been said she left Jozi because of the stabbing). Dolly quickly discovered that Welcome was the most prominent playboy of the Eastern Cape and that he already had a horde of illegitimate children and mistresses who weren't too charmed that he'd married a Soweto woman.

Her absence left a gap in the music scene that new would-be divas were flocking to fill. Miriam Makeba and the Manhattan Brothers were a sensation and their song, 'Lovely Lies' was already a hit in America. There was also Johanna Radebe, the husky Abigail Khubeka, who had been directly inspired by Doll's deep sweet voice to launch her own career, Thoko Thomo with her overtly sexual shows, and Dorothy Masuka. Dolly wasn't going to take it lying down. She made a comeback, appearing in the Township Jazz shows and it wasn't long before Alf wooed her back to African Jazz, performing with Thandi Claasen and Hot Dot Masuka.

In 1957, Dolly gave birth to a son, Smilo, and two years later, a daughter, Nontsikilelo (or Ntsiki). The pregnancy cost her a movie role in *Come Back Africa*, which Miriam Makeba starred in instead. Unhappy in her relationship, Dolly left Welcome shortly thereafter, but the travelling showbiz life wasn't exactly conducive to raising kids and Dolly still didn't have a stable home. Although she was a devoted and deeply principled mother, the demands of her career meant that for much of the time she was forced to leave Ntsiki and Smilo to be raised by relatives. She married again – to John Smith, a New Orleans jazz hound working aboard a ship who she met in Durban, but her family were dead-set against her moving to the States and they eventually divorced amicably.

Dolly sang with all the top bands, calling out, '*Thata inja!*' ('Take it, dog' in Zulu) when urging a bandmate to take a solo. She toured with the jazz-marabi style Elite Swingsters in the early '60s and the Manhattan Brothers, even travelling to Lourenço Marques (now Maputo) in Moçambique. But the landscape was changing and Dolly, with her jazzier style, couldn't keep up.

The township music scene had already been diminished when many of the top stars, such as Miriam Makeba and Thandi Claasen left to perform in the Broadway production *King Kong* in London in 1959. After the Sharpeville Massacre in 1960, the government cracked down, making it illegal for black performers to do their thing in venues that sold alcohol, eliminating the white nightclubs and concert halls and much of the audience that might have sustained the jazz greats.

Worst of all, by the mid to late '60s, musical tastes were shifting more towards mbaqanga groups such as the Mahotella Queens and later, disco and soul. Alf's shows were criticised for being too imitative of American styles. In 1976, the scene suffered another blow when riots flattened many of the township halls, writing off most of the venues.

In around 1966, Dolly retired from the chaos of the music scene. While Miriam was in exile in America and then Guinea, performing at

President Kennedy's birthday, writing songs in New York and testifying before the UN about apartheid, Dolly kept the home fires burning. She moved to Cape Town, without her children, and survived for several years by running a shebeen in the back room of her house in Elsies River and selling dagga on the side. As her lifelong friend Abigail Khubeka says, 'It was a business. It wasn't like she went downhill. She always maintained her style.'

Dolly eventually moved back to Johannesburg and settled in Mabopane, just north of Pretoria, reclaimed her kids – by now all grown up – and started another shebeen business. She had one last romance that lasted some 15 years, but her family and friends won't talk about it; all Smilo will say is 'that gentleman had an attitude to her kids and he was dismissed'.

While she was still intermittently involved in acting in the 1980s, starring in *Mapantsula* and the remake of *Cry, The Beloved Country* as the lead, this time, opposite James Earl Jones, her singing voice might have been lost if it weren't for the providential intervention of that *Drum* photographer, Jurgen Schadeberg. In 1990, he and his wife Claudia were trying to make a movie about Henry Nxumalo and the heydey of *Drum* magazine in Sophiatown. The couple wanted an authentic soundtrack, so they recruited Dolly, bringing her out of mothballs and reunited her with the Elite Swingsters, who hadn't played a gig for around ten years.

Unfortunately, when *Cry, The Beloved Country* premiered, the apartheid government flipped out and promptly shut down all film projects that could be considered 'anti-South African' or subversive, including Jurgen's. The film was never made (Zola Maseko's recently released *Drum* is an entirely different vision), but Dolly's comeback had already picked up an irresistible momentum with the new multiracial audiences. Her friend Queen Mdaba convinced her, 'The whole world needs you again.'

The Elite Swingsters' leader, Peter Mokonotela, devised arrangements to showcase Dolly's vocals, which had by then, according to Rob Allingham, the band's road manager for four years, taken on an even smokier timbre, like a fine wine maturing with age. The band released three albums, combining big band jazz, blues and marabi sounds, *Woza* in 1991, *A Call for Peace* in 1993 and *Siya Ganda* (We Are Going) in 1995 with Dolly belting out sizzlers like 'Kofifi', 'Sip'n Fly', 'Amagama', 'Emalangeni' (Jail) and 'Ten Ten Special'.

Nelson Mandela was a huge admirer of hers and Dolly, with her magnificent sense of humour, was known to joke, 'I don't know why he didn't marry me.' Nelson had known her since the days of *Drum* back in Sophiatown and told the Elite Swingsters that during his interminable imprisonment, he believed he'd never hear African jazz again.

In 1994, she performed at his inauguration as well as at a private party at his Houghton house, and later went on to play at several of his birthday parties. Once, when he was speaking in Toronto, Dolly was flown out as a surprise special guest to sing Xhosa songs. As a gesture of love and admiration and because she struggled with public transport, Nelson bought her a car in 1994. She was terribly proud of it, but because she couldn't drive, she was chauffeured by a neighbour, Lucas Makhubela.

Dolly and the Elite Swingsters landed international gigs, performing at the MASA Festival in Abidjan in the Ivory Coast and at the Nantes Festival in France, both in 1998. Dolly performed in the US for Prince Charles and also travelled to Germany, France and Amsterdam, sometimes accompanying and promoting the documentary Jurgen and Claudia made, *Dolly And The Inkspots*. In 2001 Miriam Makeba, who called Dolly 'our first lady of song' organised a tribute concert for Dolly at Felicia Mabuza-Suttle's Back O'The Moon Restaurant at Gold Reef City, which took its moniker from an old Sophiatown jazz joint. Abigail Khubeka recalls that it was an amazing reunion. 'All the girls from the '50s and '60s were there. It's good to do things for people while they're still alive and Dolly enjoyed it. The honour we gave her kept her alive. It made her happy.'

Dolly used the money raised by the concert to start Meriting kwaDolly – (Dolly's Retreat), a community hall at Mabopane started in 2001 and officially opened on Women's Day 2003. Meriting kwaDolly provides a space for the rural community's elderly to collect their pension grants without having to pay a surcharge and where they are sheltered from the elements.

Dolly began to enjoy real success and recognition that allowed her to command good fees – significant for her as the sole breadwinner for her children and grandchildren. In 2005, she was booked to perform at Carnegie Hall and do an eight-month tour of Europe. She told Smilo, 'I'm so excited! In eight months I'm going to be a millionaire.' And then, completely unexpectedly, she was struck down by a stroke. Miriam took her to hospital and when she died shortly thereafter, it was Nelson Mandela who made the announcement to the world from his Houghton home.

Before she died, Dolly asked to be buried in Soweto with 'al daai clevers' from Sophiatown. There were three funerals to commemorate her passing, one at the Market Theatre, one at her centre in Mabopane and one in Soweto. To commemorate her, Avenue Road in central Johannesburg was renamed for her (and the girl whose name she once 'stole') – Dolly Rathebe.

Unfortunately, Dolly's family dissolved into ugly infighting over her will, which she had amended shortly before her death to leave everything to Smilo. He says he was the only one close to her and is now struggling to keep Meriting kwaDolly running.

Her legacy is also curtailed by the shortage of recordings. According to Rob Allingham, between 1950 and 1956, she made about 20 recordings, but didn't see the inside of a studio again until 'Woza' in 1991. She told him it simply didn't pay enough, but the result is a dearth of her throaty purr today except on those Elite Swingster records and a few Dolly and the Inkspots recordings.

Dolly loved to be called the first African film star and in the sharp tsotsitaal she still used throughout her life, she always maintained, 'Ek is die ousie van die stuk' (I'm the leading lady).

The Brothel Queen & The Alabama

Black Sophie

Harvesting guano was a shit job. It was such a shit job, in fact, that sailors had to be conned into it or ambushed by heavies or 'crimps', who would spike unwitting sailors' drinks with the 19th century equivalent of Rohypnol or just bonk them over the head and bundle them onboard while unconscious.

The mid-1800s proved to be a boom time for bird droppings. When it was discovered (one would hope by accident) that guano was not only a splendid fertiliser but also a potent component in explosives, the previously worthless, disgusting gunk was suddenly worth as much as £10 or more per ton in London.

This 'white gold' rush took off when some loose-lipped sea dog revealed that there were craggy islands off the west coast of southern Africa coated in a thick and rancid icing layer of the stuff. The race was on and the prime destination for the muck madness was Ichaboe Island off Namibia, which was reported to be 25 metres deep in it. At the height of the rush, some 450 ships and 6 000 men descended on the tiny rocky outcrop to *donder* the crap out of each other.

It was bedlam. Rival crews would assault each other with whatever was available: fists, boots, knives, seabird eggs and even the occasional African Penguin, if one came to hand – and never having encountered humans before, they were so tame that they sometimes did. The penguins quickly learned to avoid the humans. And for their part, the humans tried to avoid the guano jobs.

Spending months scraping up foul and reeking thickened globs of bird turd was clearly never going to be pleasant work, but on the desolate islands, there was little to eat, except penguin, and no respite from the salt-barbed wind and spray, the storms and fogs and the hostile sun that cooked brains as well as skin. One convicted murderer allegedly opted to return to prison rather than continue and those sailors who'd been caught out once by the promise of easy and lucrative 'shore work', swore they'd never go back to it for love or money.

Black Sophie thought she could work with that equation. After all, she was used to trading love *for* money, as the reigning brothel queen on the seediest street in Cape Town. While land-bound ships' officers hung out in the comfort and civility of the Captain's Rooms on Heerengracht, the most ribald of entertainments were to be found on Bree Street, where the common folk could be found getting sloshed and maybe shagged among the cheap and nasty bars, brothels and boarding houses. A *dop* of brandy would set you back six pence a bottle, and if you needed a little something to battle the *babalaas*, there were stalls selling boiled penguin eggs (if you hadn't had enough of those) for a penny, as well as sour figs, fish frikkadels and watermelon konfyt.

Black Sophie was born in Graff-Reinet in 1827 under the rather more staid name of Sophia Johanna Werner. 'Black Sophie' was better suited to her coffee complexion and her personality, which was as cheerfully overabundant as her waistline. Unlike many of the other Bree Street proprietors, Sophie seemed to have a genuine fondness for the raucous sailors who rolled through her doors and into bed with her girls. She even married one – a Scandinavian skipper by the name of Charles Ludwig Nelson and years later they would sail off into the sunset together.

According to popular historian Lawrence Green, Sophie was an equal opportunity employer with an assortment of girls in all shades, and a savvy wheeler-dealer, to boot. When the men working the guano on Dyer Island off Gansbaai threatened to strike over the shortage of women, she was the only proprietor of an ill-reputed den to dispatch two ox carts of lovely ladies to make the long haul over Sir Lowry's Pass to meet the demand.

Together with her Liquorice Allsorts girls, Sophie would canvass for business by driving round the city in open-top carriages, throwing out catcalls and calling cards to potential suitors. They would also flock to the docks on sailing days, one of the few social occasions when the authorities wouldn't send them packing, to bid farewell to departing ships and 'allo to new customers among the gathered crowds.

Her establishment at number 26 Bree Street was as wild and rowdy as Black Sophie herself – and not only for the rambunctious clientele who crammed into the saloon.

It was decorated to a somewhat schizophrenic nautical theme, decked out with all manner of curiosities that had been presented to Sophie by grateful patrons on various occasions. There were beaded curtains and brocade, and ships' lanterns festively lit, immaculate miniature bone model ships, a flower bowl made from a compass stand carved with dolphins and a weather glass barometer that Sophie would consult before her clients rolled out to sea. The walls were covered in a disorderly tapestry of ships' flags and colours; any white spaces were quickly filled with sailors' signatures and the names of their ships, as well as fanciful doodles of well-rigged vessels and equally well-racked girls.

The saloon boasted a selection of biological marvels and monstrosities from albatross feet to shark spines and sperm whale teeth, intricately engraved with whaling scenes. But the most grisly relic of all was kept inside a box under the bar, displayed only by special request and only after the patrons had steeled their nerves with hard liquor.

It was a souvenir of Ichaboe – a gift from one of the island's taskmasters, Jack Gove.

The box was roughly man-sized, like a rough-hewn coffin and if you were to open it, you would find inside, indeed, a corpse, with the withered skin shrivelled about the bones and the hair dyed a quite unnatural red.

The desiccated unfortunate was once a labourer who had toiled and died amongst the mounds of white putrescence. But the curious thing about those interred on the island was that their remains underwent a peculiar change. The ammonia in the guano-rich soil had the effect of bleaching their hair and practically mummifying them. The effect was so convincing, that one such corpse allegedly ended up in a New York fairground, displayed as a genuine pharaoh, supposedly fresh-plundered from the pyramids, rather than a shitty little island off Namibia.

It's unlikely that Black Sophie's mummy would have made an appearance on a fateful night towards the end of September 1863, when Jack Gove pulled into town and after weeks of abusing the Cape governor's hospitality, the good ship, the *Alabama*, finally pulled out.

A month prior, Sophie and her girls were probably cruising for business amongst the sea of people gathered to watch on the balmy day in early August that the *Alabama* steamed into port. It was the highlight of a dreadfully tedious year, characterised by a gloomy economic depression and tiresome politicking – and besides, it wasn't every day you got to see a notorious marauder.

The *Alabama* was an American vessel, a Southerner rebel raider, although she never actually saw a Confederate port. Built in England by Lairds of Birkenhead and with a crew drawn mainly from the grog houses of Liverpool (apart from the Captain, Raphael Semmes and Southerner officers), she spent much of her career harassing Northern ships and trying to lure them away from the nautical blockade Abraham Lincoln had installed. When that stopped being fun and productive, she turned to hijacking on the high seas. She was small, speedy and bristling with cannons and in piracy, she'd found her calling. She went on to take down 64 ships during her short career, without the loss of a single man, until she was finally sunk outside of Cherbourg, France, in 1864.

Seized with *Alabama*-mania, hordes rushed for a view, lining up along Kloof Road and scaling Lion's Head, clambering onto rooftops, cramming the jetties and even setting out in small boats. As if aware of her expectant audience, and being the show-offy kind of southern belle, the *Alabama* made a suitably grand entrance, appearing in Table Bay in fierce pursuit of a Yankee barque, the *Sea Bride*. A brash battle ensued, but the Alabama was smaller, faster and decidedly more vicious than her opponent. Within an outrageously short time, she pounced and clipped the *Sea Bride's* wings just off Robben Island. The *Alabama* came prowling into Simonstown victorious, her dejected enemy in tow in full view of the cheering crowds.

Not quite sure how to handle the political ramifications of hosting a Confederate ship, never mind the legalities of the *Sea Bride's* capture in South African waters, the Governor of the Cape extended a very guarded welcome to the *Alabama*, to the spitting fury of the US Consul. It was a rather indelicate situation, but after that little display, the *Alabama* was an instant *cause célèbre* and while the politicians heckled over the raised hackles, the ship's crew swanked around town like heroes.

The ship came and went for several weeks, always returning with tales of adventure (Captain Semmes was good enough to let a reporter see his log book) and with a further 12 captive ships in her wake. Inevitably though, it became all too much for the city's officials. With international pressure mounting, the governor crisply informed Captain Semmes that the *Alabama* had overstayed her welcome.

Semmes was quite willing to go, were it not for the blasted inconvenience that much of his crew had deserted. In his journals, he blamed it on the sabotaging shenanigans of the Yankee Consul, although he admitted that some of his men had fallen foul of the law. He didn't make mention that others had fallen into the sweet and greedy clutches of Black Sophie and her girls.

The word on the street was that Semmes wasn't going to wait about for his prodigal strays to return. And, ostensibly to celebrate, Black Sophie threw a huge bash with an open bar. The saloon was rocking, with a full Cape orchestra, including a piano, a concertina, a violin and guitar to accompany the strains of a little ditty that had become recently popular, '*Daar kom die Alabama, ver, ver oor die see*'. But that night, the *Alabama* wasn't coming, it was going.

When the news came in that the *Alabama* had sailed off without them, the deserters weren't too fussed. They had a girl in one hand, a beer in the other and none of them were American anyway. Of course, they'd have to find work, but something would come up – especially if Black Sophie had anything to do with it.

Sophie was a bit of a crimp herself, although she never resorted to violent means to rope in crews for skippers like her husband or the reprehensible and very hairy Jack Gove. She'd discovered that a formula of a copious amount of brandy plus a little hot-and-sweaty beneath the sheets could be very a persuasive combo.

Sophie strolled over to introduce Jack to the former *Alabama* men. All liquored up with free booze, they were happy to hear his pitch. Old Jack was a silver-tongued spin doctor of note, although it helped that his audience were well in their cups. It was shore work, he said. Easy work, he assured them. Good money, he plied. Easy money. Harvesting guano.

One old hand pegged it right away and said he'd rather go back to fighting Yankees, but the rest of them fell for it like an anchor with a cut line. And Black Sophie sealed the deal by generously offering to cash in their advance money right now. Who could resist? They could buy brandy and tobacco as well as the appropriate gear – boots and oilskins. And when they returned, she'd charge them again for the privilege of having her girls peel them off.

The men, who were by now totally sotted as well as besotted, drank to Sophie's generosity! And the departure of the *Alabama*! And their new jobs! They may still have been in the throes of toasty self-congratulation as they shambled down Bree Street towards Jack Gove's ship, and maybe even still as they sprawled out in the hold to sleep off their stupor, while the ship swiftly set off into the night – towards Ichaboe.

There is a rock named for Sophie near Ichaboe and one also near Dyer Island, just off the coast of Kleinbaai (which also once boasted a bar by the same name, although it was never as deliciously seedy nor as prosperous as Sophie's saloon). The islets are also not much like the ebullient madam they're named for. They are grim outcroppings and spiky, surrounded by treacherous waters. The name may have been inspired by Sophie's own sneaky duplicity, but her reputation was such internationally that it's much more likely it was a tribute than a warning. In the long months away, sea-farers dreamed of returning to her riotous revels and back in Black Sophie's company and in the arms of her girls, the sailors and sealers and even the guano-collectors immediately forgave her all wrongs.

The Reluctant Amazon

Sarah Raal

In 1900, at the height of the Anglo-Boer South African War, the newspapers were atwitter with the news of Boer Amazons: ferocious fighting females no longer prepared to rely on the 'weapon of prayer' their leaders advocated.

Swarms of women did indeed regularly descend on the front. But, for the most part, they just visited the laagers, stocked up supplies for husbands or brothers, tended to the wounded or sought refuge from their burnt farms. A handful did take up arms, but not *en masse* as the tabloids liked to imagine.

Such tales were spurred by the daring, true exploits of young women such as Sarah Raal, who drove more than one British commander to distraction with her quick wits and insolence. By the time she was captured she received gift baskets from admirers and stares from the curious who flocked in droves to see her. But when Sarah first asked to join her brothers, they put her off, bemused, 'Ag, sister, how can we take you with us? Our own lives are continually in danger and full of upheaval.'

It was an attitude shared by the head honchos among the Boers, who did not approve of women being exposed to the horrors of war, although the alternative of landing up in the British concentration camps, where 6 000 women and 20 000 children died in captivity, wasn't exactly a picnic. The public didn't approve either and one indignant sceptic, writing in the *Bloemfontein Post* under the handle 'One Who Knows', said, 'If there should be such women, they should be shot down, for they have no business to be on the battlefield.'

Unfortunately, many of them were. A young British trooper wrote a letter home describing the 'fearful sight' of 16 women lying dead in the trenches at the siege of Ladysmith, while both the *Cape Argus* and the *Natal Witness* ran stories about a sharp-shooting 19-year old housewife whose husband convinced her to stay in the trenches. She was found with her husband dead beside her, a dead child in her arms and a grisly but evocative wound. Her left breast had been 'shot away', like the Amazons of lore who voluntarily cut theirs off to better draw their bows.

Some women, like the enigmatic 'Japie', disguised themselves as boys, although when their duplicity was discovered, they were often sent packing, as per Kruger's orders.

Sarah Raal never bothered to hide her gender. Even when General James Barry Munnik Hertzog joined the commando she was travelling with, it seems no-one gave her any grief or questioned her right to ride into battle with her brothers. Of course, if anyone had, Sarah undoubtedly would have let them have it. She was known for her lightning temper and lacerating tongue. Her inability to hold either in check had often landed her in the guano, but her cheekiness simply embellished her reputation.

Susarah Frederika Johanna Magdalena Raal wrote a romp of a memoir about her experiences, titled *The Lady Who Fought*, in response to a comment by a British commander. However the Afrikaans title, *Met Die Boere In Die Veld* (with the Farmers in the Veld), is probably more accurate (if less punchy), because she maintained she only ever fired in self-defence and went into battle laughing and crying at the same time, to hide her fear from her brothers.

She was an accidental action hero. She never intended to involve herself directly in the war, but she was definitely not a *hensopper* or a joiner, as those Boers who rolled over belly up or turned traitor were called. She expressed scathing disdain for the Afrikaner girls from town who swanned around with the British soldiers, oblivious to the concentration camps on their doorsteps.

Born in 1873, Sarah was barely in her 20s when she suddenly found herself alone (well, almost) on the family farm in the Free State. Her brothers had gone gung-ho commando, her father had been hauled off by the British (along with all the food in the house and some of the silverware) and her mother had gone to town for provisions and simply didn't return.

Sarah knew her parents were probably already in concentration camps, but rather than throw herself on the mercy of the English, she determined to run the farm on her own – with a little help from the farm labourers. To her consternation, she discovered her mother had been taken captive because the foreman, Andries, had informed the British that commandos made regular stopovers at the farm. Sarah was shocked that someone who had been with the family for 27 years could betray them, but she also wrote, 'It was said that the English looked after farm workers very well – they were given a rifle and a uniform, and on top of that they were well paid if they joined up.'

About a week after her mother's capture, a British patrol arrived to demand the money and food they'd been told she supplied to the Boers. They turned the house upside down, but Sarah had already taken the precaution of hiding the cash, sewing gold coins into her hatband and £500 in notes into the hem of her skirt. Cunningly, she left £6 in her purse and when the soldiers found it, she convinced them it was all she had and that Andries had taken the rest. In disgust, the officer threw down the purse and warned her that they'd be sending Andries to keep an eye on her.

When her brothers popped in some seven months later, Andries got word of it and rather than face capture, Sarah packed up some 2 000 cows, sheep and horses and as much as she could carry and set off with her loyal servants, Sam and Tryn, on a *groot trek* of her own with a mismatched team of oxen that pulled in all directions. They ended up at a creepy abandoned farm, Boomplaas, scattered with graves from an old battle 50 years prior and surrounded by forbidding mountains with dark ravines and skulking baboons. The little company did have one sinister encounter, but the rattling sound they heard one night (which had Tryn leaping into bed with Sarah) turned out to be a robber rather than a restless spook – and he was quickly scared off. Sarah saw much of her brothers who were stationed nearby, but when the British inevitably arrived on the farm and started asking questions, her quick thinking was unravelled by her siblings' gross stupidity.

Under interrogation, Sarah spun the commander a yarn about her young brother who was desperate to defect, and would be willing to betray the commando if the commander would allow her to send word to him.

To his credit, the commander was suspicious and insisted that she write the letter in front of him – in English. Standing beside him at the piano, Sarah jotted down a neutral message on her writing pad: 'Dear Brother. I have promised to let you know; an English convoy has just arrived. Try to come over at once.' On its own, that probably would have done the trick, but then Sarah took a huge risk.

While the officers chatted, she surreptitiously lifted the edge of the page and scrawled another message in Dutch on the sheet beneath: 'There is a large English force here. They're looking for you. Be careful. Don't come tonight. I've been captured.'

She held out the page so the officer could read it, 'my heart pounding like a hammer in my throat'. The commandant scanned the page and then nodded assent. He hadn't noticed a thing. Sarah very, very carefully tore off both pages together and gave them to a servant to take to her brothers.

By dusk her brother had not yet arrived and the commandant was becoming twitchy. He got twitchier still when the servant returned with a letter from her brothers, who had clearly not cottoned on to her sneaky subterfuge, boasting that they'd be there shortly to *bliksem* the Khakis. As Sarah wrote, 'How they could have done such a foolish thing, I cannot to this day understand.' Her fate was sealed. The furious commandant tried to confiscate the receipt for £1 090 he'd signed over to her for all her livestock and the contents of the house, but Sarah chirped defiantly that it had no value for her and she'd already burnt the damn thing, when really, she'd stowed it in her bodice.

When the British limped back from the skirmish with her brothers' commando, carting three wounded of their own, she asked what had happened. An officer snapped at her bitterly that they'd shot all her people dead and left them for the vultures.

The next day, she was shipped off to the Springfontein camp in an open truck in the baking heat without food or water, grieving for her dead brothers. While it wasn't Auschwitz by any means, the conditions in the concentration camps were horrific, a prototype for what was to come later in Germany. People were severely malnourished, clean water was in short supply and disease was rife. But while another maverick, the 'dumpy' English spinster, Emily Hobhouse, led a moral crusade against the atrocities of the camps, Sarah Raal got to experience them first hand.

Her initial experience wasn't too bad. The British seemed to have forgotten their threat to throw her in gaol and feeling cocky, she approached the camp commandant to ask if she might be transferred to Bloemfontein to be with her mother. Apoplectic at her insolence, he snapped that not only would she not be transferred, but that she would never have the chance to leave the camp either. 'You will die here!' Sarah shot back that at least her brothers were men fighting in battle and ridiculed him for being only a 'woman's commandant'. His aide had to intervene to prevent him from strangling her. Strangely, he calmed down after that and gave her a choice of punishment: 14 days in gaol on rice water or 14 days' worth of the camp guard's washing. Sarah opted for the latter, but even before she left his tent, she'd formulated an escape plan.

Without breathing a word of her impending sentence for fear of scaring them off, Sarah persuaded two of her friends to help her break out. It was customary to allow women out to collect firewood, but a troublemaker like Sarah would never get permission. Instead, she sent her friends to request a pass for themselves and a 'sister' and disguised herself in spectacles and a *kappie* pulled low over her eyes. The ridiculous plan worked and once out of sight of the lackadaisical guards, the trio ditched their axes and sacks and made a break for it. Halfway up, Sarah's companions were ready to collapse from exhaustion, but she nipped at their heels until they reached the ridge and were picked up by the Boers lurking up there.

Sarah was reunited with her brothers, who were not vulture pickings after all, and having nowhere else to go, joined their commando under Commander Nieuwoudt. However, they were still apparently not the brightest of sparks.

One evening, Sarah stayed behind with her youngest brother, Abram, who was suffering heatstroke. Unable to sleep, she kept watch beside him, but when she heard horses and shook him awake, he didn't believe her. By the time she woke him again, the British were right on top of them. Abram insisted on rescuing Sarah's horse, which was stabled on the farm below and in a bold move worthy of her, strolled right in amongst the British, confident that in his khaki uniform, they'd mistake him for one of their own. He brought her horse up, while Sarah herself kept a low profile, scrambling through the bushes and tearing her knees and her dress to bloody shreds.

Unluckily, her horse was white and Abram hadn't fastened the girth on the saddle properly. When Sarah mounted up and spurred her gelding to a gallop, the saddle slid crazily around her horse's back and she tried desperately to hold on. The terrifying situation was aggravated when the British spotted her pale horse, and showered them both with a hail of bullets as they fled.

The commando had their revenge for the scuffs on Sarah's knees when they encountered a lost English officer and a black guide the following day. They winged him in the side and proceeded to 'shake him out' (or *uitskud*), sending him back to his missing troops *sans* uniform, boots, gun or horse, which the Boers were quick to appropriate for themselves.

Even in the midst of battle, there were funny incidents. Sarah relates how late one night, when the scouts galloped into camp raising the alarm, one sleepy soldier scrambling into action in the dark, vaulted onto the back of an ox instead of his horse and then couldn't understand why the stubborn beast bucked and kicked and refused to move.

Sarah had her own misadventures. She courageously volunteered to run the risk of going solo up to a kopje to scout out the lay of the land and the position of the British who were closing in on them. She knew that, at worst, she'd be sent back to camp, but if a man was spotted, he'd be shot on the spot. Her brothers were dead set against her going, but when she put it that way, they eventually conceded, provided she turn over the family's money she was still carrying, in case she *was* captured. Sarah refused and borrowing a spare pair of binoculars, set off for the ridge.

She was terrified, cringing at every sound, mistaking every boulder or bush for an Englishman about to seize her. And just when she reached the top and thought she could relax after signalling the commando with the 'all clear', a steenbok leapt out at her. She got such a fright, she fell off the rock she'd been sitting on, but nevertheless yelled 'Hands up!' despite being sprawled on her back in a tangle of skirt, legs in the air and her revolver nowhere at hand.

But it wasn't all fun and steenbok. As Sarah wrote, 'Life was exhausting: food was scarce, we had little ammunition, the world around us was destroyed, and some towns and farms were utterly deserted, with everyone either captured or on commando.' Intent on disrupting the supply chain, the English resorted to scorched earth policy, burning 30 000 farms to the ground, and slaughtering livestock indiscriminately. In one place, the commando came across a flock of 2 000 sheep that had been rounded up and burned alive. 'These animals were a terrible sight to see. Those not burnt to death had legs deformed by the heat, and were crawling about on their knees. Some of their eyeballs had burst, while others' lips had curled back over their teeth. Had I not seen it myself, I would never have believed that people existed who were capable of such cruelty.'

There were also fight scenes sufficient to satisfy the requirements of any action flick. Sarah's uncle was killed in battle and her brother Jacobus was shot in the shoulder – there was nothing but tepid water with which to clean the wound. He joined the damaged in the back of groaning wagons that jolted around so much that the wounded men screamed in pain and sometimes had to be carried in blankets when they couldn't endure it any longer.

And although Sarah was occasionally swept up with blood lust, she recognised it as just 'big talk'. In the heat of the action, she was terrified, but was careful never to show it. Her modus operandi in battle was to shelter herself as best as she could and then join in the back-slapping afterwards, as if she'd been in the thick of it.

One particularly ugly incident involved two black soldiers who shot one of the Boer scouts. The entire unit moved to retaliate. They ambushed the English camp and captured around 100 men, but there were still stragglers lurking in the bush and when one of them was shot in the head, his friend rushed to his side, oblivious to the pelting bullets. He knelt beside him, weeping, trying in vain to wipe away the blood. 'Oh, I promised mother I'd look after you, what am I to do now?' Sarah's exhilaration vanished immediately and she wept with him.

The commando shook out the English soldiers of their possessions, but they'd also rounded up five black soldiers and threatened to kill them all, if they didn't reveal who had killed the scout. The Boers singled out the culprit, led him up the ridge and summarily executed him. Sarah shed no tears for him.

Race relations, which were already tenuous, were mutilated by the war. Black soldiers – recruited by the British for a quarter of the pay and with big promises that they would get their own farms at the end of it – were set to do the dirtiest of dirty work that the British balked at, burning farms and seizing homesteads. This naturally enraged the Boers.

Of course, there were atrocities committed on all sides, including sexual assault, but the lines drawn between nations during the war would foment hatred for decades to come.

After almost a year, Sarah's commando was in a very bad way. They were filthy, scrawny and many of them were barefoot, but that didn't lessen the humiliation of capture. When the British ambushed the small group of ten riders, Sarah was so angry, she smashed her rifle against a rock before she handed it over. The English were thrilled that they'd caught the infamous girl 'general' and when she was marched in with the other captives, they threw their hats in the air. Furious, she misbehaved terribly and insulted everyone she encountered.

Sarah was separated from her brothers, who were later sent to India as prisoners. Two nurses searched her in vain for the fortune she was rumoured to have stashed about her person (she'd switched hiding places to a cloth envelope in her bodice, which she sneakily let slip to the floor when they demanded she strip). Thereafter she was taken to a nearby town for a week where she was relentlessly interrogated by the commandant (although he got only lip out of her) and hassled by soldiers for photographs. Finally, she was sent off to Bloemfontein by train, but during the journey, her guard fell asleep and she snatched his rifle, yelling, 'Hands up!' He leapt like a steenbok with fright, but Sarah realised that even if she did escape, she had nowhere to go. She relented and returned his rifle. She later wrote that if she'd known what was to come, she would have shot him and run ...

In Bloem, an old family friend, Dr Krause, took her in, while the commandant figured out what to do with her, although she was always under guard. Sarah's reputation had preceded her and she made an unexpected friend in the form of one Captain Reed, who seemed to admire the young hellion. When she was presented to him for further questioning along with a letter that described her as 'the lady who fought', he advised her simply to keep quiet. 'They cannot punish you if you don't wish to speak ... Personally, I admire your courage, but I'm not supposed to say such things to you.' He visited her a few times and when she was sent away to the camps, invited her to write to him. It certainly seems that the young Captain was quite taken with Ms. Raal, but even if she had been inclined to reciprocate, she despised the *meisies* who hung on British soldiers' arms so much, that she would never have acted on it.

Before she left the Krauses, Sarah transferred her money to a new hiding place, stashed inside a pillow, which she would send back to them in the not unlikely event that she died in the camps. After a gruelling journey, with nothing to eat or drink and having curious bystanders gawk at her at every station, Sarah arrived in the concentration camp in Kroonstad. Typically, she immediately irritated the local commandant so much that he sentenced her to the worst possible punishment, to be locked in solitary confinement in the Bird Cage.

The Bird Cage was a fenced off enclosure, about a hundred square feet with space to erect a tent, set apart from the rest of the camp. She wasn't allowed to set foot outside it and the guards had to lift up the wire to let Sarah in. Her leaky tent and threadbare blanket were scant protection from the elements and she lived on meagre rations of bully beef and klinkers (biscuits so hard they could chip teeth). She took to sleeping during the day to avoid being 'bothered' by the guards at night.

The horrors happening around her seemed to dampen her spirit. She wrote later, 'My pen will not write everything I endured.' Worn out and worn down, she became terribly ill, but it was only after she collapsed in pain and hunger, apparently waiting to die, that they took her to the infirmary. Her treatment in the hospital was far superior to that in the Bird Cage and she began receiving gifts and visitors who'd come to see the 'angry, brave girl'. While she was recovering, she managed to keep her cash-lined pillow with her and even struck a deal with the commandant, who agreed to not send her back to the Bird Cage if she agreed not to cause any further trouble.

The remainder of her time in camp was reasonably uneventful. She was finally reunited with her parents in Uitenhage, where she managed to irritate the camp commander there as well. On 31 May 1902, peace was declared and while her brothers were still being held prisoner in India, Sarah and her parents were reunited and able to return to their farmstead.

They found it devastated. All the windows were broken, the grounds were lost in a tangle of overgrown vegetation and the house had been ransacked. But with the money Sarah had so carefully stowed for all her time in the veld and the camps, they were able to make a new start. Her brothers returned 17 months later and in 1906, she married one Ockert Snyman.

She only wrote her memoir some 35 years after the events that catapulted her to fame. And as Johan Wolfaardt, a researcher at the War Museum of the Boer Republics in Bloemfontein points out, she probably took some fairly major liberties. When the book was published in 1938, in time for the Great Trek Centenary celebrations it drew a heated outcry from English-speaking South Africans for its anti-British sentiment. Sarah was granted a veteran's pension in 1946 and died in 1949.

* * *

As a last note on the Boer war, it was the women survivors of the concentration camps that inspired the sparrows on South Africa's farthing coin first minted in 1923 when they petitioned Prime Minister Jan Smuts to commemorate their experiences and their worth in the eyes of God. They'd been inspired by a verse in the Bible in Matthew 10, which reads: 'Are not two sparrows sold for a penny? Yet not one of them will fall to the ground apart from the will of your Father. And even the very hairs on your head are numbered. So don't be afraid you are worth more than many sparrows.' The one cent coin, now out of use, still bears this image.

The Hungry Artist

Irma Stern

The jungle was burning when the stout, middle-aged lady artist arrived alone in the Belgian Congo in 1942. Not from the fires of revolution – that was only to come later and it's doubtful the woman armed with only an easel and paints would have noticed the sparks of unrest already fomenting – but actually, spectacularly ablaze.

Irma Stern was thrilled. She'd motored into the densest forests of the Lake Districts with only a driver, supplied by a bemused, but mostly befuddled Belgian government official at Elisabethville, to find inspiration for her art. The veld fire they passed through early in the expedition was the least of it.

In her journal, Irma riffed rhapsodic about the colours, the leaden sky, red flowers dangling from a tree 'like clogged blood', a basket of 'green oranges in the green light' as well as the extraordinary beauty of the local people she compulsively sketched and painted wherever she went.

It wasn't exactly the done thing for a Cape Town high society lady to go blundering off into the bush on her own, particularly one of Irma's breeding and taste. After all, this was the woman who had won awards for her outlandish costumes at Cape Town balls, who entertained an expensive fetish for imported hats and beautiful shoes, who threw famously decadent banquets frequented by actors and politicians and artists and travellers and other important and interesting types. But then, despite her social standing, Irma didn't ever really fit in.

She was a prodigious artist with appetites to match. It was well known that when she finished painting a still life, she would eat it. In her Rosebank home, The Firs, she employed a personal chef, Charlie, to prepare meals that had to be as sumptuously attractive as they were delicious. It was said her demands drove him to drink, but she rather huffily maintained he was a drinker when she hired him. One of Charlie's specialties was preparing colour co-ordinated dinners (pink crayfish tails in pink sauce on fuchsia-coloured tableware), for her banquets, where she'd hold court in plush throne-like chairs, specially made to accommodate her considerable girth.

She was a rather large lady. Shortly before she died of heart failure brought on by diabetes in 1966, she had become so heavy that she was unable to go upstairs and it was cruelly rumoured that she had to squeeze sideways through the carved doors she'd brought back with her from her adventures in Zanzibar.

She was terribly self-conscious about her weight and it's telling that she never painted a self-portrait, which was par for the course for her contemporaries. Even in her 20s, before she became really big (in more ways than one), she told her friend, Trude Bosse in Germany that her body bothered her. 'I am afraid of the eyes of strangers,' she wrote in one of her countless letters.

But if Irma's size topped the scales, so did her personality. She was a vivacious, fiercely intelligent and indomitable woman who tended to overwhelm whatever space she was currently occupying. The artist Walter Batiss once described her as someone who 'breathed in air and breathed out fire'.

She was also spoilt, self-indulgent and stubborn as hell. She didn't think much of other artists, apart from Picasso and Matisse, and then she couldn't afford to buy their paintings anyway. Apart from the works she'd collected on her audacious solo trips into Africa, the only art she would have in her house, was her own. She dismissed other South African artists such as her one-time rival, Margaret Laubser, out of hand.

To avoid provoking an argument or Irma's terrible temper, some of her close friends, like the Feldmans, would take down work by other artists and stash them away whenever Irma came to stay and would re-paint her room in colours Irma would find more aesthetically satisfying. It didn't always help. Irma extended her habit of decorating cupboards and doors and windows to her friends' houses too, especially if some detail offended her, for instance the Feldmans' art deco fireplace.

She had a low tolerance for boredom and required constant stimulation and attention. After the bright lights and brighter minds she'd been exposed to while studying art in Berlin in her early 20s, she would become terribly frustrated with parochial Cape Town society. She accused the mother city's citizens of being 'like commercial mineral water gone flat' and complained bitterly that she was forced to rely on profuse correspondence with smart and cultured friends such as Richard and Freda Feldman to keep her sane. However, if they didn't reply promptly to her letters, she would dash off plaintive missives that read 'Are you still alive? Why do you never write to me?' in her untidy scrawl of misspelled words and frantic dashes in place of real punctuation.

She was also an incurable romantic in her art and her private affairs. In her work, she was criticised for her idyllic depictions of Africa, even by her closest friend, Richard Feldman, who wrote in a review that he wished she'd pay more attention to the socio-political, and paint mineworkers and maids as well as the idealised Swazi hunters or Watussi royalty that were her favourite subjects. But Irma paid little heed.

She was never much interested in politics or economics and thanks to her mentor, Max Pechstein and the particular brand of German expressionism from which she'd evolved, she nurtured an enduring fascination with the exotic and the perceived primitivism of Africa in particular. But while Irma never really engaged with the context of her subjects' lives, she did connect with the people.

Irma could be very charming and she inveigled her way into all kinds of strange and wonderful places where few whites had dared to venture before. She was received by Watussi and Bakuba royalty, had sweet tea with the Sultan's wife and attended a gala for the Aga Khan. In Zanzibar, she delighted in the game of bargaining in the markets, watched nimble Arab dancers swirling about with swords and tried to crash a Swahili dance, only to find herself, 'trumpeted out, in a rude and rather obscene manner. Obscene was the dance in a high degree and it was most unwelcome that it be witnessed by a European'.

She was also guilty of being patronising. She bought a shipload of art from the Bakuba, which she described as 'magnificent pieces of sculpture carved out of wood, of fetishes and masks, grotesque and beautiful, revealing primitive Africa in all its fear-ridden phantasy, with its witch-craft and taboos, with its ancestral worship and its world alive with the spirits'. With the Bakuba chieftain she shamelessly traded acid drop sweets (which she had to eat herself to show they were not poisoned), a bottle of whisky, condensed milk and foie gras for a royal cloak masterfully woven of raffia.

She relayed to the king, through a translator, that she intended to show the Bakuba's works together with her paintings, 'so that the white people in my country may learn what beautiful things the black man in the Congo creates'. The king seemed pleased with her gifts and her intentions, but then, to her shock, he asked her to send him a Remington when she was back in Cape Town. 'I was breathless with astonishment. This king, only one generation removed from man-eating, the King of the Bakubas, with six hundred and eight wives – a typewriter!!'

Irma also had darker adventures. In the land of the Leopard Man, a figure with metal claws who was supposedly the embodiment of vengeance in the Congo, her car sprung a spring. Waiting on the side of the road for her driver, Pierre, to repair the engine, Irma was unnerved when she found that the grass had been creepily knotted together in bundles, like bamboo. She took a knife and cut the knots, writing in her journal, 'I am not usually superstitious but here the beliefs are so strong, the fears of witchcraft so potent. The air is dense with cruelty.'

While Irma may have missed the slow simmering discord in the Congo or the injustices of the system the 'natives' lived under, she was not unobservant or unmoved by her experiences. When she saw a child on the barge clearly dying of sleeping sickness, she wrote that her 'heart stood still with fright and horror and pity'.

And in her Zanzibar travelogue, she commented on how Arab women were marginalized, forbidden to go to mosque (because it was believed they had no souls), as well as the skewed pricing at the slave markets of old where a donkey went for three times the cost of a boy.

Her romantic notions weren't limited to Africa. She was also enraptured by her travels in Europe, writing that Madeira was 'to me a wordless concept of earliest delights' and describing Paris as 'a shimmering, glistening feeling, like life in a colourful maze – The women are like colourful birds twittering and fantastical'.

While art critics would later criticize her for never recording the names of the African subjects she painted, neither did she note the names of the Spanish prostitutes in *Harlots* or the women picking grapes in *Vineyard Sketch*, for example.

It was her insatiable appetite for novelty that inspired her travels and she brought the same innovation to her work. Unfortunately, it didn't always go down so well. Her first South African exhibition at Ashbey's Gallery in 1922 shocked the refined sensibilities of Cape Town society so badly that two policemen and a *dominee* were dispatched to judge whether it was 'obscene'. They reluctantly concluded that it was ugly, but not indecent.

The scenesters in the city had never heard of expressionism and certainly never been exposed to anything like Irma's bold torrent of colours and skewed forms. The socialite Lady Florence Phillips scathingly dismissed her as 'that nice girl who paints terrible pictures', although author Sarah Millin (who had covered Daisy de Melker's trial) seemed to quite like it. The show quickly gained so much notoriety that during one lunch hour, queues to see it spilled out into Long Street.

Although she'd been deliberately provocative, Irma was still hurt. In her disjointed journal, she sketched a watercolour of an artist painting with her 'heart's blood', surrounded by a mocking crowd who 'all laughed and slung mud at me'.

Even at the liberal Weimar Art Academy in Berlin where she studied, Irma had initially met with resistance to her art. When her lecturer, Martin Brandenburg spurned *The Eternal Child*, which Irma felt, quite rightly, was the first true expression of her own style, she sought out another mentor and found Max Pechstein, a member of Germany's first modernists, Die Brücke, freshly returned from New Guinea. He helped to nurture her talent and introduced her to the gallery owner who would host her first show. But while her exhibitions in Europe were very well received, it would take a little getting used to for the backward backwater of Cape Town to catch on. It was no wonder she sought escape into 'the wild and free Africa'.

Irma was never a starving artist – at least not financially. After the South African public learned to adjust to her vivid stylistic works, her shows did very well. Now, of course, her paintings, on the rare and special occasion when they come up for sale, are easily worth a million.

While Irma certainly craved success and acceptance, what she really longed for was love – a 'person who will caress my soul'. It's likely that the combination of her formidable weight and her formidable personality scared some potential suitors off, but it's also clear that Irma would have settled for nothing less than a prize catch – a beautiful man who was as intelligent and passionate as she was. She nurtured terrible crushes on her male friends who were able to match wits with her, including Richard Feldman, although it seems half of Johannesburg was after the handsome and charismatic businessman.

In 1921, Irma confessed to Trude in a letter that she had a secret love, but that her parents, who she was still living with, didn't approve because he couldn't support her. They did approve, however, of another suitor, one Dr. Johannes Prinz, the 40-year-old German lecturer at UCT, who was a regular visitor to the house. Irma had been madly infatuated with him once, when she was 15 and he was her tutor, but now, his attentions made her feel unhappy and oppressed. In her letter she wrote, 'And now I sit here – The one I cannot have – the other I do not like ...'

In another letter to Trude she declared that she was so desperately enamoured of a mystery man, recently married, she would have to clench her teeth at night so as not to scream with the pain of it. But Irma also wrote, 'Every now and then I think – "Get married to anyone – everything is lost now in any case – and you can only age because of it – and it is abnormal for you to climb into the grave as a virgin" ... Then again it makes me feel sick and so it goes on.'

To the surprise of her friends and acquaintances, Irma married Johannes Prinz in 1926, but he was a damp squib compared to Irma's technicolour pyrotechnics and there are doubts whether the marriage was ever consummated. Certainly, she never felt that he fulfilled her and his interest in art extended only as far as his collection of esoteric pornography.

The marriage lasted seven years, during which Irma spent as much time as possible away, travelling to Europe and venturing off to Swaziland and Pondoland, bringing back increasingly adventurous work that was beginning to make a name for her.

There are hints of other men in her letters, although she was always reluctant to name names and how much is fantasy, is not entirely clear. In 1923, she had a shipboard romance with a man engaged to be married, probably the Portuguese author, Hippolyto Raposo. The affair lasted only 12 days, but it seems that it only went as far as the moment when 'he came to me and kissed me, kissed me madly'. Two years later, Irma confessed to Trude that she was still in love with him.

While Irma fantasized about her good-looking intellectual friends, the relationships she had in the real world were with careless cads and inevitably led to heartache. In the early 1940s, she makes mention of a man called Prager in her letters, who was probably an ex-serviceman and seemed to have messed her around, playing hot and cold. Later, there was a rogue called Nollkamper, a retired Dutch airforce officer and alcoholic, who was sweet when sober, but acted abominably when drunk, shaming Irma in front of her friends.

Irma also had a turbulent relationship with her parents. Her father, Samuel, was very critical of her work and had once thrown one of her sculptures of a pregnant nude out the window. When he died, in 1933, around the same time her marriage to Johannes Prinz dissolved, it freed her to do as she wished, although she still had her mother with whom to contend.

Her mother, Henny, was domineering and difficult (not unlike her daughter) and being stuck together in the same house caused much bickering and resentment. Although Irma threatened to move out, she was too comfortable for the threats to be anything but idle. Sometimes their spats spilled out in public; on one occasion Irma showed her mother's portrait without asking her permission and Henny tore it off the wall and smuggled it out beneath her skirt.

By 1943, Irma's mother was bedridden with cancer and the atmosphere in the house descended into gloom and depression. In spite of this, Irma seemed to have surges of creativity and energy, but she was still shocked and sore when her mother finally died. She wrote, 'It is only now – I am beginning to understand life and all that my mother meant to me. I am feeling horribly lonely at times … I am alone all day long.'

By 1947, Irma had chilled out a great deal, if her letters were anything to judge. Her shows overseas were receiving rave reviews and she'd even sold a large still life to the queen of England. She was also happily settled with a man, Dudley Welch.

Dudley was an architect who became involved with Irma around 1939. He would help her arrange exhibitions and stretch and mount canvases, but there are suggestions that, at least initially, he was more to her than just a helpmeet. Her mother accused him of being a leech, but Irma seems to have been very fond of him in a fractured sort of way. She wrote, 'He is unreliable to a degree that it breaks my heart to think he is my best friend and I wanted to rely on him – when I am alone.'

He was a very skittish man, and if she tried to nail him down as to where their relationship was going, he'd bolt. She learned to manage him by letting go and soon he was spending most nights at The Firs until, in 1944, he moved in. He stayed with her for 22 years, and by the

1960s, Irma was signing off letters and Christmas cards from both of them and they were travelling to Africa and Europe together. But there was never any suggestion that they might get married.

In 1960, Irma's health started to deteriorate and by 1965, the doctors told her she had to stay home. She wasn't allowed to go to jaunting off to Johannesburg, let alone further afield. The restrictions made Irma very *mif*, but by then her legs had swollen up terribly and she was barely able to move around her house. In February 1966 she received an invitation to hold a retrospective at the Grosvenor Gallery in London. She believed it would make her career – and it likely would have, if her heart hadn't stalled in her chest a few months later. She died in her home on 23 August. The exhibition was held posthumously in 1967.

Irma was a diva, but unlike many artistic personalities, she had the talent to justify her outrageous behaviour. She was unhappy and desperately lonely for much of her life, but her wild travels and her wilder paintings sustained her and by the end, she'd achieved not only grand success but a measure of contentment too.

After she died, friends rallied to save her house and transform it into a museum. The Irma Stern Museum is preserved almost as it was in her life. In her studio, there are oils dried on the easel and perched on her desk, the 'Do Not Disturb' sign she used while painting, which Charlie, the chef, would occasionally nick when he wanted to keep her out of his kitchen. Doors and cupboards and even windowpanes are smothered with decorative art and many of her paintings and sculptures as well as her invaluable collection of African antiquities are on display. The only thing that's changed is that now the house also displays the artworks of other artists, with rotating exhibitions. Irma would have been either horrified or greatly amused.

The Blood Sun

Nongqawuse

It was 1857 and the Russians were coming. Or at least those were the rumours, spreading thick and fast, as contagious as the lung sickness that brought cattle to their knees across the country. Actually, there seemed to be some confusion about exactly who was on their way to rid the land of the British and restore peace and prosperity to the Xhosa nation, but *someone* was definitely coming. Nongqawuse had prophesied it.

When the 15-year-old orphan went down to the Gxarha river together with her little cousin, Nombanda, to scare away the birds from the crops, she had no idea it would be such a momentous day or that the things the spirits in the reeds were to tell her would have such ruinous repercussions for the amaXhosa.

The Gxarha is even now a bewitchingly beautiful place, the dark twisting ribbon of river hemmed in by sheer cliffs that downgrade to gently sloping green hills near the river mouth as it meets the ocean. Mists roll in from the sea, casting strange shadows amongst the reeds; it was an appropriately eerie spot for the ancestors to announce their imminent return. The strangers who appeared to Nongqawuse commanded her to tell the people that their cattle were tainted by witchcraft, that they were to slaughter their livestock and halt their cultivation in preparation for the ancestors' return and the birth of a new world, to be heralded by a blood sun rising in the sky.

The great cattle-killing her words inspired resulted in the deaths of over 40 000 Xhosa from grim starvation and was to become one of the most contentious events in South African history. But was it suicide or murder? A culling of sick beasts that got out of control? A grand conspiracy of chieftains to drive their people to war? Or a sinister plot by the British governor Sir George Grey to finally crush the Xhosa once and for all? Or the manipulations of a conniving missionary uncle? And where the heck did the Russians fit in some 100 years before the official *Rooi Gevaar* had white South Africans looking for commies under the bed?

The idea that the Xhosa ancestors would arise from the dead to make the world 'right again' had first sprung from the lips of the great prophet and war doctor, Nxele, in around 1818. He'd been educated in the ways of Christianity on the farm he grew up on in Cape Town. He claimed to be Christ's younger brother and it may have been the missionaries' disbelief and disapproval or perhaps the visions that plagued him that spurred him to develop a new theology, setting up a black God, Mdalidephu, in opposition to Thixo, the God of the whites, who were such disrespectful savages that they murdered their God's son by nailing him to a cross.

Nxele's preaching inspired at least one insurgence against the British and they responded by shipping the troublemaker off to Robben Island at the first opportunity. He drowned trying to escape in 1820, but 30 years later, there emerged a new prophet in a time of terrible drought and famine, who many considered to be Nxele reincarnated. As prophets go, Mlanjeni, the 'Riverman', wasn't an impressive specimen – a sickly, skinny, uncircumcised boy of 18 – but what he lacked in physical stature, he made up for with obtuse predictions of a better world and extraordinary witch-hunting demonstrations.

A tenet of Xhosa belief at the time was that all disease, sickness and ill in the world (including drought) were not part of the natural order but a sign of the ancestors' displeasure. Like his predecessor, Mlanjeni claimed that if the people only rid themselves of the evil magic or *ubuthi* the ancestors would be appeased and the people's suffering and quite possibly death itself would come to an end.

He encouraged people to burn their charms and kill all dun- or yellow-coloured cattle, which were supposedly an abomination to the Earth. Those who wanted to clear themselves of suspicion could walk between two witchcraft poles. If they were innocent, they would pass through unhindered, but any guilty of witchery would be stuck fast, unable to move. Rather than kill the offenders, Mlanjeni used his divine powers to cure them of the affliction of evil.

The British didn't like any of this. Governor Harry Smith, a deplorably arrogant toss whose idea of diplomacy was humiliating the local chiefs by forcing them literally to lick his boots, was on a mission to rid the Xhosa of their uncivilised backward habits, including this ridiculous witch-hunting notion. The self-proclaimed 'Great White Chief of the Xhosa' thought the cattle killings smacked of anti-white sentiment considering dun was the colour of the English, and was decidedly nervous about the Xhosa servants and labourers abandoning their posts in the Colony to return home to await the great event Mlanjeni prophesised.

Attempts were made to arrest Mlanjeni, but he evaded the British at every turn and started preparing medicine intended to turn the enemies' bullets to water and make the Xhosa warriors invulnerable. Clearly there was a big-time battle brewing, incited by Harry's botched attempts at keeping the peace, such as deposing one of the chieftains, Sandile, practically on a whim.

The War of Mlanjeni, also known as the Eighth Frontier War, kicked off in 1850 and raged for three years. It was an ugly confrontation characterised by atrocities on both sides. The Xhosa disembowelled the corpses of their victims to prevent the supernatural force of *iqungu* from slithering out of the body and attacking them, hacked out organs believed to have magical properties as war medicines and slow-roasted to death any enemy soldiers unlucky enough to be captured alive, a torture normally reserved for suspected witches.

For their part, the British under Colonel Eyre, delighted in killing unarmed refugees, including women and children, and stringing their corpses up in trees. Soldiers cut off ears as trophies and sent home human skulls as mementos or specimens for scientific study, boiling the flesh off the decapitated heads in their cooking pots, which the Xhosa, understandably, perceived as acts of cannibalism.

Mlanjeni's reputation grew. As war doctor, he took the credit when the Xhosa were victorious and Sir Harry Smith's abrupt recall to England and the wreck of the Birkenhead, en route to battle with some 300 British reinforcements, were both attributed to the prophet's powers. But he deftly avoided the blame for failures. When the British troops' bullets did not dissolve mid-air into harmless drops of water, as promised, but ripped through the warriors en masse, the prophet claimed it was because they had defied his command to remain celibate when preparing for battle. Blaming the people for not obeying the letter of the law was to become a popular refrain in time to come.

In the course of the war, some 16 000 Xhosa died compared with just 1 400 settlers, but while the chieftains were sorely battered, they were not yet defeated. Nevertheless, in 1853, an uneasy peace was settled by the new governor, Sir George Cathcart. In keeping with a long tradition of settler treaties, it ripped off the Xhosa wholesale, claiming their lands for the Crown.

Mlanjeni was undeterred and told his people that his ancestors had told him the time was not yet right, but that they would still return and bring with them all the dead killed in this war and reclaim the stolen lands. Then he died abruptly of tuberculosis.

In 1854 Cathcart was relieved of his duties in the Cape and, in doing so, inspired the rumours of Russians. He was dispatched to the Crimean War where he was killed in a skirmish. His last words before the Russians cut him down, were, 'I fear we are in a mess.'

Word of the slaying of the despised governor spread with incomprehensible speed through South Africa, but no-one was quite sure who these Russians were, or even where Russia was. The British explanation that they were white – and losing – was dismissed with scepticism as more of the same propaganda the Xhosa had heard for years. Word quickly got around that the Russians were, in truth, a black nation, possibly even the embodied spirits of fallen Xhosa warriors returning to avenge their deaths. Men were dispatched to watch for the imminent arrival of the Russian ships, surely carrying the new people of the prophecies.

In the meantime, possibly inspired by the news of the Russians, at least five new prophets sprang up throughout British Kaffraria. But it was the girl prophet, Nongqawuse, in the free lands of the great Xhosa King Sarhili, across the Kei River, who was to prove the most important and the disruptive of all the seers.

Not much is known about her. She was an orphan, possibly as a result of Mlanjeni's War, and she may have been witness to some of the bloody horrors of that conflict. Shortly after her parents died, she was taken in by her uncle, Mhlakaza, and was living with him in the village of Qolorha when she first heard the voices. Significantly, before 1853, Mhlakaza was someone else entirely.

When he lived in Grahamstown, Mhlakaza went by the name Wilhelm Goliath. He was the first Xhosa to be baptised and became the trusted servant of the Archdeacon Nathaniel James Merriman, tramping all over the Eastern Cape for 18 months with his missionary master, spreading the word of God. They were idyllic days and Mhlakaza/Wilhelm was treated as an equal, but when they returned to Grahamstown in 1850, he was relegated to servant status and it didn't sit well with him. The Merrimans came to regard him as a lazy nuisance and were concerned when he claimed to experience religious visions. They were grateful to see him go. He returned to his village in 1853, reclaimed his Xhosa name and began to preach his own gospel in such a way that people felt compelled to listen – if not to him, then to his wild-eyed imaginative niece.

On that fateful day when Nongqawuse ran to report the message from the spirits, she was met with scepticism and dismissed for telling fairytales. Dejected, she enlisted the aid of her uncle Mhlakaza to win over the tribal elders. It just so happened that he was the one who would interpret the meaning of her prophecies, which with all this talk of reincarnation, sounded a lot like a mutant amalgam of Xhosa and Christian beliefs.

Word quickly spread and soon the great king Sarhili came down from his Great Place in Hohita to see for himself what all the fuss was about. He left a believer. While Nongqawuse was dishevelled and distracted, almost incoherent at times, it was in keeping with 'the call' from the ancestors that any *thwasa* or sangoma initiate went through and only added to her credibility.

Nongqawuse reportedly showed Sarhili wondrous things – a fresh ear of corn out of season as proof of the new people's crops and his favourite horse and beloved son – both returned from the dead, glimpsed among the shadowy figures that rose and fell on the surface of the ocean in the distance.

Admittedly, Sarhili was in an emotional state at the time. Although much loved by his people and a fair and just ruler, he was an indecisive man and had suffered much. The lung sickness that entered South Africa at Mossel Bay with a shipment of Friesland bulls on a Dutch ship, was destroying herds despite all attempts to contain it through culling sick animals. Almost 5 000 Xhosa cattle a month collapsed, unable to breathe and dying in a drawn-out agony of starvation. To make matters worse, a crop blight had destroyed much of their corn. The Xhosa had never experienced such terrible damage to their livelihoods and Sarhili felt powerless to stop it.

He was also burdened by personal pain. His father, the great king Hintsa had been killed by the British some years before and Sarhili's only surviving son had sickened and died at the age of 12. Worse, when one of his trusted counsellors was accused of bewitching the boy, he didn't intervene to save him even though he believed he was innocent. The man was executed and Sarhili was tortured by his own inaction.

Now, having witnessed Nongqawuse's miracles, Sarhili became an instant convert. He returned home and started killing his own cattle and commanded the nation to do the same. Many followed his lead and made their own pilgrimage to the banks of the Gxarha to see these marvels, but while some came away convinced they had heard cattle lowing and seen the tips of horns grazing the surface of the water, a sign of the other world's oxen impatient to come forth, others were sceptical. Sarhili's first cousin, Chief Ngubo, called Nongqawuse an imposter and beat her, while another chieftain said he'd see her right with a tussle in the grass, implying that her visions were delusions inspired by an adolescent girl's sexual frustration.

The Xhosa rapidly divided into believers or *amathamba* and unbelievers, *amagogotya*. The *amathamba* described themselves as 'soft' because they were willing to sacrifice their own material interests for the benefit of the nation, while the *amagogotya* were regarded as 'hard' for their selfish and unbending stance in refusing to co-operate, which could, Nongqawuse said, compromise all.

While the *amathamba* slaughtered their cows or sold them off for ridiculous prices, throwing away their seed, rethatching their roofs and building bigger kraals to accommodate their visitors and the oxen they would bring with them, the *amagogotya* simply shook their heads.

The resurrection was expected to occur at full moon in June 1856. When the day came and went without incident, many were understandably greatly disturbed. But when Sarhili confronted Mhlakaza and Nongqawuse, they claimed a misunderstanding, and under pressure, said the arrival would actually take place in August when two red suns would arise in the sky and collide, bringing forth darkness and a terrible storm that would sweep the unbelievers and the English into the sea. Needless to say, this didn't happen either.

Nongqawuse, speaking through Mhlakaza, predictably blamed the First Disappointment on the people, because even the believers held back on killing all their cows, and worse, sold them off, which was clearly not the same as sacrifice. Sarhili visited the riverbanks once more and once again came away convinced that he had seen irrefutable proof. He redoubled his efforts and sent men to guard the roads to prevent people from selling their cattle.

Meanwhile, back in the Colony, Cathcart's departure in 1854 made way for a new governor, the redoubtable George Grey, fresh from civilising the Maori in New Zealand. Grey promised to be a more liberal Imperialist who took a great interest in the culture of the people he lorded over. While his predecessors held by bludgeoning the local peoples into submission by force, George believed the 'natives' would leap at the chance to become willing converts to the civilised ways of capitalism if provided with the right incentive.

Unfortunately, dear George was a tad unhinged and fiercely ambitious – a dreadful combination in any circumstances, but especially in people in power. Throughout his life, Grey suffered terrible depressions and on at least one occasion returned to the Cape in tears, having suffered a breakdown and hallucinations. However, some historians suspect his odd behaviour might have been a side effect of the opiates he supposedly dosed himself with to treat the pain of an old spear-wound, administered by an aggressive Australian Aborigine who didn't want to be civilised, thanks very much.

Apart from his personality disorders, Grey was a lying, cheating skunk with a proclivity for exaggeration that happened to suit his purposes. In New Zealand, for example, he rid himself of a troublesome Maori chief by slapping him with trumped up charges that the man had been conspiring to kill settlers and rape white women. On arriving in the Cape, one of the first actions Grey took as new governor was to use the unsubstantiated rumours of a conspiracy between the Xhosa and the British-allied Mfengu as an excuse to extort huge amounts of money from the British government to avert another expensive frontier war. Grey claimed he needed £40 000 a year, delivered post-haste, to be able to distract the Xhosa by employing them in his civilising labour schemes.

When he heard about this cattle-killing, he was initially very alarmed at what he believed was superstitious savagery and sent a message to Sarhili demanding that he cut it out at once. Sarhili replied that his hands were tied. 'There is a thing which speaks in my country and orders me and my people to kill all our cattle, eat our corn, and throw away all our witchcraft wood, and not to plant and to report it to all the other chiefs to kill their cattle.'

Grey was livid that Sarhili had defied him and he became paranoid when he heard that the BaSotho king, Moeshoeshoe, had sent a delegation to investigate the commotion, even though he eventually decided not to kill his own cattle. Always one for conspiracy theories, Grey decided this was clearly evidence of a sinister plot between the Xhosa and the BaSotho, who were using Mhlakaza to stir up the people. If they killed all their cattle and destroyed their crops, the Xhosa would be freed up from guarding their herds and the ravages of hunger would inspire them to attack the British.

An attempt to put these impertinent chieftains in their place backfired spectacularly and gave new life to the prophecies, just when they should have died out. Grey inveigled the captain of a warship, the *HMS Geyser* to detour en route from Durban to Cape Town and call in at the Kei River mouth near Gxarha in November 1856 to give the Xhosa a little demonstration of the might of the British. Unfortunately, the captain was drunk and neglected to procure a pilot. When the ship entered the river by the wrong channel, the Xhosa gathered on the banks, shouting war cries, convinced this was going to be an attack. However, when a boat set off for shore, it overturned almost immediately, nearly drowning the five men in it. One of them swam ashore and bluntly refused to return to the boat, choosing instead to walk all the way back to East London. The *Geyser* slunk out with its tail between its rudders and soon rumours were rife that the new people, whether Russians or the ancestors, had intervened on behalf of the Xhosa.

Even while children passed out from hunger and dogs were too weak to bark at strangers, the believers tightened their *lambiles* or hunger belts specially designed for times of famine, and staged raids on the unbelievers, burning their crops and killing their herds. But Mhlakaza became nervous and tried to pass the buck. Nongqawuse and Nombanda began calling for the return of their chief, Nxito, ostensibly, they claimed, because the spirits wanted to speak through a chief rather than a lowly ex-missionary. Although Nxito was a vocal unbeliever, he heard them out, but wasn't convinced. Unfortunately, the news of his return together with the failed 'attack' of the *Geyser*, seemed to be proof positive to the believers that the rising would occur at the next full moon.

The Second Disappointment was soon to follow. On 11 December 1856, the anxiously awaited dead again failed to arise, the skies did not darken and no great storm swept anyone out to sea. This time Nxito was the scapegoat. When he interfered by planting a scout to ensure Mhlakaza could not resort to chicanery at a meeting for the chiefs, he had insulted the ancestors and yet again, they refused to come.

By now the threat of starvation was dire indeed. It was too late to sow seed even if they wanted to and many of the people were living off mimosa bark and scrounged roots, having already killed off their chickens and their goats. The Xhosa still believed because they had to, because there was no other choice. The alternative was facing up to their terrible mistake and certain death.

Another flurry of excitement ensued when a new young girl prophet emerged to corroborate Nongqawuse. In early 1857, Nonkosi, a girl of about eleven, met her own set of strangers and along with the command to kill cattle, also advocated that believers must shave their eyebrows. People rushed to conform.

After yet another postponement, the final day was announced to be 16 February 1857. People spent their time frantically preparing for the arrival of their ancestors. Remarried widows abandoned their new husbands to wait at their old homesteads for their long lost loves, others lit signal fires to show the way and the last straggling survivors of the great herds that once covered the plains were put to death.

The sun shimmered over the horizon at dawn, but to the dismay of the waiting crowds, it was *not* blood red. They sat through the following sunrise, in the hope they'd merely got the day wrong. And on the day after. And the day after that. By 21 February a storm opened up the skies and the people rushed inside, but it was still not the great day of the rising. Not then. Not ever.

The fallout was horrific. In some respects the prophecy had come true, because the emaciated survivors did indeed resemble the walking dead. Unbelievers died by the thousands. Years afterwards, sad little clusters of skeletons were found – of families who had just given up and sat down beneath a tree or in their houses to wait for death. Believers attacked unbelievers and settlers for food, parents snatched food from their childrens' hands, and horses and well-fed settler dogs became fair game. Some were so desperate and crazed from hunger they turned to cannibalism, an atrocity that was harshly punished.

Some found succour with the Mfengu, until George Grey, in his infinite wisdom, warned his allies that the British did not approve and would punish any found harbouring the Xhosa. The Cape Governor took a hard line, even shutting down a charitable British organisation set up to help the starving, called Kaffir Relief. Partly it was to punish Sarhili for his insubordination and to expand the borders of British Kaffraria into the free Xhosa territory, but he believed it also fit in perfectly with his scheme to civilise the Xhosa. Grey wasn't against charity, just the kind that wasn't usefully applied in the service of the Colony or that encouraged the well-known 'laziness' of the indigenous population. If they didn't have to work for aid, how would they appreciate it?

The Colony was drastically short on skilled labour and in return for providing such, Grey promised assistance to the suffering believers. Those who accepted the offer were issued with passes and contracts binding them to three or five years of lowly paid servitude. By the end of June 1857, some 13 000 Xhosa had made the move to the cities and towns, compared with the more than 40 000 who had endured the awful lingering death of starvation outside.

Despite a suicide attempt (using his father's assegai, supposedly restored to him by the ghost of King Hintsa himself in one of his sessions on the riverbank), Sarhili still held out hope. It was only in November, after Mhlakaza himself died of the famine he'd helped bring on, that Sarhili finally realised just what he had wrought. He returned to his homestead a broken man, but determined to start again.

He sent a heartfelt plea for aid to the Cape Governor, calling on the spirit of *ubuntu* but once again Grey was to show what a 'merciful' man he was. The British attacked, forcing Sarhili to flee. He sought refuge in a remote and impenetrable valley, but his brethren were not so fortunate. Those chieftains who were captured were sent to the already notorious Robben Island, imprisoned together with the lepers and lunatics and the other unwanted flotsam of the Empire.

Nonkosi, the new prophetess was captured and after months of interrogation, the eleven-year-old 'confessed' that it had been a grand plot to attack the British all along. On the flip side, many Xhosa came to believe that it had been Governor Grey himself hiding in the bushes, confusing a naïve girl with his conniving whispers so that he could subjugate the chieftains and steal their land.

And what of that naïve girl? Nongqawuse survived and was sent to stay with Grey's faithful servant, Major Gawler in East London, together with Nonkosi. A photograph of them survives. In October 1858, the prophesying pair were sent to Cape Town and installed in the former Pauper's Lodge that housed female prisoners, although some reports state that they too served time on Robben Island.

It's not entirely certain what became of the vague and dreamy girl who was at the centre of the fall of the Xhosa nation caught between the wily schemes of duplicitous men and the fervent hopes of her people and their king. It's said that when she was finally released, she made her way to Alexandria in the Eastern Cape, where she settled after being chased from Port Elizabeth when the people discovered who she was. The biographical data available thereafter is this brief: she married, had two daughters and died in 1898. Ironically, her grave on a farm in Glenshaw is surrounded by herds of happily grazing bovines.

Qolorha, the village on the banks of the Gxahra on the wild coast has become a tourist attraction. Visitors taking in the wrecks and the birdlife stop to throw coins in Nongqawuse's pool for luck and the people who live there are reportedly still divided between believer and unbeliever.

The Ship's Cat

Rifles, the leopard

The shameful secret of Simonstown's most celebrated pooch, Just Nuisance, is that the so-called 'Able Seaman' never actually set out to sea. He was infamous for riding the trains round the peninsula and was occasionally even taken on illegal flips in a reconnaissance plane. However, the closest the navy mascot ever came to the ocean proper was sprawling on the decks of vessels docked in the harbour, usually right in front of the gangplank to the exasperation of the crew, whose rather polite expletives (these were sailors after all) inspired his name.

Rifles, on the other hand, was an all-paws-on-deck-kinda gal. Twenty years before Just Nuisance was even a pup, and about the same length of time before the Royal Navy officially accepted women as sea-going crew, the handsome and devilish leopard who prowled the decks of *HMS Hyacinth* was a favourite of the Simonstown sailor set.

Rifles was brought on board the *Hyacinth* as a cub in 1916 when the cruiser stopped over in Mombasa on its way to the Cape of Storms. It was fairly common practice for the navy to take on exotic furry shipmates – at least until such time as they became too troublesome, but Rifles proved to be a natural seadog. Growing up on board, she became quite accustomed to the lilt and tilt of the ocean and could usually be found above decks in all but the worst of weather.

As with any respectable cat, she was highly mischievous and while the leash she was kept on gave her full range of the quarterdeck, she would often slip it, in order to hide behind bits of structure and machinery, tail lashing, waiting to pounce with a happy growl on any unsuspecting unfortunate who happened to walk past. She was also known to bat ankles. Although she was pretty good about not playing too rough, on those rare occasions when she got out of hand, the crew was forced to box her ears, leaving her with a look of outraged astonishment.

Only once did her antics lead to near disaster. A new recruit, who was unaccustomed to dealing with the perils of a large and fearsome feline on board, got such a shock when she leaped out at him, that he, sensibly, leapt out of her way with a shriek of terror, sending Rifles plunging over the railings and into the icy South Atlantic.

The officer on watch called a halt to the ship, but it takes a good while for even a light cruiser to stop, even at full reverse thrust and the crew had to keep the bobbing furry head in sight above the swells. Rowboats were dispatched to rescue the frantically paddling leopard. When she saw the boats, she changed course towards them and was pulled out of the drink, terribly bedraggled yet still hissing and spitting with furious indignation. Surgeon-Commander Allan Bee, who wrote the only surviving history of Rifles (his rollicking tale is available in full at the Simonstown Museum) said he'd never seen so 'blasphemous' an animal. 'She damned everybody from the Admiral downwards.'

By all accounts, Rifles was a rather spoilt, over-sized kitty. She had a cat house, but usually slept in the hammock vacated by the signalman when he went on duty. And while the crew had been advised not to feed her raw meat, because it would turn her wild, they found she became so sick on half-cooked food that they ignored the warning.

She was so accustomed to being the sole female on board that she would become terribly jealous of potential rivals for her crew's affection. When lady visitors dared to set dainty foot on her ship, she had to be held on a short and straining leash, or was bundled into her little house and locked in, to the hissy hussy's bitter disgust.

In her two years as able seacat, Rifles never attacked anyone with anything more than a playful nip, but while reports that she snubbed any officers who wore more gold than the *Hyacinth*'s commander are probably exaggerated, she did cause a stir with civilians when the ship pulled in to dock. According to the Surgeon-Commander, she hated the noise and the dockyard hands even more, sending them bolting back to shore with a vicious growl and cries of 'Blimey, it's a tiger!' She attracted a crowd of spectators so thick that no work could be done and the crew had to resign themselves to the fact that she had to go.

She retired with full honours to the London Zoo in 1919, where she lived out the rest of her life in comparative peace and quiet until 1923. Unfortunately the zoo doesn't have detailed records of her stay, so whether she ever got over her loathing of lady visitors or found a mate whose landlubbing ways she was able to overlook, is unknown.

The Feminist Farm Girl

Olive Schreiner

Olive Schreiner needed to get laid. Preferably by a man who was her match in both intellect and liberal idealism, a man whose conversation and profound ideas would set her mind sparking with neural lightning storms. But alas, while she shook up prim Victorian society with her shocker of a novel, *Story Of An African Farm*, as well as her radical theories that women's libidos were quite the equal of men's, Olive never managed to escape her missionary upbringing and consummate her ideas on willing flesh.

Quite the opposite. She did everything within her power to suppress her own desire, which she believed had an 'aberrant effect on the intellect', especially for her brilliant male friends, Havelock Ellis and Karl Pearson.

Her letters to them loudly proclaimed that they should treat her as a man and that their friendship was purely intellectual, but an aching, lonely subtext seeped through the pages like a watermark. When straightforward denial didn't work, she took to dosing herself with a pharmacy's worth of drugs to suppress any stirrings of the passions that so terrified her, including – at Havelock's suggestion – potassium bromide, noted for deadening the central nervous system.

Olive was a knot of contradiction. She was one of the leading feminists of her time, expounding revolutionary theories in her book *Woman and Labour*, that called for women to be usefully employed lest they be forced to resort to 'sexual parasitism'. And yet she was known to remark wistfully that she wished she'd been born a man and sympathised with the maxim she'd heard from black South African women who said, 'God cannot be good, otherwise why did he make women?'

Her parents, Gottlob and Rebecca were missionaries so puritanical that when her older sister, Kate, committed the cardinal sin of exchanging a wink with her fiancé in church, Gottlob 'excommunicated' her from receiving the sacrament during his services. They never approved of the young man anyway.

The Schreiners came out to South Africa from Britain in 1837 to run a missionary station for the Wesleyan Church. Rebecca gave birth to 12 children over the next 24 years, five of whom died in infancy, including three boys, all called Oliver. Olive was the ninth child, born in 1855 and named in memory of her dead brothers.

She was a striking child, with large dark eyes and a fierce intellect that drew adults to her for her insights, and children for the wild stories she wove. But she could also be retiring and strange, apt to languishing in her thoughts. When she was in trouble for misbehaving, she had the distressing habit of beating her head against the wall until she was nearly unconscious.

Life on the mission station was hard and made harder still by Rebecca's strict domineering nature. The children were forbidden from speaking Dutch and once, when Olive accidentally slipped out with 'ach, how nice it is outside', Rebecca caned her 50 strokes for that one discordant syllable in the *verboten* tongue. Rather than turn on her mother, the beating inspired the little girl to a 'bitter wild fierce agony in her heart' against God and man.

It was the beginning of her falling out with her faith. Apart from three short years of schooling from 12 to 15, the only education Olive received was from her sharp mother and the Bible. She was particularly moved by the philosophy of the Sermon on the Mount, but she started questioning her family's unstinting belief in God at a young age after her favourite little sister, Ellie, died at the age of two. Keeping watch over the infant's dead body incited Olive to devise her own philosophy about how reality worked and what eternity was. She felt the world *more* beautiful for having spawned and then reclaimed such a precious gift as Ellie.

When she was 12, Gottlob was thrown out of the Wesleyan Church in disgrace, after 27 years of service, for breaking the regulation that ministers were not allowed to engage in trade. He tried to start his own business but the venture was so spectacularly unsuccessful that the family were left destitute and forced to split up, sending the three youngest, Ettie, Will (who would become prime minister) and Olive to live with their older brother, Theo, a headmaster at a local school in Cradock.

No-one in Olive's family shared her religious scepticism or even understood her ideas, and it was only when, at the age of 15, she briefly met a young 'freethinking' government official called Willie Bertram that she discovered she wasn't alone in her dissatisfaction. He lent her his copy of Herbert Spencer's *First Principles*, a philosophical treatise that tried to balance religion and science in light of Darwin's new theories of evolution that caused such a furore. It changed her world.

After Theo left to join the diamond rush in Kimberley, Olive's life became most unstable as she was shunted between relatives. During one stay in the little town of Dordrecht, she became involved in a casual social circle of bright young minds, including a young man by the name of Julian Gau. Quite improperly, he accompanied her on a 160-km trip and at the end of August 1872, she sent her sister Kate a letter announcing, quite abruptly, that she was engaged, although she was noncommittal about setting a date. Some biographers speculate that Julian seduced her on the pretext of engagement and that she had a pregnancy scare, but there is little evidence to support such a theory; Olive was always secretive about her romances. Nine days later, she wrote to Kate again, but made no mention of the engagement and by September, judging by Olive's black mood and the maudlin poetry she wrote in her journal, the engagement seems to have been off.

It was around this time that she developed asthma, possibly as a psychosomatic response to her disastrous love affair and the flak her family gave her about her anti-religious stance. She'd always been robustly healthy, but now she suffered attacks that left her fighting for breath and crushed her chest with pain.

She dreamed of going to America to study medicine, but in 1874, in light of her family's desperate poverty (Gottlob had resorted to wearing Will's cast-offs), she resigned herself to becoming a governess at the age of 19. However, her first post turned ugly when her 33-year old employer, George Weakly, the father of the house, tried to kiss her and worse, although she never did reveal exactly what he did that induced her to leave.

Later, she admitted to her friend Havelock that she was attracted to several of her employers and suffered terrible ambivalence about the situation. When her brother Will became engaged, she declared that she felt that the ability to love was 'burnt out in her' and that she would never marry unless she found someone who could 'make me lose myself utterly'.

She enjoyed teaching when her charges responded to her, but resented the time it took away from her writing. Still, over the next seven years while she worked in various households, she completed two novels, *Story of An African Farm* and *Undine*, an autobiographical work about a 'queer' girl struggling to come to terms with her life and love, only published posthumously.

Story of An African Farm tackled similar themes, with the protagonists Waldo and Lyndall questioning everything, especially gender roles and the tyranny imposed on girls. It was considered shocking because Lyndall gives birth to a baby out of wedlock and her would-be lover, Gregory Rose, assumes the disguise of a woman to look after her.

She also started a third book, *From Man to Man* about two sisters, Bertie, a naïve girl who ends up a prostitute, and Rebekah, a married woman who finds herself in a not dissimilar situation, forced to put up with her husband's infidelities for the sake of economic survival.

At 21, she received word that her gentle father, Gottlob, on whom she based *Story's* compassionate Otto, had died. She entertained the idea of moving in with her mother to care for her, but they were too different and their relationship too conflicted.

She sent *Story* to friends in England to forward to a publisher, who remarked that the tale showed promise, but needed to be cut before he would consider it. She also asked them to send her the application forms to train as a nurse at the Royal Infirmary in Edinburgh.

Olive set off for England in 1881, but her dreams of entering the medical field were unrealistic. She lacked the necessary formal education and when she tried out a stint volunteering in a local woman's hospital, within five days she came down with inflammation of the lungs.

She was terribly despondent and became extremely ill, as she often did during times of stress. During this time, she also started an involvement with a man who was a sadist and discovered, to her horror, that he fulfilled a masochistic need in her.

Like the advances of various employers such as George Weakly, she found it terrifying and demeaning, but also, to her shame, exciting. Her tension about the affair, which she only mentions once briefly in her letters, exacerbated her condition.

She started hawking *Story* and found a willing publisher, Chapman Hall. The latter suggested she add a line whereby Lyndall secretly marries the father of her child or else, it was feared, the book would be condemned as wicked, the booksellers would refuse to stock it and it would impugn on her reputation as a young lady. Olive refused to change a word.

The book, published under the pseudonym Ralph Iron, went on to become a roaring success, although admittedly some of those roars were of moral outrage. Her brother Fred wrote to her to say he couldn't have anything more to do with her (although he later recanted) and at least one reader made a big fuss about having burned her copy, after she finished reading it, of course. *Story* sold 100 000 copies by the turn of the century and it quickly became widely known that Olive was the writer behind the very masculine nom de plume.

The book served her well, catapulting her to fame and acting as a potent introduction to high profile people with whom she became friendly over the years, including Gandhi, Rudyard Kipling, Oscar Wilde, Cecil John Rhodes and the man she was to marry, Samuel Cronwright – all great fans of her work.

The book also spurred a young trainee doctor, Havelock Ellis to write to her in 1884, kicking off a lifetime correspondence. Havelock was to become a leading sexologist and social reformer and, like Olive, had also lost his faith at a young age in 'an empty and mechanical world'. Over the course of their exchange, the pair discovered that they had so much in common, they were virtually reflections of each other. Surely, this was the kind of man of Olive's dreams?

But while their correspondence was deeply intimate and, at times, in their heated discussions of gender issues and sex, deeply provocative, they never got it on.

Olive felt that she was being 'cruel' and 'untrue' if she came near him or kissed him and dared not give in to her feelings, while he, in turn, claimed he was only interested in a 'realisation' of her. He advised her on her work and acted as confidante and part-time therapist and said he felt most fulfilled when she was ill, plagued by her asthma as well as nausea, dizziness, fever and crying jags that might have as easily been a result of all the drugs she was mixing and matching as any physical ailment.

Olive claimed she felt Havelock had abnormal needs and the fact that he remained a virgin until he married at 32, despite an overwhelming interest in sex and homosexuality in particular, lends some credence to her theory.

There was someone interested in her at the time, a very sweet doctor, Bryan Donkin, who was bowled over by her book and the woman who wrote it, but she was unable to reciprocate his feelings. In her book *From Man to Man*, she wrote that when a man touches a woman, he touches her 'soul, her brain, her creative power. It is putting his fingers into her brain and snapping the strings when he draws her to him physically and cannot take her mentally'.

There has been some speculation that Olive was a lesbian, but although she loved her female friends fiercely, it seems it was never erotic. The word doesn't seem to have been part of her vocabulary of thought and although she acknowledged male homosexuality, she never made mention of Sapphic love in any of her writings.

Still living in London, she became embroiled in another intellectual crush on a barrister and mathematician, Karl Pearson, through an elite group called the Men and Women's Club that met regularly to discuss gender relations and sex quite openly, although they vetted their members carefully. Formed in 1885, members presented discourses on anything from venereal diseases to the inferiority of girls' education and how Buddhist men treated women.

Olive was one of the committee members and her outspokenness on the stupidity of celibacy and how women's sex drive was just as natural an animal force as men's, ironically earned her the label a 'free woman'. In theory, she could regale Havelock that 'I would base all my sex teachings to children and young people on the beauty and sacredness and importance of sex,' but in practice, it seems she was more buttoned up than most.

She and Karl started corresponding regularly, but from the outset, he laid down the law that their friendship should be the 'free open friendship of man to man'. Olive tried to play by the rules, but she was strongly attracted to him. They had a falling out when he disclosed some of her private letters to a mutual friend and in the resulting fracas, her health broke down completely.

Bryan Donkin, who was Olive's doctor as well as her would-be suitor, blamed her breakdown on hysteria caused by sexual repression, a common theory at the time, and wrote Karl a letter to that effect. Olive sent a missive hot on its heels, claiming Bryan was wrong and that she'd never felt 'sex-love' for him and if he really felt she did, why had he never confronted her about it? He didn't reply and her worsening condition thereafter belied her claims. Through 1877 and

1888, she travelled around Europe, staying in Switzerland, Italy and Paris and tried to get over Karl.

She was still writing furiously, working on an introduction to proto-feminist Mary Wollstonecraft's *Vindication Of The Rights of Woman* and trying to complete *From Man to Man*. She pursued her interest in prostitutes by spending time with working girls and was even mistaken for one when walking one night with a male friend. Her landladies may have entertained similar suspicions considering the number of male visitors she had in the boarding houses in which she stayed. (Later, during World War I, they would give her grief for having a German surname.)

She returned to South Africa in 1889 at the age of 34, sweeping into the country with an aura of celebrity slung around her shoulders like a mink stole, but she was still depressed and wrote to Havelock about 'feeling dead', which was only made worse when she heard that Karl had married Marie Sharpe, one of her acquaintances from the Men and Women's Club, in 1890, the same year she published her book of allegories, *Dreams*. In 1891, Havelock also married and Olive wrote to him that she felt that she might be able to now marry too without sacrificing her individuality, though she scoffed that she would never find the right man. She met her husband a year later.

Olive moved to Matjiesfontein, where she hoped the dry air of the arid Karoo would relieve her asthma. She felt the place was perfectly balanced between civilisation, with its wild natural surroundings offset by the larney hotel catering to the high society folks who holidayed there and the railway that connected her to Cape Town.

She was much sought after in social circles, but she considered the people who surrounded her to be parochial philistines compared with her brilliant friends in England. There was one exception – 'the only big man we have here' – the prime minister, Cecil John Rhodes. She met him through her brother Will, who was employed as his legal advisor. She admired him greatly, at least initially, for his genius. She compared him to her questing character Waldo in *Story* with his avid mind but clumsy child's body. For his part, he was a huge fan of her book and the two became fast friends. It became quite the social coup to have both of them at a party, but they soon fell out, predictably enough, over politics.

Olive was a great supporter of the Boers and was also deeply interested in the 'Native Question' and how to bring the black population into the white social system. She was horrified when she learned that Cecil had supported the Flogging Bill, which proposed that 'natives' could be whipped at the slightest provocation. She was also outraged by rumours that she was trying to catch him as husband and by the end of 1892, she was so disillusioned that she snubbed him at the Matjiesfontein station, refusing to shake his hand.

At the end of that year she visited her old friends, the Cawoods, for whom she had once worked as a governess (and by whom she had once been rejected for her free thinking ways that made her in Mrs Cawood's words, 'God's enemy'). The manager on the neighbouring farm was a 28-year-old ostrich farmer and self-proclaimed freethinker, Samuel 'Cron' Cronwright who was also a fan of *Story*. He always said when he met 'Lyndall' he would marry her. And so he did, two years later.

Many of Olive's friends felt Cron was beneath her, but Olive said she'd never felt like this before about anyone. She had convinced herself she wanted to marry a 'man of action' and with his admirable physique, jet-black hair and cropped beard, Cron fit the bill. She wanted, she said, a relationship where she could provide her man with a 'moral education', while he would adore and idolise her as a 'saint'. Again, Cron was a prime contender for the role and while he wasn't a Havelock or a Karl, he was still intelligent and liberated enough to suit Olive, and sufficiently savvy to go on to a career in politics. When they married in 1894, in keeping with their freethinking ways it was a simple ceremony and they wore everyday clothes. She kept her name and he changed *his* to Cronwright-Schreiner. Cron was highly supportive of her writing and gave up his lucrative job on the farm so she could move to Kimberley, where her asthma wouldn't plague her so terribly, and continue with her work.

By then, she was pregnant. Delighted, she started preparing a little book for her baby-to-be, writing in it every day and preparing a reading list on the off chance she should die and not be able to share all the things she wanted to with her child. Her macabre preoccupation with death was misplaced. It was not she, but the baby who died.

After a delivery involving forceps and chloroform, the infant was taken away from her so she could rest. She heard it cry once during the night, but in the morning, 16 hours later, her baby girl was dead. Weeping, Olive cradled the child for ten hours, before relenting and allowing her to be taken away. A photograph of the tiny body was taken, held in a grim-faced Cron's arms.

The baby was buried in their garden. Olive wrote 'you don't know what that little brown heap is to me'. Thereafter, whenever they moved, they took her with them in a tiny lead coffin, first to Johannesburg, then Hanover, and later De Aar.

Olive kept trying and during 1896, she had three miscarriages. The doctors told her she would have to take to her bed for six months if she wanted to have a baby, but she deemed it impossible.

She was becoming increasingly involved in the political sphere through Will, who was now the attorney-general in Cecil John Rhodes' cabinet and through Cron, whose political career was also taking off. She was furious with Cecil for his part in the Jameson Raid, a conniving plot to take over the Transvaal Republic. But when he was forced to resign and set off to pacify Rhodesia instead, Will was elected into power to take his place as prime minister.

Olive reacted to the scandal of the Jameson Raid by writing an unfortunately preachy parable, *Trooper Peter Halket of Mashonaland*, which was a criticism of Cecil and his policies and featured a gruesome photograph on the cover of the hanging tree in Bulawayo, weighed down with the bodies of executed black men. The book and Olive's outspoken criticism of Cecil caused much dissent in her family and there were later rumours that the Transvaal government had paid her to write it, which upset her greatly.

By 1898 Cron was broke. He had supported Olive over the last two years in her writing, but wasn't convinced she was ever going to finish *From Man to Man*. He determined to become an attorney and they moved to Johannesburg, which Olive described it as a 'great fiendish hell of a city' that crushed her creativity.

It was clear that war between the British and the Boers was imminent. Olive landed a commission as war correspondent for *The New York Journal* and was about to set off for the Boer frontlines when she suffered what was probably a heart attack and had to abandon her plans. When the war *did* finally break out, she was recuperating in Cape Town, but that didn't prevent her from joining what was pejoratively known as the 'shrieking sisterhood' of women who took a stance against it, including Emily Hobhouse.

While Cron was overseas stirring up anti-war sentiment, Olive delivered ferocious speeches and was harassed by minor officials for her pro-Boer campaign. She was living in Hanover, then under martial law, which she found damnably irritating. She wasn't allowed to travel without a permit, news was scarce and her letters from her friends, which kept her sane, were heavily censored. She consoled herself by lavishing attention on her beloved fox terrier, Nita, and the tame meerkats she kept as pets. But she was again on the edge of a nervous breakdown, taking to bed for long hours at all times of the day and writing very little.

She was upset by the farm burnings and concentration camps and tried to use her influence to intervene in an execution of four Boers she believed wrongfully accused of attacking a train. It was to no avail and the men were shot.

In 1900 the Schreiner ministry fell and by 1902 the war was over. Olive and Cron returned to Johannesburg, but when they arrived there, they found their house had been looted and burned, and the manuscript of her new book *Woman and Labour* had been destroyed. Cron was later to claim in his rather one-sided biography that she was delusional and had spent so much time thinking about her book that she imagined she'd already written it, but this seems unlikely.

In 1903, Olive's mother died and she had her father exhumed so they could be buried together. She told Cron she wanted to be buried on Buffelskop in the Karoo with her baby girl and her dog Nita.

After the war Olive turned her energies to exploring the question of labour and black politics and kept in regular contact with Gandhi's peaceful resistance movement in India and the Women's Enfranchisement League in the UK.

She was also hard at work rewriting her lost manuscript and *Woman and Labour* was finally published in 1909. Known as her 'sex paper', it was considered a major feminist work. Olive argued that with modernisation, all the traditional jobs done by women such as making bread, beer or clothes was now outsourced to factories, and though she believed marriage and the family were sacrosanct, she felt if women could not be engaged in work that had a useful role in society, they would fall back on 'sexual parasitism'. Women needed to be provided with training and useful labour, she argued. Unfortunately, the book was only really relevant to the middle and upper classes, especially in South Africa where black women did all the manual work.

She made a final trip to England in 1914 at the age of 58, but Cron refused to leave his business and they spent the next five years apart. She travelled in Europe for a while before the outbreak of World War I rendered it impossible and then she struggled to find accommodation back in London with her German name. Havelock saw her occasionally and reported that she was more dogmatic and cantankerous than ever. She was depressed again and asked Havelock to burn all the letters he had from her as there was no-one to whom she could leave them.

Cron went to see her in London in 1920 in London, after Will had died, and was shocked to find how much she'd aged. The couple had a falling out over an affair Olive insisted he was having with an acquaintance of hers. He denied it and told her she was crazy and that if she pressed the point, he would not visit her at all. On this point, she does seem to have been delusional.

Certain that the end was near, Olive decided she wanted to end her life in her own country, despite her doctor's warning that it was madness to undertake such a long journey. Cron stayed behind in England and back in Cape Town, Olive found accommodation in a quiet little boarding house in Wynberg.

Despite all, she couldn't resist becoming involved with social issues and politics and when 19 black workers were killed during a strike led by Cape ANC leader, Samuel Masabalala, Olive raised money for his defence and wrote prime minister Jan Smuts a scathing letter reminding him what had happened to the czars in Russia after so many centuries of oppressing the serfs.

Her health worsened and she was suffering regular small heart attacks, so it was no surprise when on 11 December 1920, the maid found her peacefully dead in her bed, the book she'd been reading resting on her chest.

Back in London, Cron received a telegram advising him of her death only after he'd already read about it in the papers. For several weeks thereafter, he still received letters from her that she'd posted before she died.

She was buried in a simple ceremony in the Maitland cemetery, but in 1921, when Cron returned to South Africa, he had her exhumed together with the bodies of her baby girl and her dog, Nita. He commissioned a craftsman to construct a sarcophagus on the top of Buffelskop with its panoramic views of the Karoo wilderness that had so inspired her. The ground at the peak was ironstone and too hard to be broken; it took two months to cart materials up the 2 000 feet to build Olive's final resting place.

On 13 August 1921, a small and very informal procession set off early in the morning for the summit. A group of black labourers carried Olive's coffin, which Cron deemed appropriate because 'she had always been their champion'. Just before they reached the top, Cron saw an eagle flying overhead that he couldn't identify. It seemed to him, and two of the people with him as if it was the embodiment of the Bird of Truth Olive had written about in *Story of An African Farm*.

The parable, related to Waldo by a mysterious Stranger, told of a Hunter who went in search of the Bird of Truth. Along the way, he encountered many perils and distractions and people who mocked him or tried to lead him astray, but he struck on and reached the mountains of stern reality. He started to climb, but the path grew narrower and steeper and finally disappeared. The air was thin, he spent years hacking steps into the rock with bleeding fingers, but refused to give up. At the end, when he realised he was dying, it didn't matter because he knew others would follow in the steps he'd cut and find the Truth through him. He died holding a feather from the Bird, never realising how close he'd come.

It was an appropriate metaphor for Olive's life.

The Snake Charmer

Glenda Kemp

*I*n 1973, at the height of South Africa's *verkrampte* sexual repression, the little *dorpie* of Volksrust, on the edge of KwaZulu-Natal, was afizz with the news that the notorious Glenda Kemp would be performing. With her gyrating limber hips and the python she coiled around them, she had already inflamed the moral outrage – and desire – of white South Africa, but no-one could have been prepared for *this* show. When the lissom and mischievous showgirl got wind of the uproar, the emergency prayer meetings and the cops lying in wait to arrest her if she showed even a hint of dusky nipple, she rose to the challenge by getting down on her knees and praying to God for inspiration.

That evening, despite the *dominee's* seething warnings to his congregation to stay away from that 'dark hole of evil', the Olde Barn nightclub was packed with a thrall of people, including wives primped and preened for the occasion, prominent townsfolk, church elders, two magistrates and several cops.

The lights dimmed, a hush fell on the room and to the rhythmic tattoo of African drums, the woman they had all been waiting for shimmied into the spotlight – as they'd never seen her before. Gasps rippled through the assembled crowd.

Glenda's shows had a reputation for being quirkily creative. Unlike the lithe young things twisting themselves around a pole in strip clubs today, Glenda didn't just take her clothes off. She had audiences coming back week after week not because they wanted to see her naked (she only stripped completely in Lesotho and Swaziland) but to see what daring and imaginative thing she would to do next.

Some show were re-envisioned fairy tales, only in her version of Beauty and the Beast she was carried off by a gorilla, while in her bastardised Nutcracker, she took on the role of a mannequin come to life, oiling her limbs, surrounded by her immobile fibreglass sisters.

There was her legendary strobe dance, where she'd strike a pose between flashes of light, her Little Devil puppet who caused one policeman blushing embarrassment when he was forced to testify that he'd found her topless and 'busy with it' during a performance and, of course, her most famous co-star, Oupa, the snake. But *this* took it too far as she skirted dangerously close to a contravention of the Immorality Act, laying bare poor repressed white South Africa's darkest taboo.

When Glenda stepped onto stage that night, she was wearing the bare minimum required to avoid arrest – a cuff of springbok fur folded around her ankle, a matching G-string and homemade nipple caps, but she was also slathered head-to-toe in black body paint and wearing a tightly coiled Afro wig. When the audience caught their collective breath, one man, beside himself, burst out, '*God, dis 'n meid!*' (God, it's a maid!)

'They wanted to be shocked, so I gave them what they wanted,' Glenda says with one of her signature dulcet giggles, sitting in the threadbare lounge of her modest Durban home overlooking the ocean. Now 57, with a practical pixie-cut that long ago replaced the flowing locks she flung around with such abandon, it's still possible to see in her features the incandescent young woman who electrified a nation. Her alter-ego, the demure teacher, is now all that remains.

It's taken the schoolteacher-turned-stripper-turned-schoolteacher (and now devout Christian) some 30 years to shake off the last vestiges of her scandalous reputation, which even after she gave up the gig, snagged around her ankles like one of her casually dropped G-strings. It still occasionally trips her up.

She tried to quit stripping in the late '70s, but when she applied for a job at a school in Goudstad, the principal creepily pulled out a file full of clippings on her, together with a strongly worded letter from the Minister of Education suggesting that her type was not the sort the department wanted to employ.

In a more recent job interview, Glenda rendered the principal at a Durban Christian school speechless when she came clean about her past. 'She was so shocked. I remember going home and I was actually crying that she could be so prejudiced.' But the principal got over it and now Glenda uses her flamboyant imagination to entertain – and educate – five-year-olds. Of course, 30 years ago, grown men might have argued that seeing Glenda perform was an education in itself.

Glenda is not proud of her past – 'Is that my claim to fame?' but claims that she was never a bad girl, she just played one on stage, which, she says, is like vilifying an actor for portraying a murderer. She maintains she still doesn't understand what all the fuss was about. 'I felt I was so innocent. What were the police doing? You know, it was really very stupid that they arrested me. It was just an act. I had a good show.'

Even the arresting officers were forced to agree and the arts community, including incendiary critic and artist Walter Batiss, rallied to support her during one of her many trials for indecent exposure, adamant that her shows were legitimate theatre. That's not to say she didn't court controversy, but for Glenda, it was never about a cause. 'I'm sorry,' she says, 'I would disappoint people, because I didn't do it to make a statement about anything. Here was an opportunity to create my own stage and do my own thing. If anyone had approached me to say rather come be in our play, I would have done that. With all my heart I wanted to be an actress.'

Glenda was always a dreamer, a trait that was to irritate the authorities like a bikini rash throughout her life, from the matrons at the orphanage where she spent three years as a teenager to the magistrates and ministers who decried the moral degeneracy they claimed she provoked.

She was born 'somewhere in the Cape', the youngest of six, but after her father, Dirk, died, her mother Martie was forced to send her children to orphanages or into foster care. Martie tried to hold on to Glenda as long as possible, but at 12 she too was shipped off to the Abraham Kriel orphanage.

During the first year her older sister Joan was there to look after her and keep her out of trouble, but once she turned 18 and matriculated, Glenda was left to her own devices. She remembers it as a hard and regimented place where they called the kids by numbers rather than their names – she was number 16 – and she often cried herself to sleep.

She says, 'I was permanently in trouble when I did nothing wrong. I would forget my toothbrush in the bathroom or I'd be late because I had gone for a walk and I was such a daydreamer I didn't know what the time was. They'd accuse me of things – like meeting boys in the mealiefields, but I was just dancing and singing and talking to my imaginary friends.' Her flair for fantasy had some advantages; despite her shyness, she used to trail children behind her, rapt in her stories.

At 15, she went on a church camp with the other orphans and something about her caught the attention of one of the camp leaders, Magriet Baumbach, who despite her age (she and her husband, Tino, were pushing 60 at least) was moved to take Glenda in as a foster child on their farm in Swartruggens, near Rustenburg.

Although she always kept in touch with her mother and her siblings, this was a completely new life for her. She was free to wander at will in her beloved nature, spending hours on the riverbank or curled in a tree, reading, dancing and acting – because while she had considered becoming a teacher or a vet, more than anything she dreamed of becoming an actress. Under her foster parent's influence and her new-found Christianity, Glenda's school career underwent an about-turn: from shy underachiever she became head girl at Rodeon School and was already developing a reputation for theatrics and puppet shows in school plays.

At 20 she went on to attend the Teacher's Training College at Potchefstroom and then Goudstad, where she was subjected to humiliating initiations in her first year. The older girls forced her to wear the same dress for three weeks, shouted at her every time she used the word 'I' and prevented her from sleeping. It was a huge blow to her fragile self-confidence, built entirely on the creaky foundation of those three brief years in the Baumbach's care.

It was only when she started clubbing in Hillbrow, then the bee's knees of the trendy nightlife scene, and landed a job at the Marrakech as a go-go dancer for R5 a weekend that she realised she could win approval and affection through her creativity. Just as she was never merely a stripper, she was also never 'just' a go-go girl. She started acting out the words to the songs and then dressing the part. She moved on to cabarets and one day she pretended to take her clothes off. And then she stopped pretending.

In *Glenda, My Life Story*, the 1975 movie based on her life in which she starred, director Dirk de Villiers came up with a motivation for her to take up stripping – that her brother was in dire need of money – but in reality, Glenda says, 'I don't know why or how or where it came from. I just enjoyed it.'

She performed at various clubs, private parties and cabarets such as the Westerwald, and her shows gradually became increasingly outrageous and suggestive. When a teaching post became available in Koringfontein, she declined on the basis that the town was so remote, she couldn't find the place on the map and, besides, why go back to teaching when she could make the equivalent of a month's salary in two performances?

She was already garnering a reputation for herelf, when, at 24, she was swept off to Boston by an American club owner who saw her dance. Once there, however, Glenda discovered to her horror, that La Boheme was a little *too* bohemian for her tastes, requiring its dancers to include private performances under the sheets. Glenda deftly avoided intimate contact with the patrons by running upstairs to 'wash her hair' after every show, a task, which, curiously, seemed to take her most of the night. Eventually the management took the hint and left her alone.

After a couple of months, and a brief, aborted stop in New York (which she found way too intimidating), she returned to South Africa, her dignity intact.

Despite the eroticism of her shows, off-stage Glenda was as conservative as 'an office girl'. When a church group picketed one of her shows brandishing Bibles, for example, she joined in the hymns because she knew the words. On another occasion, while relaxing on the beach in East London, a young man starting chatting to her and invited her to attend the Glenda Kemp show with him that night. She declined and 'he immediately apologised, saying he could see I wasn't *that* kind of girl', she laughs.

This duality perplexed the fans arriving at her home to pay the advance deposit for her appearances at their private parties and they refused to believe that the diffident young woman holding open the door could possibly be 'Glenda Kemp the stripper'. Likewise, if someone walked in on her after a show, she would cover up and chase them out, absolutely mortified, despite their protests that they had already seen her naked. 'I was different on stage,' she explains, 'I was playing a part. I was an actress, that's all.'

That air of innocence was very much a part of Glenda's appeal. She was a delectable gamine with a hint of ingénue, like an Afrikaans Audrey Hepburn – if Audrey moved like J.Lo and took off her clothes. She was part belly dancer, part erotic ballerina with a heavy dose of orgiastic disco groove. Even when her shows were clearly contrived, as she bucked her hips against the thick coil of snake between her legs or had her coy devil hand-puppet tweak a nipple and try to tug down her panties, before hiding away behind her shoulder, she moved with unaffected joy.

'I think I was a very strange package,' she says, 'Obviously it was suggestive, but it was funny, like the Sunday school teacher wrapped up in a stripper's package. People couldn't understand it.' Some men must have found it discomfiting, not entirely sure whether they wanted to take her to bed or put her to bed and tuck her in. One cop who was ordered to arrest her did exactly that. Instead of carting her off to jail, he took her home, introduced her to the wife and kids and installed her in the spare room for the night.

In all the years she performed, she says she never had a bad experience with anyone trying it on, although she did occasionally hear rumours that one of the drivers who picked her up for her private shows and dropped her off again afterwards would intimate that they'd 'had a good time'. She shrugs it off. 'It didn't bother me, because we both knew the truth.'

The truth was she was strictly a one-man woman and that man was Karl Koczwara. She met him after one of her go-go gigs when she was still a teaching student and he offered her a lift home to the hostel. They were together for almost 20 years; although Karl was never thrilled about her line of work, he was apparently content that while others could look, he was the only one who took her home.

Her shows were more playful than pornographic, often starting and ending on an anticlimactic joke, like Glenda pulling on a billowing pair of bloomers (although this also conveniently got around the law in place at the time that you weren't allowed to leave the stage wearing less than you came on in). While her foster parents expressed disappointment in her, Glenda's biological mother Martie was very supportive and even made an impromptu debut on one occasion when Glenda handed her a blazing firestick that stubbornly refused to die. Martie mistook her intentions and instead of removing it for her, got up on stage and did a prancing circuit with it.

The snakes happened by chance. Encouraged by her brother who kept them as pets, Glenda took a mole snake along as a prop for one of her shows. She had such an overwhelming reaction to what was, after all, 'such a small snake', it became a much imitated mainstay of her act. She gradually upgraded to bigger and bigger snakes until she acquired Oupa, who was actually not one python but 20, all going by the same name because she only had one licence. While some have interpreted the name as a sly satirical dig at the old men who decried her, Glenda says the truth is more banal. 'He just looked like an old man, with that grumpy down-turned mouth.'

Glenda would twist the snake between her legs and simulate fellatio, but unfortunately, one of Oupa's incarnations didn't take kindly to her sliding its head suggestively in and out of her mouth and one night, it bit her in the face. She clamped its jaws shut with elastic bands thereafter. On another occasion, en route to a show in Ladysmith, her snake died abruptly in the car. Nonplussed, Glenda did the show anyway, throwing the dead thing around as if it were alive. The audience was oblivious and on the way home she tossed it unceremoniously out the window. She never did like snakes.

When she went to London, at 29, to work in the classy Paul Raymond Revue Bar and the famous Windmill in 1978, she was elated when they told her to ditch her little reptile friend and she gave Oupa away to the first person who asked. Her show focused on her African dancing sketch, always her favourite, dancing naked to the transfixing rhythm of the drums, with the occasional schoolgirl number and a washing routine that had her pulling on a wet T-shirt and lathering on suds, thrown in for good measure.

She'd been photographed for *Scope* and *You*, and even the *Financial Mail* in South Africa (to the consternation of her foster mother, who was especially upset that she was wearing a bonnet a family friend had made for her), but in London, she declined to be photographed by a men's magazine, claiming they were only interested in 'her vitals'.

While the newspapers trumpeted her triumphant taking of the city, Glenda was desperately lonely in London. Never a big party girl, despite her love of dancing, she felt she didn't fit in with the other women who worked at the club and she was cut off from all the 'normal' people who worked during the day. She was genuinely a naïf. She never drank and was shocked when her companions passed around a joint. Likewise, when someone offered her a button, she thought they meant she'd lost one on her blouse. Although not the oldest, she found herself taking on a motherly role; she baked cookies for the other dancers and acted as a confidante.

Glenda returned home in 1979. She'd given up dancing intermittently over the years to try her hand at other work including a stint as a relief matron at the Epworth Children's Village in Germiston, part-time teaching, modelling for magazines (with and without clothes) and had tried to break in to 'real' acting or TV presenting.

But by then, she'd finally had enough. She'd stopped enjoying it and as she says, 'You have to know when to stop. There's a season for everything and the season for that was over. I felt that everyone had seen me and I wanted to get married and become a mother.' And so Glenda Kemp hung up her G-string.

Possibly to escape from the whispering scenes and black looks she inspired whenever she stepped out in public, Glenda and Karl went to Botswana for three years to run safaris, where she managed to avoid snakes, but tangled with troops of monkeys instead, come to raid her bushveld kitchen.

She and Karl married in 1983, when she was already pregnant with her daughter Kim. She was so delighted by the birth of her baby that she licked her all over 'like a little kitten'.

After a stint working in her sister's scrap shop and a friend's boutique, Glenda moved to Durban where she ran a small puppet show business with Kim, entertaining quite innocently at children's parties. She and Karl separated in around 1992; while Glenda had always remained faithful, it seemed her husband wasn't able to return the favour.

She'd saved enough money from her career as South Africa's highest paid stripper to buy security in the form of a house with a sea view and a ten-minute walk to the beach, which she eventually sub-divided and let out. One of her tenants was a man by the name of Peter Harper and in 1998 she married him.

The Glenda in Dirk de Villiers' biopic meets a grisly end, strangled to death by her snakes, which the real Glenda always saw as symbolic of the end of her career, although she adds wryly, 'Now that I think of it, it was a stupid ending, but the Afrikaners love to do this in their plays and movies. Everybody dies and it's all tragedy and I don't like that. I like happy endings.'

In life, Glenda has found her happy ending, one that involves leaving her provocative past behind. The day before our interview, she received the final physical clearance she'd been waiting for – a presidential pardon expunging her criminal record. The three-page letter, dated 8 August 2005, bearing the state seal and Thabo Mbeki's signature, absolves her on three separate counts of 'contravening section 19B of the Sexual Offences Act 1957 by exhibiting herself in an indecent dress or manner in full view of the public'. 'It's official,' she says, 'God cleared me long ago, but now the country has cleared me too.'

The Struggle Sisters

Lilian Ngoyi and Helen Joseph

Repressive regimes are not known for their rationality, but the apartheid government's actions against a pair of 'little old ladies' at the height of the struggle seemed unreasonably vindictive – even by despotic dictator standards.

After all, what danger could a stylish Sowetan seamstress and an aging ex-Brit with breast cancer possibly pose to the might of the National Party that could warrant their transmogrification into non-persons, forbidden from leaving their homes or speaking in public? Even though their banning and house arrests drew much heat, inspiring a torrent of sympathy and outrage, even unsettling some devout NP supporters, the irony was that the government had good cause to panic.

With the legendary 'raging lionness' Lilian Ngoyi in one corner, and 'that red bitch' Helen Joseph in the other, these were hardly toothless doddering old dears. On the contrary, despite their fashionable appearances, Lilian in her black hat and Helen in her cat's eye glasses, they were dangerous inciters, compatriots and friends, so close that they would later be buried 'side by side' in Soweto.

The government tried everything to get them to shut the hell up. They were banned, barred from attending meetings, jailed and tried for treason together with 154 other troublemakers. Their words were deemed too inflammatory for public consumption. It became illegal to quote or disseminate anything they said or wrote.

They had to report to the police station on a daily basis and they were imprisoned in their homes. The solitary confinement of house arrest is a particular brand of lonely limbo hell, although it pales in comparison to the atrocities committed behind closed doors; of wet bag torture and cattle prods and 'suicides' from fifth floor windows. But while the full picture of those horrors was only to be exposed like a gruesome Polaroid during the agony and the apathy of the Truth Commission, the house arrests and bannings happened in open view. Like a public flogging, they were designed to serve as a warning as well as a means of rendering the troublemakers in question powerless.

In the case of Lilian and Helen, it was to have the opposite effect. The two might have been cut off from their friends and family and their involvement in the struggle, but the glaring blank spaces of their absence only served to draw more attention to their cause.

The Special Branch must sorely have regretted not doing more to silence them for good as they did with Ruth First – although that's not to say they didn't try. Both women endured much misadventure during their long careers (as when Lilian posed as a pregnant woman, her fake tummy stuffed with political pamphlets to get through a road block) as well as the occasional attempted assassination, such as the bomb strapped to Helen's front gate.

The two had beginnings as disparate as the conditions in the black and white women's cells they found themselves in during the Treason Trial in 1956. Unfortunately, while Helen wrote three books, *If This Be Treason*, *Tomorrow's Sun* and *Side By Side*, maNgoyi as she was respectfully known didn't leave much of a paper trail behind her. Even before she was banned and it was illegal to quote her or record her words, her thunderous and magnificent speeches that would rivet the room were made off the cuff and she seldom resorted to making notes.

Lilian Masediba Matabane was born on 25 September 1911 in Pretoria, one of six children in a family that teetered on the brink of abject poverty. Her father, John, who was vehemently anti-white, worked in the platinum mines, while her mother, Anne, was a one-woman laundromat, washing clothes and sheets for white families in the suburbs. Lilian often accompanied her mother collecting or delivering the laundry, but was disturbed when she saw that dogs were better treated than black people, allowed inside the house to eat their food in the kitchen, while Lilian and her mother were forced to eat on the pavement outside. She said later, 'I used to think that compared to white people, we were made of second-hand stuff.'

Lilian's grandfather, who relinquished his position as a Pedi chief to become a church minister, promised that God would save them, but Lilian came to realise that prayer alone was not going to cut it. Despite all her fervent prayers, the family's financial circumstances deteriorated to the extent that their only food was mealie meal porridge and a small serving of meat once a month. Poverty also put paid to her hopes of becoming a teacher and she was forced to leave school at the Kilnerton Training Institution in Standard Two.

A continent away, Helen Beatrice May Fennell was born in Sussex in 1905 and lived with her middle-class parents and her older brother Frank in a small house in London where she attended convent schools. Her father was called up to fight in World War I and Helen's most vivid childhood memories were the screeching sirens, blackouts and fires in the sky that heralded the violent barrage of air raids on the city.

In 1927, she graduated from King's College, University of London, with a not very useful second-class honours degree in English that qualified her only for teaching overseas in countries where the schools didn't require a teaching certificate. Helen set off, most reluctantly, for India at 22, and spent the next three years at Mahbubia School in one of the country's wealthiest and most oppressive states, Hyderabad. Although she was in the country when Gandhi led his passive resistance campaign against the salt tax that saw massive strikes and imprisonments, Helen didn't pay much attention; she was as apathetic to the campaign for independence from British sovereignty as she'd been to the General Transport Workers strike that paralysed England while she was at university.

Towards the end of her three-year contract, she was promoted to assistant principal and became engaged to the young Hugh Powell whose job at the Imperial Tobacco Company had him heading out into the rural areas to teach the villagers how to smoke. They intended to marry after two years and return to England, but following a riding accident Helen sustained a head injury severe enough to prevent her from continuing with any strenuous work, including her current position. In desperation, she wrote to a friend in South Africa, who found her a less demanding post at a boys' school in Durban. Helen was naïvely oblivious to the racial segregation in South Africa and by the time her Indian friends warned her, it was too late to change her plans.

She never returned to India or her fiancé. In Durban, she met a dashing dentist, Billie Joseph, 17 years her senior. She married him, despite her father's disapproval because he was Jewish. Over the next five years, she learned to adjust to the 'shock' of the racist society and although she had Indian friends, the closest she came to intimacy with black people was through the servants in her home.

Because Billie didn't want her to work, she became quite the socialite, playing bridge and tennis, and riding horses. He didn't want children either, with two kids already from his previous marriage, the oldest barely ten years younger than Helen. Helen too was reluctant, considering how shaky their marriage had become. Spurred by Billie's blatant infidelities, Helen sought out her own, and while they kept up the façade of a happy couple, she later wrote that they 'gradually sank to a very low level'.

With the advent of World War II, Helen's brother and father in England signed up for active duty, while Billie joined the Dental Corps in South Africa. Inspired by an ad calling for Welfare and Information Officers for the South African Army and Air Force, she drove to Pretoria for the training course. It was to change everything.

Helen was charged with disseminating information to new recruits and female officers, but she found that there were mortar-size gaping holes in the notes she was given that depicted a shiny, happy South Africa preserved by the racist system. For the first time she found herself questioning the policies and rationales of her adopted home.

Back in Johannesburg, Lilian landed a job as a trainee nurse at City Deep mine hospital, where she fell in love with a van driver, John Ngoyi who shared her passion for competitive ballroom dancing. They soon married and Lilian gave birth to a daughter, Edith. Their life together was quietly content and then John died of tuberculosis in 1942, leaving Lilian on her own to care for their daughter and her parents. In 1943, a friend of Lilian's passed away, leaving behind her eight-day-old daughter. Lilian raised Memory Mphahlele as her own child.

During the forced removals of the mid-1940s, the little family was uprooted to a one-roomed shack in The Shelters, an especially grim slum in the Soweto suburb of Orlando. Lilian found a job working as a seamstress for a sympathetic Austrian woman who had fled the war, and joined the Garment Workers Union Number Three (African Clothing Workers Union Branch) headed up by the spitfire Solly Sachs, where she rose through the ranks to officialdom.

When 1945 swung round, bringing with it the end of the war, it also saw the end of Helen's marriage. She considered returning to England, but an Air Force colonel she worked with reprimanded her, 'Oh no, people like you will be needed in South Africa.'

She stayed and took on a job managing a community health centre. Realising that she wasn't qualified, she enrolled for a part-time diploma in sociology and social work at Wits to fill the gaps in her experience. She was increasingly troubled by the disparities between white and black and was thrilled when a job opened up at a coloured community centre in Cape Town. She spent the next two years working in Elsiesriver in the Cape Flats, but came to realise that social work was only treating the symptoms and not addressing the inflamed core of the problem, affecting every capillary of society like a diseased heart – apartheid.

In 1951, she became the Secretary-Director of the Medical Aid Society of the Transvaal Clothing Industry, working closely with the Garment Worker's Union's notorious General-Secretary, a man who described himself as an ugly Jew with a rough voice, a Lithuanian accent and everything against him. Helen initially found Solly Sachs' pockmarked discoloured skin repellent, although she was fired by his ideology. In turn he called her a 'wishy-washy liberal'. Nevertheless, the two became lovers and eventually moved in together, although they never married. Helen felt she would always come second to his work and Solly was apparently looking for a more 'epic' woman. Little did he know.

In 1952, Solly was banned under the new Suppression of Communism Act, even though he'd been expelled from the Communist Party 20 years prior. Thousands of union members came out in protest and Solly defied his banning orders to address them on the steps of Johannesburg City Hall. The police reacted with the blunt-eyed brutality that was already par for the course, bursting through the doors to drag Solly away. When the protestors – who were almost entirely all women – surged forwards in outrage, the police beat them to their knees with batons and broken chairs, chasing them bleeding into the streets. It brought home the reality of the repressive state and Helen was shocked to her core.

Solly was released, immediately violated his banning orders again and was hauled off back to jail. When his case came up in court, the judges maintained that his banning was all in order. Defeated and unable to continue his work in politics or the unions, Solly decided to leave the country. Helen remonstrated with him to stay, already firm in her own commitment to change, but he was unmoved and left for France.

1952 was also the year Lilian sealed her commitment to the cause when she joined the African National Congress. Together with the South African Indian Congress (SAIC), the ANC launched the Defiance Campaign, a passive resistance against the pass laws and segregationist regulations that separated toilets, entrances and even park benches according to race. Although Edith was critically ill in hospital at the time, Lilian joined four other women at the 'whites only' counter at the post office to send a defiant telegram to the prime minister. Hers read, 'Doctor Malan, will you please withdraw your bills. South Africa has been a peaceful country. If not, remember what happened to

Hitler in Germany and Mussolini in Italy!' The five were arrested, but later acquitted, thanks to their canny lawyer, Oliver Tambo.

Helen joined the committee of the newly formed Congress of Democrats, a white organisation allied to the ANC with many ex-Communist Party members involved. At 48, she had come to politics late and with typical self-deprecating humour, described herself as a 'late bloomer', but she was inspired by her friendship with the ANC president Chief Albert Luthuli, who also entered the field at ripe middle age.

Lilian's political career also flourished and within a year of joining the ANC, she was sitting on the executive and was elected president of the ANC Women's League. Her rapid rise was thanks in part to MaNgoyi's evocative speeches. She had a flair for dropping genius soundbites such as, 'My womb is shaken when they speak of Bantu Education!' and claimed the effect of the inferior schooling was that 'we women are like hens that lay eggs for somebody else to take away'.

On another occasion, at an anti-pass meeting when someone suggested using violence, she put him down with a scathing, 'Shed your own blood first and let's see what stuff it's made of.' And also; 'Freedom does not come walking towards you, it must be won.'

Helen and Lilian met through a 1954 conference arranged by Hilda Bernstein and Ray Alexander, to set up a new organisation for women of all races, the Federation of South African Women (FEDSAW). Lilian, natch, became vice-president and two years later, president, while Helen took on the role of national secretary, a powerful position, which she dismissed with her usual modesty as a 'dogsbody' role. Both women worked in Johannesburg and would occasionally meet for a quick bite in Helen's car during lunch, cementing their friendship.

In 1955, both Helen and Lilian were invited to attend the World Congress of Mothers in Lausanne in Switzerland. Lilian and another ANC leader, Dora Tamana, had endless hassles just getting there. Neither were in possession of a passport and although it was legal to travel without one at the time, it was a bit dodgy. When two black women were discovered hiding in the toilets on board the Union Line ship they'd legally bought passage on, *sans* official documents, the captain dumped them summarily back on dock.

Undaunted, they made their way to Johannesburg and caught a flight to London, but the hostile reaction and whispering of the white passengers onboard prompted the disgusted pilot to make an announcement that there would be no apartheid on his plane.

The conference was an eye-opener for Lilian, but her travels afterwards were the real revelation. While Helen was *mif* that her skin colour seemed to exclude her from the glut of international speaking invitations going round, Lilian was invited to go to Uganda, London, Germany (where she was horrified by the concentration camps), China and Soviet Russia.

In the UK, she was taken aback to see whites employed as manual labourers in London and more so when two white men on a crowded train stood up to offer her and Dora their seats. In Uganda, she went to the movies with a mixed-race audience and in Rome, when an Italian opened the door for her, she was expecting to be shown to the kitchens. Instead, he offered to buy her a drink. Although she found the USSR daunting in its scope and technological advancement, she was inspired by Lenin's resolution despite being banned ten times. But it was in the peasant society of communist China that she found a model that seemed achievable for Africa; she returned bolstered with new conviction in 1955.

In her absence, Helen was involved with the Congress Alliance meeting of 3 000 people at Kliptown on 26 June 1955, to sign the Freedom Charter – a manifesto that laid out the demands that South Africa belongs to all who live in it, that the people shall govern, that there shall be equal rights, work and security and housing and peace for all. Right on cue, the police stormed in to disrupt the peaceful gathering, but neither their show of force nor searching and seizing hands could disrupt the proceedings.

The government retaliated by introducing pass laws for black women and Helen hit the road in a beat-up little Ford, christened 'Congress Connie' that admirably weathered the worst rural roads, together with

Robert Resha and Bertha Masheba, who tried in vain to teach her protest songs. She resorted to 'la-la-la-ing'.

Helen and Lilian were involved in various campaigns to educate women about the pass laws. When the ANC top brass balked at the pass burnings they inspired, Lilian shot back with, 'We don't want men who wear skirts under their trousers. If they don't want to act, let us women exchange garments with them.'

Was it any wonder that there was some speculation that Nelson Mandela, the Transvaal President of the ANC might marry her? Although she was older than him, the two were spotted out and about together, but eventually he chose to marry a young social worker, Winnie Madikizela instead. Winnie admired Lilian hugely and always said that every woman aspired to be her.

Inspired by the Black Sash, the white women's resistance organisation, which had demonstrated on the lawns of the Union Building, and the success of a protest by 2 000 women led earlier by Helen and Lilian, FEDSAW was moved to launch a national demonstration.

On 9 August 1956, now commemorated as Women's Day, together with notables Rahima Moosa and Sophie Williams, Helen and Lilian lead 20 000 women in the biggest demonstration yet. They found a way around the hurdle of bus permits by relying on public transport and slipped through a loophole in the law that forbade large public protests by turning it into 20 000 individual protests instead, furnishing every woman with her own petition. The petitions were piled up outside Prime Minister Strijdom's door, because he had wisely fled the building.

No speeches were made – to avoid turning the gathering into an illegal meeting. Instead, more provocatively, the thousands of women gathered on the Union Building steps stood in unwavering silence for a full 30 minutes, arms raised in the clenched fist of the Congress salute. Helen wrote, 'I looked at those many faces until they became only one face, the face of the suffering black people of South Africa. I know that there were tears in my eyes and I think that there were many who wept with me.'

At the end of the half hour, Lilian softly began to sing the opening bars of 'Nkosi Sikelele i'Afrika' and was joined by thousands of voices. They followed it up with a new number, composed to mark the occasion, *Wathint' abafazi / Wathint' imbokodo / Uzokufa'* ('You have tampered with the women / You have struck a rock / you shall be destroyed') and then peacefully dispersed.

The prevailing mood was that victory and an end to apartheid was not far off. The government realised it had to suppress these bold ideas as soon as possible and in December 1956, police swooped on private homes around the country, scooping up 156 Congress Alliance members, including Lilian and Helen, who was waiting with her suitcase already packed, to be put on trial for high treason.

The trial was a farce, in the bleak mould of Kafka. When the prisoners arrived in court for the first time, they were shown into a huge wire cage that would prevent them from having contact with the public. Their lawyers were outraged and insisted the cage be removed, but the trialists, who included Ruth First and Nelson Mandela, reacted with irreverence, putting up hand-written signs that said, 'Don't feed the wild animals!' and 'Dangerous!' to the roaring appreciation of their supporters.

The cage was removed the next day, but the trial dragged on for an interminable four years, although after the first two years, all but 30 of the defendants had charges dropped against them. Lilian and Helen were among those remaining together with Nelson Mandela and Walter Sisulu.

The prosecution couldn't decide what it wanted to prove and relied on dubious evidence including placards seized from a meeting that were marked 'soup with meat' and 'soup without meat', which Helen laughingly dismissed as proof of 'treason soup'. The garbled nonsensical records of speeches scribbled down by detectives were a particular source of amusement.

At other times, when the Special Branch actually recorded the words correctly, the speeches proved not how dangerous the movement was, but how reasonable, such as a quote from one of Lilian's speeches, 'We have thousands and thousands of coloureds with Afrikaner parents.

What's the good of apartheid in the streets if there's no apartheid under the blankets?'

Bail was granted and most of the trialists were able to continue with their lives in a stunted sort of way. Helen, who still worked at the Medical Aid Society, would work in the morning, before racing through to Pretoria to sit through the long and tedious hours of the trial and then return to the office at night. But Lilian lost her job and took to sewing at home, providing a space in her little house for another trialist, Dr Alfred Letele to set up his practice.

While most of the accused travelled to Pretoria in a specially assigned bus, Helen bought a new car for the occasion, nicknamed Treason Trixie, big enough to fit five. One of her passengers was Nelson Mandela, who sat beside her in front, thanks to his long legs. Over the years they grew so close, they became 'like family'. Later when Nelson was imprisoned and Winnie was on the run, Helen provided a home for their children Zindzi and Zenani (as well as white lawyer activist Bram Fischer's daughter, Ilse).

In 1957, Helen was issued with a five-year banning order, prohibiting her from leaving Johannesburg or attending any gatherings outside of social ones. In 1960, the outrage over the Sharpeville Massacre, where 67 peaceful pass protestors were killed by police, inspired the government to declare a State of Emergency and ban all organisations deemed to be a threat, including the ANC.

Lilian and Helen, together with the other treason trialists, were rearrested and taken to Pretoria Central Prison, where they kept up their morale by calling to other prisoners through the walls and singing hymns.

To Helen's bitter shame, she discovered that she and Lilian had vastly different facilities. She wrote, 'It was as Lilian had said: my pink skin brought me a bed, sheets, blankets. The mattress was revolting, urine stained, but Lilian slept on a mat on the floor with only blankets. My food was better. I had a sanitary bucket with a lid. She had an open bucket covered with a cloth. I learnt to hate my pink skin, but I could not change it nor expiate it.'

The trial finally wrapped up on 29 March 1961. Lacking sufficient evidence or a coherent argument from the prosecution, all the accused were found not guilty and released. But what was left for them with their political structures banned? The ANC made the uneasy decision to establish a military wing prepared to use violence, Umkhonto we Sizwe – the Spear of the Nation.

In 1962, Mandela was arrested, and sentenced to life imprisonment at the Rivonia Trial in 1963, only to emerge from prison 27 years later. Despite this blow to the movement, Lilian and Helen threw themselves back into their work, as outspoken as ever and formed the Human Rights Welfare Committee to very inconsiderately dig up the troublemakers the government had gone to a lot of trouble to banish to remote areas where no-one spoke their language. Lilian visited several people in the Northern Transvaal, but was then slapped with another banning order confining her to Orlando.

Helen was determined to continue the fight, and in a brief period of grace between bannings, together with two friends, Joe Morolong and Amina Cachalia, travelled 13 000 km over two months to meet with 36 banished people and hear their stories. Helen wrote a book, *Tomorrow's Sun: A Smuggled Journal From South Africa*, the title inspired by a passage in Olive Schreiner's book, *Trooper Peter Halkett*, but the first draft was rejected, the criticism coming back that she'd tried to include too many stories and too many people – with unpronounceable names. Helen saw this latter point as typical of English chauvinism and the publisher conceded that he felt 'I was standing at his elbow, saying "Listen, listen!" and he had to listen'. She rewrote the book and it was finally published in 1966.

The government reacted by smacking her down immediately with a new banning order preventing her from writing anything more, nor was she allowed to enter any building that housed a trade union or publication, which included her office at the Medical Aid Society. At 61, she was fired from her long-time job and the handicap of her political affiliations and her banning caused prospective employers to 'freeze in silence'.

Both women endured the desperate isolation of house arrest and the surprise visits of Special Branch popping in to ensure that they weren't up to any mischief like meeting with more than one person at a time. Helen also had to deal with anonymous death threats phoned through late at night, shot gun blasts fired through her front window (which she later conceded to bullet-proof), a bomb strapped to her gate and pranksters who arranged for large quantity deliveries of anything from building sand to booze to be made to her door, C.O.D. Once, two very confused morticians arrived to collect the body of 'Mrs Joseph'. Helen shut the door on them, laughing bitterly.

She also had run-ins with the police and on one occasion mightily embarrassed – and pissed off – an undercover officer who used to tail her in his car when she turned the tables and started tailing him. He drove off in a huff, tyres squealing. However, when she forgot to report in to the police station one day, as she had to do every lunchtime, she confessed to the precinct captain rather than get the officer on duty into trouble.

While they could have easily gone into exile, both women chose to stay. Lilian told one reporter, in a very brief respite between bannings, that her spirits had not been dampened. She said, 'You can tell my friends all over the world that this old girl is still her old self, if not more mature after all the experiences. I am looking forward to the day when my children will share in the wealth of our lovely South Africa.'

However, it's an indication of how hard and terrible their lonely existence was that when Helen found a lump in her breast, she didn't do anything about it for months, justifying her decision that it might be easier to just die. She came to her senses and her third ban was temporarily lifted in 1971 for her to have a mastectomy. Helen abused the suspension by jumping up on the podium to speak at universities almost as soon as she was discharged from the hospital.

Helen gave up her British citizenship in 1973 to prevent the government deporting her, but at 75, was jailed for two weeks in 1976, when she refused to testify against Winnie Mandela, causing a new international commotion that the government could imprison a frail old lady.

While Lilian's 18 years of confinement never broke her spirit, it did break her health and in 1980, barely two months before her banning was due to expire, she died at the age of 68 due to heart problems. Helen was one of the thousand mourners who attended her funeral in Soweto, fearlessly festooned with the illegal ANC colours. Two years after her death, she became the first woman to receive the liberation movement's highest award, Isitwalandwe.

Helen was banned again, for the last time in 1980, but even after the ban lifted in 1982, she was still a listed person and while she was able to give speeches, nothing she said was allowed to be quoted in the media. Articles that were written about her university talks pointedly noted that they couldn't quote 'the granny down the road' may have had more impact than anything she could have said.

Helen continued to stir, giving speeches and visiting Nelson Mandela in prison, right up until her third and last stroke in mid-December 1992. She died in hospital while her friends celebrated the last of the legendary 'Helen Joseph Christmas Parties' that had become an institution, this time without her.

Nelson expressed regret that she didn't live to see the new democratic South Africa for which she and Lilian had strived so long. But perhaps Lilian's words encapsulate it best. Before her death, she said, 'When I die, I'll die a happy person because I have seen the rays of our new South Africa rising.' Helen was buried in the Avalon Cemetery in Soweto next to her old friend.

The Interpreter

Krotoa-Eva

Translating is a tricky gig. Translators are constantly having words put in their mouths and must live with the raw deal that anything other people say can and will be held against them. It's not only words that have to be interpreted, it's also the intentions behind them and being stuck in the middle is part of the job description. For Krotoa-Eva it meant being caught between her family and the devils from across the deep blue sea. It's no wonder she eventually turned to drink.

In her short lifetime, Krotoa-Eva racked up a number of significant firsts. She was one of the first go-betweens between the Khoekhoe and the Dutch, with the unenviable task of negotiating the political intrigues of the time. She was one of the first Khoekhoe to actually live in Jan van Riebeeck's fort, although she'd often ditch her clothes and go back to her people for extended visits.

She was among the earliest Christian converts in southern Africa and acted as part-time missionary spreading the word and encouraging Khoekhoe children to pray around the campfire. And, before some dogmatic idiots decided it was both immoral and illegal, she was also one of the first South Africans to enter into an inter-racial marriage and have mixed-race babies.

Krotoa-Eva has been hauled out and paraded around like Sara Bartmann by various historians, journalists and academics, interpreting her as proof positive of all kinds of pet theories; an apartheid-era *Huisgenoot* article in 1942, for example, concentrated on her tragic downfall as evidence that any attempt to civilise black peoples was doomed to messy failure. More recently, academic papers have held her up as the original mother figure or the very embodiment of colonialism's metaphysical rape of the indigenous population. But with her torn allegiances, if she was anything, psychologically speaking, it was one of the earliest Oreo cookies or coconuts.

The term (which for the blissfully naïve is a very disparaging reference to someone black on the outside and white on the inside) is ugly and plain distasteful. It's the very antithesis of any spirit of conciliation across the colour line, but if the words had been around in the mid-1600s, there's little doubt that Krotoa-Eva's main detractor and rival, Doman (another Khoekhoe interpreter), would have delighted in adding 'em to his vocabulary of insults along with 'lick spittle' and 'traitor' and the occasional death threat he threw at her.

Krotoa-Eva's identity was as split as her double-barrelled name. In the Dutch East India Company's Fort, she was Eva and she would wear an Indian sarong (the closest she was prepared to come to the confining couture of the Dutch ladies), attend church, do household chores and babysit the Van Riebeeck children. Outside it, she was Krotoa, a Khoekhoe girl clad in skins, with powerful connections as both the niece of Aushaumato, leader of the Goringhaikona and the sister-in-law of Oedasa, chief of the mighty Cochoqua.

Many of the Khoekhoe at the time took on English or Dutch names for the convenience of the uri-khoi! (white men) who couldn't be bothered to learn all those accursed clicks. Even Jan van Riebeeck, who knew seven languages, couldn't wrap his tongue around Khoekhoe. So, Krotoa was known as Eva and her uncle Aushaumato was known as Herrie to the Dutch and King Harry to the English.

Krotoa was brought into the Van Riebeeck's household as a servant in around 1652 at the tender age of ten or 11. She'd already picked up a little Dutch from her uncle Aushaumato, who as leader of a straggling cattle-less tribe of outcasts known as the Watermen or Strandlopers, made a passable living by trading with the ships that popped in for fresh supplies ever since the Portuguese first rounded the Cape in 1488.

The family, especially Jan's 21-year-old wife, Maria de Quellerie, warmed to her quickly and made every effort to civilise this young 'savage' in their midst, including teaching her Dutch, which it was noted, she spoke with the tang of Jan's eloquent enunciation.

Krotoa was no stranger to the idea of servants. Rich Khoekhoe cattle-owners employed servants themselves, sometimes captured from other tribes. The work she was employed to do – milking cows, cleaning the house and looking after the kids – would have been familiar too.

They also introduced her to Christianity and the vengeful God of the Dutch who was trotted out regularly as a warning to the locals not to mess with them or face His wrath. Organised religion wouldn't have been an alien concept to her either. The Khoekhoe engaged in ritual praise dances at new moon and full moon, appealing to that scarred silvery orb or the earth spirit Tsui-Goab to bring rain and fertility to the land. Furthermore, this Jesus Christ the missionaries went on about seemed to have a lot in common with the legendary chieftain Heitsi Eibib, who arose from the dead himself on regular occasions and was commemorated with stone cairns scattered around the peninsula (not unlike the Moslem kramats today).

There's been some speculation that Krotoa was sent to live in the fort to spy for her uncle, but if that had been the case, he would have placed a huge deal of faith in a little girl. He probably did envision it as a tactical advantage, as a way of tying himself to the Fort and its commander, and for a time he did indeed enjoy the status of favourite intermediary between the Dutch and the Khoekhoe traders before he mucked it all up.

Krotoa's Dutch seemed to be considerably better than Aushaumato's and by 1657, at the age of 15, she was being regularly roped in to help translate, to the disgust of Doman, who saw her as a threat to his job security and the safety of the Khoekhoe.

He had good cause to complain on the first charge. On at least one occasion, Jan van Riebeeck called in Krotoa to translate Doman's words into 'better Dutch'. Although she was just a girl, she was one of the most proficient translators in the new colony and had quickly picked up Portuguese as well. Doman's rebellious nature, not to mention his blatant role in the cattle raids on the settlement and later in the first Khoekhoe-Dutch war, didn't exactly endear him to the settlers.

As for the second and more serious accusation, there is evidence that as a young girl Krotoa was sometimes so eager to please that she may have bent the truth. In his journals, Jan van Riebeeck remarks, 'Occasionally we do catch Eva drawing the long bow a little, for she knows well by now how to introduce a little flattery and to say the sort of thing she imagines one would like to hear.'

One of the subjects the Dutch couldn't get enough of was Monomotapa, the fabled city of gold far to the North, which was supposedly inhabited by a tribe of white peoples, the Chobona. Krotoa was happy to oblige her hosts with tales of the fantastical kingdom and spurred on by her words, an expedition set off to find it.

They didn't get further than the mouth of the Berg river, but even later explorers, including Krotoa's husband-to-be, never turned up a trace of it. In her defence, the legend may have been rooted in truth; in earlier centuries, civilisations in Zimbabwe and Mapungubwe had produced fabulous golden artefacts as well as stone cities similar to the ones of which Krotoa spoke.

She was occasionally guilty of shocking indiscretions, revealing too much about the Khoekhoe and the various alliances and enmities for some of her tribesmen's liking. Doman sneered, 'I am a Hottentot and not a Dutchman, but you, Eva, you try to curry favour with the Commander.' But that wasn't strictly accurate. Krotoa might not have always played fair or true, but she knew exactly where her loyalties lay – with the people she cared about. And besides, Doman wasn't exactly non-partisan himself.

Jan quickly picked up that in a dispute, his translators sided with their own tribes. Krotoa would push for alliances with the Goringhaikona and the Cochoqua, while Doman tried to sway agreements in favour of the Goringhaiqua or Kaapsmans and their chief, Gogosoa, known as the Fat Captain. They were both quick to blame the other's tribe for any trouble. However, Krotoa was unique in that she extended the same allegiance to her adopted family at the Fort as to her real relations on the outside.

The first time Krotoa left the Fort was under dire circumstances. Aushaumato's relationship with the Dutch had soured. They blamed the sly social climber for the shortage of Khoekhoe bringing in cattle to barter and accused him of stirring up trouble and purposefully fouling negotiations. 'Herrie' naturally denied it, but secretly plotted to break with the Dutch and rustle a whole corral of cattle. Some of his men waylaid a Dutch herd boy and made off with his cows, which were Khoekhoe cattle anyway, Aushaumato probably reasoned. But the boy put up a fight and in the scuffle, he was accidentally killed.

Terrified of Dutch retribution, Aushaumato fled for the hills, taking the cattle – and Krotoa – with him. He was intercepted by Osinghkhimma, the son of the Goringhaiqua chief, who confiscated all the cattle for himself. Herrie was left in a precarious political position. He'd lost everything – the herd and the coveted status that came with cattle ownership as well as the trust of the Dutch.

Krotoa returned to the Fort after several months, during which Jan and Maria assumed she'd been held captive, and tried to make a case for her conniving uncle. Not yet embittered by years of such betrayals and desperate to maintain good relations with his suppliers, Jan let it pass. For the moment.

Krotoa made several more trips to see her people and seems to have been quite conflicted as to whether to stay or go. She was allowed to travel pretty much as she pleased, acting as an official ambassador to lure more traders with cattle to the fort. However, the Dutch weren't always happy to see her leave and there were occasional rumblings in the ranks that she was spying on them. Doman certainly did his best to bring her into disrepute and even tried to claim the credit – and the commission of beads, brandy, copper and tobacco – on the new batches of cattle traders regularly arriving at the Fort.

When she left the Fort, Krotoa would cast off her clumsy Western clothes and slip back into her old lifestyle almost as easily as she did her skins.

The Khoekhoe were largely nomadic, with the exception of poor tribes such as the Goringhaikona who mostly kept to the shore, foraging for herbs, roots and fish, and scavenging dead whale. The cattle owners, on the other hand, moved between seasonal grazing grounds with portable huts carried on the back. This was a big part of their beef with the Dutch who had laid claim to perfectly good grasslands when they arrived, thinking it unoccupied. The Khoekhoe had used the land for centuries and when the Dutch started fencing it off and ploughing it up, they were not impressed. It was to become a sticky point between the two civilisations.

On the plus side, the Khoekhoe did enjoy the Dutch music. They loved dancing, not only in celebration and praise of the moon, but also re-enacting herding and hunting scenes, playing the roles of animals, to tunes coaxed from a long musical bow similar to the Xhosa *uhadi*. Their weakness for music was such that when Krotoa went to visit her brother-in-law Oedasa with a Dutch goodwill delegation bearing gifts, she insisted that Jan also send a delegation of fiddlers to entertain them.

They were also fond of the glass beads and copper wire the white traders swapped for cows. The women adorned themselves with necklaces, bracelets and anklets strung with beads and metal, and sewed bright patterns of glass onto their leather aprons.

They were into cosmetics of a kind too. Both men and women smeared their skins with butter mixed with ochre and buchu, as protection from the elements, although this primitive sunscreen had the rather unfortunate side-effect of turning rancid and producing a smell the Europeans found dreadfully offensive, even while their own skins reddened, blistered and peeled. They would have done well to pay more attention – better to be malodorous than suffer malignant melanomas.

Krotoa was always welcomed back into the fold. She was respected for her role as the Dutch interpreter and some may have tried to court her favour in an attempt to win the Commander's. But Doman and the Goringhaqua still despised her and on a trip to visit her brother-in-law, riding on an ox like royalty, she was robbed of all the pretty trinkets the Dutch had paid her for services rendered.

Her relationship with the Dutch may also have indirectly landed her in a hot spot with her family. Oedasa set out at her request to bring back ivory and 'wild horses' or zebra for the Dutch when a lion leapt out from the rocks and savaged his arm. His men fell on the beast, wrenched open its mouth and speared it to death, but not before he lost much blood. This near-disaster may have caused some bad blood in the family and Oedasa certainly lost all interest in appropriating tusks and zebra for his sister-in-law or her uri-khoi! taskmasters.

She remained very close to her sister, whose name was never recorded by the Dutch, but a fictionalised account calls her Kabatsu, which is a splendid name, so we'll use it. Once, when Kabatsu visited the Fort, Krotoa was so happy to see her, she was rendered mute with joy and spent the rest of the day with her arm slung around her shoulder.

Kabatsu was also Krotoa's first convert. Krotoa found her people were receptive to the good word, especially the children who quite enjoyed the hymns and prayers, but it may have remained only sociological curiosity until the moment the Dutch God apparently intervened to save Kabatsu's life. During one of her visits, Kabatsu took deathly ill. Krotoa took charge, treating her with the traditional remedies taught to her by the elder women, but also praying over her every night religiously. Kabatsu made a marked recovery and consequently God made a tribe of converts. Oedasa asked Krotoa to instruct his children in the Christian ways and when she returned to the Fort again, it was ostensibly because she had been sent to learn more.

Life back at the Fort was more complicated than life outside. The political intrigues and back-stabbing verged on Shakespearean in their tangled drama. Jan van Riebeeck seems to have been tolerant of some of the goings-on. Of course, his primary goal was to keep the peace to ensure a steady supply of fresh food for the Dutch East India Company ships passing through, but Aushaumato and Doman would have tried his patience sorely, especially when he kept forgiving them their misdeeds and they kept betraying him. Which is not to say that the Dutch weren't conniving scoundrels themselves. The agreements they made were inevitably in their favour and Jan wasn't above claiming that the ordinary fare he served the Khoekhoe notables who dined at his house, was the cuisine of kings.

Political one-upmanship and cattle theft were the main issues between the Dutch and the Khoekhoe, but Doman proved to be a real firebrand. Some historians have pegged him as the first freedom fighter, predating the formation of the ANC by some 350 years. He was definitely one of the most outspoken and active campaigners against the white interlopers. Doman was sent to the more settled Dutch settlement of Batavia to get a better grip on the language and the customs. He came back, only slightly more fluent in Dutch, with a new name, Anthony, new clothes, and, to Jan's bitter remorse, an intimate knowledge of firearms.

The killing of the herd boy came up again in 1658 when Jan, at Krotoa's secret suggestion, took three of Gogosoa's sons hostage to try to force a resolution over the issue of several slaves gone astray. The tactic had worked before in coercing the Khoekhoe to return stolen cattle and it was hoped that the pressure would lead to the runaway slaves being similarly turned in. Doman blamed Krotoa for the outrage and threatened that the Kaapsmans would have her killed. The Dutch were forced to cover for her, claiming it was their idea all along.

Doman insisted, in fairness, that Aushaumato and some of his men be held as well. Jan was only too happy to oblige, seeing it as the perfect opportunity to play the tribes off against each other and expose the truth of the murder.

Aushaumato was captured peacefully when he answered the summons to the Fort without question. Unfortunately, the same could not be said for his men. When the Dutch tried to impound his herd of cattle, his followers resisted and one was shot dead – the first recorded instance in the settlement's history.

Tempers flared all round and negotiations disintegrated into a frenzy of finger-pointing. Finally a truce was settled on over the murder of the Khoekhoe man, but this was one of many treaties that went dismally wrong. As for the matter of the stolen cattle and the dead herd boy, Aushaumato and several of his men were implicated and imprisoned on Robben Island. To placate Krotoa who pleaded for her uncle 'as Esther did Mordecai', Jan said he would be able to spend the rest of his life 'in peace' there. She wasn't convinced, but neither was he and so Aushaumato remained on the island until he made a daring escape in a leaky scuttlebutt of a boat in 1659.

In the meantime, tensions mounted. The Khoekhoe were regularly raiding cattle to bulk up their herds and the free burghers retaliated in kind, sometimes stealing back the same cattle that had just been seized. Worse, the Dutch continued to encroach on Khoekhoe grazing lands, interfered incessantly in Khoekhoe affairs (which they knew all about thanks to Krotoa) and were making moves to extend their influence inland to trade. The Goringhaiqua believed they had no choice; they had to drive the trespassers out.

At Doman's provocation, they launched into the First Khoekhoe-Dutch war which dragged out over most of 1659 and into 1660. Armed with Doman's insider information about the settlement, and, more importantly, the functioning of firearms, they planned their attacks for rainy days when the gunpowder was damp and often failed to go off. They staged lightning raids, destroying crops and stealing livestock. The free burgher wives fled to safety in the Fort, while the men tried to hold their farms as best they could and resorted to arming their slaves. It was an unprofitable business all round. The Dutch lost a fair amount of trade with passing ships and although the Goringhaiqua had gained many cattle, they'd lost the war and now the Dutch were demanding double their losses back. Doman, who had been wounded in battle when a bullet pierced his shoulder, had lost his position as trusted interpreter and lost face with his people, having critically failed to draw other powerful tribes into the fray. Oedasa brokered the peace, through Krotoa who begged Jan to 'forgive these poor wretches'.

Aushaumato and Doman resolved their differences and arrived at the Fort together to state their case. They argued, quite reasonably, that the grazing pastures belonged to the Khoekhoe by dint of having been theirs for centuries and demanded to know if they'd be allowed to come in and take over as the Dutch had done, if they went to Holland. Jan was impressed by their 'telling points' but riposted, disingenuously, that the land had 'justly fallen to us in a defensive war, won by the sword … and we intend to keep it'.

The Khoekhoe had no choice but to accept and daily life and trade resumed relatively uneventfully, with a great deal of help from Krotoa, until Jan's commission at the Cape ended and he departed its shores with his family on 7 May 1662. One of his last acts before he left, at Maria's prodding, was to ensure that Krotoa was baptised. It's safe to say she missed her foster family of ten years.

The new governor Zacharias Wagenaer was not so well disposed to Krotoa and was particularly incensed by her habit of wandering off without so much as a by your leave. His diarist recorded his irritation, complaining, 'this naughty thing … this lewd vixen … has often played us this trick.' Compared to Jan van Riebeeck, who was always a gentleman and open-minded, even when conspiring to shape events in his favour, Zacharias was downright rude and in his journals likened a group of visiting Khoekhoe to 'dead hedgehogs' under their 'filthy stinking skins'.

Krotoa's circumstances had changed dramatically and now she was drinking regularly. While the Khoekhoe shared dagga pipes as a favourite social indulgence, only men were allowed to drink the mild honey beer they brewed. At the Fort, on the other hand, some of the Dutch thought it tremendous fun to allow her the odd tipple, behind the governor's back. She probably had her first taste of brandy as a reward for a job well done. The other translators typically got a nip after negotiations were wrapped and she may well have insisted that she was deserving of one too.

She also already had two children out of wedlock by Pieter Meerhoff, a respected, very white Danish surgeon who arrived in the Cape in 1659 onboard the *Prinses Roijael* from Copenhagen. Between 1659 and 1665, he set off on six expeditions into the hinterland, driven to find Monomotapa. He was obviously unsuccessful and Krotoa never disillusioned him but he did gain a reputation for bravery and perseverance and would have had the pick of the Colony's single ladies. His engagement to Krotoa was announced in April 1664, when she was 21 and he was 27. It was to be the first Christian marriage involving a 'native' and considering his good standing, there can be little doubt that it was a love match.

They were married on 2 June inside the Fort and Krotoa was awarded 50 rix dollars and a 'little marriage feast' in the Commander's house as a wedding gift, although considering her long service and free labour to the Company, it was pretty skimpy. Wagenaer held out high hopes that marriages such as this might bind the Khoekhoe closer to the Dutch. The Khoekhoe obviously felt differently and Oedasa, who had always promised to give Krotoa's husband 100 cattle and 500 sheep, skipped out on their agreement, possibly annoyed that she had married a European or simply distanced from her since Kabatsu had died and she no longer visited.

Just over a year later, Pieter was appointed as the superintendent of Robben Island – a prestigious promotion, although some historians believe it was a way to keep the inter-racial couple out of sight and out of discomfited mind, especially considering the previous man to fill the post had also had a black wife – Jan van Riebeeck's freed slave, Angela of Bengal.

There wasn't much to do on the island and when Pieter was busy managing the prisoners and quashing rebellions, Krotoa may have turned to the bottle as a distraction. She started experiencing regular fainting spells (drunken black-outs?) and on one occasion, when she fell and struck her head, was comatose for three days.

In 1667, her brave and dashing adventurer husband who had served the Company so well before, was shipped off to find new trading opportunities along the east coast of Africa. He was killed, together with eight men, in a skirmish with the locals at Antongil Bay in Madagascar, although Krotoa only got word of it eight months later when his ship, the *Westwoud*, returned. This was the beginning of the end.

In Khoekhoe culture, strong family bonds ensured that the poor were looked after and lone women were often taken in as concubines, but Krotoa had broken her ties and at the Fort she had to rely on the good will of the governor.

Initially, this wasn't a problem. When she returned to the mainland with her children, Soon, Pieternella and Salamon in September 1668, she was granted a piece of land with a house and assigned her husband's slave, Jan Vos. But she couldn't maintain order. Probably devastated by the loss of her husband, she turned to drinking in a big way and, it seems, prostitution.

Unimpressed by the 'adulterous and shameful behaviour' of 'this drunken swine', the Church Council threatened to take away her children but the final straw was when she caused a Brenda Fassie of a scene one night at the governor's hall. She fled in fear of punishment, leaving her children 'naked and destitute' and took up with some indigent Khoekhoe scrabbling together a living on the downs of Mouille Point.

Her children were put into the rather dubious care of Barbara Geems, a known prostitute and allegedly a madam as well. While this wasn't exactly a step up when it came to providing the children with an fine upstanding upbringing, it's quite possible that Barbara was the only one in the small-minded white community who was prepared to take in mixed-race children – for a small stipend, of course.

Krotoa may well have entertained a desultory plan to rescue her children, but she failed to carry it out and when a further scene erupted on a sedate Sunday afternoon, which some have claimed was the result of her resisting an attempted rape, soldiers were sent to 'hunt up that Hottentoo pig'. As a consequence, she was banished to Robben Island in March 1669 and despite several attempts at reforming her, she continued to drink and sleep around, giving birth to three more illegitimate babies.

When she died on the island five years later on 29 July 1674, she was accorded a Christian burial in the newly finished Castle. According to author VC Malherbe in *Krotoa, Called 'Eva': A Woman Between*, her epitaph read:

July 29th. – This day departed this life, a certain female Hottentoo named Eva, long ago taken from the African brood in her tender childhood by the Hon: van Riebeeck and educated in his house as well as brought to the knowledge of the Christian faith, and being thus transformed from a female Hottentoo almost into a Netherland woman, was married to a certain Chief Surgeon of this Residency, by whom she had three children, still living and some others which had died. Since his death, however at Madagascar, she had brought forth as many illegitimate ones, and for the rest, led such an irregular life, that for a long while the desire would have existed of getting rid of her, had it not been for the hope of the conversion of this brutal aboriginal, which was always still hovering between. Hence in order not to be accused of tolerating her adulterous and debauched life, she had at various times been relegated to Robben Island, where, though she could obtain no drink, she abandoned herself to immorality. Pretended reformation induced the Authorities many times to call her back to the Cape, but as soon as she returned, she, like the dogs, always returned to her own vomit, so that finally she quenched the fire of her sensuality by death …

Unfortunately, this racist diatribe against her inherent savagery were the last words we have on her. Like Sara Bartmann, her own voice was never recorded, except when it affected Dutch business dealings. While several academics and novelists have taken a bash at speaking for her, as she did for so many, she never had the opportunity to speak for herself.

As for her legacy, the records show that her three children by Pieter were adopted by a Batholomeus Borns and his wife, who took them to Mauritius. One of her sons returned to the Cape where he died of 'wild habits', and we don't know what happened to the other illegitimate siblings. Pieternella married a Dutch white man, Daniel Zaijman, who became one of the wealthiest plantation owners on the island, before they returned to Cape Town in 1709, settling in Stellenbosch with their eight children, including a daughter called Eva. Krotoa's bloodline runs through branches of many South African families, including Saayman, Botha and Oosthuizen.

The Woman Who Loved an Alien

Elizabeth Klarer

This is a love story; of an interstellar romance that spanned space, time and credibility.

But it's also a mystery story tangled and clotted with verifiable facts, close associations with top brass military personnel, experimental plane testing sites and a four-month vanishing. What really happened to Elizabeth Klarer?

Elizabeth Wollatt was born the youngest of three daughters on 1 July 1910, most auspiciously in the same year Halley's Comet inched its blurry way across the night skies. She was into horse riding and music and the stories of the farm's induna, Ladam, which he related to her in Zulu.

She had her first encounter when she was just seven. As Elizabeth tells it in her book, *Beyond The Light Barrier*, she and her nine-year-old sister, Barbara, were playing outside on the family farm in the KwaZulu-Natal Midlands, when they saw a pock-marked meteor hurtling through the upper reaches towards the farm, viscous smoke trailing in its wake. Suddenly a silver disc appeared, coruscating with a lustrous pearly light.

It swooped out of clear skies to intercept the meteor. In fear, the dogs ran yelping for cover.

The children tumbled into the house to tell their parents of the narrowly averted disaster and the spaceship that had saved them. Elizabeth's father, Samuel Bankroft Wollatt, was sceptical, while her aristocratic mother, Florence, who dressed in glittering evening gowns for dinner – even in rural KwaZulu-Natal, accepted them at their word. But it was Ladam who was the most supportive of their wild-eyed claims.

In Zulu legend, there is a creature known as the lightning bird, but although most references depict the *impundulu* as a witch's familiar that summons thunder with its wings and lightning strikes with a kick of its talons, Ladam painted it as a herald of the Sky Gods with metallic iridescent wings that shifted colour, coincidentally much like the ship Elizabeth had seen.

Her second sighting came several months later. She was outside with Ladam, when a flattened, black cumulonimbus cloud bristling with jagged flashes of lightning suddenly heralded a tornado that twisted down over their heads. Again, a silvery craft swept in to the rescue, intervening between Elizabeth and the pulsating funnel that spun away to vent its fury on a pine tree and an abandoned shed instead.

Ladam called her *Inkosazana* (chieftainess) and *Hlangabeza* or 'one who brings together' and claimed that her golden hair would call down the *Abelungu* (white people) from the sky and that there would be a meeting. And a mating.

By comparison, the next few years were uneventful. After matriculating from St. Anne's Diocesan College in Pietermaritzburg, Elizabeth moved to Italy to study art and music in Florence, and then on to Cambridge University where, compelled by her fascination with the skies, she completed a four-year diploma in meteorology.

She returned to South Africa in 1932, married a Royal Air Force pilot, Captain W. Stafford Phillips, and gave birth to a daughter, Marilyn, a year later. Stafford taught her to fly and she would often serve as navigator during flips in his Tiger Moth. In 1937, they were en route from Durban to Baragwanath airfield in a Leopard Moth when a huge pulsating sphere with a slightly raised dome pulled level with their plane over the Drakensberg. Elizabeth tapped Stafford on the back of the neck. When he looked over his shoulder to see what she was on about, he immediately launched into evasive manoeuvres, ducking and banking away. The ship paced them easily, cyclically flashing through white, blue and yellow, before it flipped on its side, rolled away like a wheel and then, with a burst of light, vanished. As soon as they landed, Stafford filed a detailed report to headquarters in Pretoria. Unfortunately, the South African Air Force has no record of it.

Shortly thereafter, Stafford was redeployed to the DeHavilland Experimental Station in Hatfield, England. Elizabeth was employed by the Royal Air Force as a meteorologist and was trained to observe aerial anomalies, as many women were during the war. It was around this time that she claimed she met Air Chief Marshal Sir Hugh Dowding (who later led the defeat of the German Luftwaffe in the Battle of Britain in 1940 and was consequently upgraded to Lord).

Hugh, or 'Chief' as Elizabeth was wont to call him, a keen spiritualist and student of unexplained phenomena, was very interested in her experiences. Just before the outbreak of World War II, the Chief recruited Elizabeth to do research on flying saucers, perhaps as an early precursor to a quite real secret committee set up after a rash of sightings in the late '40s.

Under pressure from top brass such as the Chief, as well as Earl Mountbatten and Sir Henry Tizard – a leading scientist who helped develop radar technology, the British Ministry of Defence initiated the unfortunately named 'The Flying Saucer Working Party' in 1950. Their findings (recently released in February 2005 under the Freedom of Information Act, according to London's *The Times* newspaper) were cursorily dismissive of the sighting reported by people like RAF Flight Lieutenant Hubbard who had seen an oscillating 'flat disc, light pearl grey in colour'.

If Elizabeth was privy to that very secret information, it didn't dissuade her in the slightest and she maintained regular contact with the Chief until 1960, ten years before he died.

During the war, Elizabeth said she did decoding for the RAF as well as research into what the pilots called 'Foo fighters' and the radar monitors 'angels'; small bright lights that used to pace the planes. It was originally thought that the mysterious lights were some kind of secret German weapon, until it was discovered that the Luftwaffe was reporting them too.

In 1943, Elizabeth moved back to South Africa and allegedly continued her work in air force intelligence. She was hospitalised in Groote Schuur after an accident on the Ysterplaat airbase when a fire broke out in one of the hangars and a petrol tank exploded, catching her and Stafford in the blast as they tried to rescue one of the planes. (SAAF records recall a fire in 1944, apparently an act of an Afrikaner group with Nazi sympathies, but no injuries were noted.)

The couple divorced soon after, quite possibly because Stafford didn't share her passion for flying saucers, or perhaps Elizabeth was subconsciously trying to make way for the alien assignation she claimed later she psychically knew was to come. However, she married again in 1946, this time to Paul Klarer, an engineer in Vereeniging. She gave birth to her son, David, in 1949, but Paul proved too level-headed to handle her all-consuming passion for the unexplained and by the mid-1950s, the marriage was over.

Elizabeth still holidayed habitually in the Drakensberg on the farm, which by then belonged to her older sister May and her husband Jock. In 1954 she experienced something that would shift her reality forever.

According to her, she was standing on what has come to be known as Flying Saucer Hill when the same silver ship that haunted her childhood scudded through the sky, using the clouds as camouflage. It descended lower and lower until it hovered barely a metre from the ground, its pulsating hum reverberating through her head until her ears popped. It was a massive ellipse of a ship, 18 m in diameter with a rounded dome dotted with portholes in the centre – the quintessential flying saucer. Staring at her from one of the portholes, a man stood, arms-folded – the most beautiful man she'd ever seen with a shock of white hair.

In her book, which takes on a decidedly Mills & Boon tone after this point, she writes, 'I studied his face, the most wonderful face I had ever seen and I felt a sense of affinity and love. A slight smile softened the aesthetic lines of his face, a gentle smile that caused my heart to miss a beat; a smile I knew had softened his eyes too and I dared not look again into those eyes.' After a few brief minutes, the ship abruptly rose vertically and with a flash of light disappeared, leaving only a heat wave shimmer in the sky behind it.

It was to return 18 months later. Elizabeth sensed its imminent arrival (she'd spent much of her life developing her telepathic skills by practising on animals, plants, machines and 'anything with the spark of life'), but this time, when she rushed up Flying Saucer Hill, the ship was parked, the tall man standing beside it clearly waiting for her. She ran to him and he swept her into his arms and swung her round, laughing.

'Not afraid this time?' he asked.

'I have known your face within my heart all my life,' she answered.

He took her onboard and introduced himself as Akon, a scientist from the planet Meton in the Alpha Centauri system. He had light grey eyes, fair golden skin, aquiline features and straight white hair that reached the nape of his neck. He wore a tight, shimmery one-piece suit. Elizabeth said the suit had a matching headpiece with slanted, slit eyeholes and a slit mouthhole, although he rarely wore it.

He told her he had been watching and waiting for her all his life and that while his kind only rarely mates with Earth women, when they do, they keep the offspring to strengthen the race with the infusion of new blood. Then he whisked her away beyond the reaches of the atmosphere to the awaiting mother ship.

He showed her the marvels of his immaculately utopian civilisation by way of an 'electric mirage', a type of holographic screen. He introduced her to his colleagues and they quickly provided explanations of how their ships worked (they're moulded from pure energy and based on an electro-magnetic gravity field that creates the shifting colours). They also revealed their peaceful space-faring society, discussed technology, philosophy and that ultimate force of the universe – love. But while Akon and Elizabeth shared electric kisses and he revealed to her that she was truly a Venusian and the reincarnation of long lost soul-mate, she had to wait until the following occasion for their love to be consummated.

Back on earth, the Zulu villagers gathered on the hill, the women ululating and the men shouting about the *umlingo* 'wagon in the sky' in a scene that her sister May described as cinematic. May was admirably stoic about the news of Elizabeth's would-be alien lover, but the Chief was so ecstatic, he flew out immediately from London to see her, although he advised her to let the hubbub calm down before she tried to see Akon again.

The story was already out in the press and when Elizabeth returned to Johannesburg; she was bombarded by journalists, enthusiasts and sceptics wanting a piece of her. At the time, alien intrigues were all the rage along with the perils of the communist *Rooi Gevaar* and there were several people at the time claiming to have seen UFOs, possibly inspired by a 1953 movie *Invaders From Mars* that was the first to dramatise alien abductions.

Elizabeth was very critical of her rivals and wrote, 'Societies flourished like fungi in the bracing warmth of the highveld summer, watered by the fanatical enthusiasm of many misguided individuals whose egotism far outweighed any good they attempted to do.'

Indeed, a few years later, Elizabeth was to have a very public falling out in the newspapers with another self-styled specialist, Ann Grevler, whose book, *Operation Broomstick* claimed that she had experienced a close encounter of her own on the astral plane with an enlightened being called Ashtar.

Back in 1956, Elizabeth claimed she was threatened with abduction by shadowy military organisations and possibly the Russians if she didn't hand over scientific details of the ship's propulsion systems. When she appealed to the authorities, presumably the Chief or his local cohorts, she claims they assigned an ex-policeman to guard her Parktown home and accompany her wherever she went.

Unfortunately her book is sketchy on the exact dates, but when Akon's ship appeared over Johannesburg in about 1958, she says, inspiring the

Air Force to scramble jets from the Waterkloof Air Force Base, she knew it was a sign and left for the Drakensberg immediately with David and her two dogs in her MG.

Akon was waiting for her when she arrived – but, she claimed, so was a curious Air Force helicopter. Fortunately, Akon bent the light rays around the ship to render it invisible and took Elizabeth to the heights of Cathkin Peak, where they would not be followed.

Inside the ship, alone at last, Elizabeth removed her practical gillie shoes and her thick tartan kilt and luxuriated in an exotic green foaming bath rich in minerals and cleansing agents. When she stepped out, Akon presented her with a ring of beaten silver and green enamel set with a stone of light and then … 'I surrendered in ecstasy to the magic of his love making, our bodies merging in magnetic union as the divine essence of our spirits became one.' Afterwards, they enjoyed a tasty meal of fresh vegetables and fruits grown onboard and Akon returned her to Earth. Already his seed was growing within her, at the ripe age of 49.

Rather than return to Johannesburg, May and Elizabeth decided it would be best for her to lie low in the Drakensberg. Marilyn was already at university and David attended boarding school nearby, although Elizabeth claims he was with her on a ride up the mountain to meet Akon, when Russian cosmonauts ambushed her with the intent of kidnapping her and her unborn baby in their vertical-landing spacecraft equipped with a death ray. She made a narrow escape and galloped off on her horse. In frustration the cosmonauts fired at her and the death ray melted a nearby sandstone boulder, which may well still be up there. The brewing storm drove off the cosmonauts back to their orbiting spacecraft, while Elizabeth raced to one of the stone camping huts along the trail, where David was waiting for her, quite calmly with a meal prepared.

David remembers none of this. He has no recollection of his middle-aged mother being pregnant. Nor does he remember her being away for four months, when Akon supposedly took her – and, conveniently, the MG – into space so she could give birth on his planet in 1959. However, he admits that he simply might not have noticed her absence, being at boarding school. Or he shrugs, reluctant to be blatantly disloyal to his mother, his memory may have been erased.

While Elizabeth (and her car) were supposedly only gone from Earth for four months, that time equated to nine years on Meton. The planet was a truly wondrous place, with dome homes arranged in private gardens where the grass never needed cutting, amazing birds and horses and silkworm plants that produced the silvery clothing everyone wore. There was an abundance of everything and, Elizabeth noted, a marked absence of violent movies or comic books, alcohol, cigarettes or drugs.

When the time came, she had a natural birth, remarkable only for being utterly painless, and she called the child Ayling. Curiously, in her book while she lavishes pages on Meton's incredible white horses, she spares only a few paragraphs on the nine years of her son's life, describing him as a perfect gentle child, full of life and intelligence, who would sleep in her arms and ride on Akon's back when they went for walks or rides.

Unfortunately, the planetary vibrations affected her heart and Akon gently explained that while they could implant a timing device to regulate her pulse to Meton's electrical frequency, she would never be able to readjust to Earth and her heart was too unstable to endure the shock of a device that could normalize the effect of multiple time-fields.

She reluctantly returned to Earth, glowing with her startling new revelation that would put anyone else's alien encounter to shame, but her health was never the same. After May and Jock died, she moved back to Johannesburg and started work in one of CNA's bookstores. However, she struggled for money and her tachycardia plagued her to the extent that she ended up in hospital.

In 1963 she became romantically entangled with Major Aubrey Fielding, an ex-British intelligence officer who Elizabeth maintained the Chief had sent to look after her. Certainly he was there to take care of her when she was hospitalised, but David maintains he was much more than just a bodyguard and that his poised and elegant mother did love the gentle major. However, one of her surviving friends now claims Aubrey was a member of MI16 (as opposed to MI5 or MI6), and that when he died in 1980, it was an assassination by lethal injection because of Elizabeth's interests.

Whether he was still an active agent or not is debatable but Aubrey was, as proprietor of the Aubrey Fielding Gallery, most definitely an art dealer and Elizabeth, ever the culturati, delighted in being part of the hip Jo'burg art scene as well as the alien one.

And what did Akon think of all this? Elizabeth believed he was not only supportive, but that he'd helped to arrange it. For his part, Aubrey had only this to say to the newspapers, 'Well, my wife has been in love with a spaceman for 20 years. That's all right with me – as long as he stays in space where he belongs.'

Despite his gruff rebuff, Aubrey, unlike Paul Klarer, was very much a believer. He was involved on the sidelines in Elizabeth's work and the flying saucer society she chaired, Contact International, which held monthly meetings well into the '80s.

Elizabeth was quite the activist, travelling the country, giving talks to interested groups. Apart from the heckling she received at the Jo'burg MENSA society meeting, she was generally met with open-mindedness or, at worst, polite scepticism. She also attracted international attention and had correspondences from all over the world, including a post card from Professor Valerii Sanarov at the Soviet Academy of Medical Sciences in Novosibirsk, Siberia, who read about her in a copy of *The Sunday Times* that was mailed to him, and a letter dated 17 January 1968 from America's Library of Congress in Washington DC, requesting a copy of her book, then still in manuscript form.

In 1975 she was invited to attend the 11th International Congress of UFO Research Groups at Wiesbaden and received a standing ovation from the 22 assembled scientists. She also apparently gave a speech at the House of Lords in London in 1983 and one of her papers was read at the UN, although hard evidence of these latter two appearances is not readily available.

What is readily available, in a trunk in David Klarer's house in Durban, is a ton of newspaper articles. Ever since the 1950s when she first came forward about her experiences, the papers have loved her – and loved to ridicule her. She was a favourite of human interest columnists and journalist Jani Allen (best known for her affair with the riding-challenged AWB leader, Eugene Terreblanche) did several pieces on her over the years that were mostly friendly. But other journalists couldn't resist the opportunity to make light of her light-years-away romance. Juicy headlines in the entertainment section read along the lines of: 'My Stepfather Is An Alien', 'Liz Is In Love With A Harmony From Space' and 'A Romance That Is Out Of This World'. Elizabeth took it on the chin, claiming bad publicity was better than none, and she needed all she could get to spread Akon's message of peace, love, understanding and environmentalism that would save the planet.

When her book, *Beyond The Light Barrier* was finally published in English in 1981, it inspired new flurries of publicity. Following her coup at Wiesbaden, the book had already been published in German in 1977 and the first two print runs had quickly sold out, but in South Africa, publishers treated her autobiography as science fiction and it was only several years after completing it that Howard Timmins Publishers stepped in to bring it to light.

The book is an uneasy combination of autobiography, emphatic New Agey philosophical treatise, complicated science that sounds most convincing and wild adventure love story. It includes many photographs of the family farm in the 'berg, pictures of various dogs, horses and family, and Elizabeth receiving a bouquet in Wiesbaden, as well as several authentic-looking photographs of ships in motion streaking across the sky, which Elizabeth took with her Brownie box camera. But apart from a painting of Akon, there are no images of her family in space or close-up shots of the ship when it had landed.

While Elizabeth was in regular telepathic contact with Akon, she never saw Ayling again other than in holographic projections. She claimed it was too dangerous for him to come to Earth considering the violent barbarism of its inhabitants.

She always maintained that Akon would come back to fetch her. He never did, although her friends will tell you that she's with him now.

In 1994, at the age of 84, Elizabeth died of breast cancer, leaving her second book, *The Gravity File* unfinished.

She purported that her second book would fill in many of the gaps of the first and would also provide a detailed breakdown of Akon's electro-gravity propulsion technology. The manuscript is not lost, however, just incomplete, and attempts are being made to reconstruct it.

Was it all hokum, a convenient format to propagate her free spirit philosophies, a way for a middle-aged woman to bask in the glow of public attention? Or did she really see something in her youth and just go overboard at the end as Zimbabwean UFO authority Cynthia Hind apparently claimed? Or are we simply not capable of understanding?

David says he now regrets not 'cornering' his mother on some of the things she wrote in her book. There are certainly glaring plot holes; for instance that there just happened to be beautiful white horses on Meton, which Elizabeth just happened to love, or that Akon took her MG onto the ship because he wanted to adjust the engine, despite not being familiar with piston engines, let alone the purple prose or the biological logistics of having a baby at 50.

On the flip side, Elizabeth had the hard evidence of photographs, Akon's ring and a piece of space rock (although it was never analysed), which are all in the keeping of her family, as well as ties to high-ranking British military personnel. She is still taken very seriously by UFO societies today.

The descriptions of technology in her book read convincingly, at least to a layperson, although her relationships with the Chief and Stafford at the DeHavilland test site would have placed her in a position privy to speculation about new technologies. Based on currently available technology, it would take *all* Earth's energy resources to power a ship to reach the closest star, Betelgeuse, let alone Alpha Centauri. And it would take 250 years to get there.

As for her claims to working for the South African Air Force's 'UFO division', a highly placed archivist I spoke to (who requested anonymity) says he's never seen any documentation to that effect and all the SAAF's secret files cross his desk, including the ones on the

Helderberg. It helps that he has a special interest, having experienced a sighting himself outside of Kimberley.

However, he wasn't prepared to dismiss it entirely either. 'Just because I haven't seen anything doesn't mean it didn't exist – it could have been shredded,' he says. 'I know many pilots who have seen things and the SAAF once scrambled a Mirage to check out a sighting in Thaba Nchu. In the '70s at the radar base in Devon [outside of Pretoria] the guys saw stuff on that James Bond shit of theirs that was moving too fast to be anything we know of.'

In her book, *Abducted: How People Come to Believe They Were Kidnapped by Aliens*, Harvard psychologist Susan Clancy poses the theory that abductees' memories are often a combination of a nasty, but quite normal sleep paralysis, which many people experience at least once in their lifetimes, combined with a vivid imagination, and an already established interest in the paranormal, that work together with tricks of memory and emotional investment and are often complicated by suggestive hypnotherapy.

On the flip side, even Britain's Ministry of Defence isn't prepared to deny flat out that UFOs exist. The press release that accompanied the declassifying of The Flying Saucer Working Party in February 2005, stated, 'The MoD does not have any expertise or role in respect of UFO/flying saucer matters or to the question of the existence or otherwise of extraterrestrial life forms, about which it remains totally open-minded.'

Or as Elizabeth cannily wrote in the introduction to *Beyond The Light Barrier*, 'The Cosmic scale of this book will be lost and misunderstood by many whose intelligence cannot be expanded in this epoch of time, to a conscious awareness of our Cosmic connections.'

The Outcast with the Heart on Fire

Bessie Head

Bessie Head spent too much living inside her head and consequently lost it. Southern Africa's most intense writer was damned to Greek-level tragedy by the circumstances of her birth in a mental asylum, which was presented to her as a prophecy by a callous school principal who told her, 'Your mother was insane. If you're not careful you'll get insane just like your mother.' Bessie took it to heart and in a sense, went out of her way to ensure that it was self-fulfilling.

But even while she alienated friends with her increasingly paranoid delusions and the seething venom in her letters, her unravelling mind sparked magnesium-fierce and bright before it burned out and her most compelling and harrowing novel, *A Question of Power*, was a thinly veiled fiction exploring a mental breakdown from the inside.

Bessie was born in the Fort Napier Mental Institution in 1937, the unwanted mixed-race, bastard child of a white woman, 'Toby' Bessie Amelia Emery, and a black man whose identity has never been uncovered. Bessie grew up believing that her mother was committed to the asylum for the unforgivable sin of sleeping with a black stable hand, but the truth is that no-one suspected her father might be other than white until she was born. And Toby had started on her downward spiral into schizophrenia long before.

Toby was unhinged by the death of her first-born son, Stanley, who was killed at the age of four, crossing the road in a hit and run in 1919, probably one of Johannesburg's first-ever car accidents. Toby's husband, Ira, never forgave her, although it was hardly her fault. After ten years of bitter resentment widening the gulf between them, he divorced her in 1929, leaving her with their younger son, Ronald. In the wake of their separation, Toby disintegrated entirely and her mother, Alice Birch, was forced to step in to manage her affairs. She dispatched Toby to a mental hospital for a year from 1934 to 1935, where she wrote rambling, disjointed appeals to the authorities, begging them to let her out.

Toby was eventually released into her mother's care, but in October 1936, she approached a solicitor and asked him to draw up a will, leaving everything to Ronald. The will was later deemed invalid because she wasn't in her right mind, but it's significant, because this would have been around the time when Bessie was conceived and a love affair – or a rape – may have been exactly the kind of dramatic event that would have incited Toby to start thinking about her death.

She was already six months gone when her sisters noticed she was pregnant in April 1937. The signs had been disguised by her plump build, a characteristic she was to pass on to her daughter, together with her name, her expressive eyes, her creative bent, her love of gardening and, possibly, the faulty connection in her brain.

She was admitted to the psychiatric hospital almost immediately and Bessie was born there two months later. Toby was in no fit state to care for her child and Alice Birch arranged an adoption for her illegitimate granddaughter. Although the birth certificate clearly stated 'white', the foster family took one gander at her and sent her back, claiming that with her dark skin and black eyes, she looked 'strange'. Bessie was finally placed with the only people who would take her – Nellie and George Heathcote, a coloured couple in Pietermaritzburg who received the princely sum of £3 a month for her care.

Alice visited Bessie occasionally and paid for her upkeep, but Toby never saw her very beautiful little daughter again and strangely, while she wrote Ronald countless letters, not once did she make mention of his half-sister. Toby died in the asylum in September 1943 of abscesses on the lung and mental degeneration typical of schizophrenia. Embittered by the ravages of the scandal on the family name and worn out by Toby's long degeneration, Alice abandoned her granddaughter with a £300 inheritance and forbade anyone from ever mentioning Bessie's name in her presence again.

The closest Bessie came to discovering the truth of her circumstances was in her 20s, when a journalist friend, Dennis Brutus, liaised on a project with Ira Emery, Toby's ex-husband who had since remarried. Bessie couldn't have failed to notice that they shared a name, but she didn't follow up. Perhaps she was afraid of what she might find.

For the first 13 years of her life, however, she was totally oblivious to the bleak soap opera of her reality. The Heathcotes were decent sorts, but limited by lack of education and poverty, especially when George died in 1946, around the time Alice made her last visit. Nellie couldn't understand Bessie's devouring obsession with books and would clip her ear if she found her wasting time nestled in a corner reading instead of doing her chores or being sociable.

In 1950, Bessie went to St Monica's Home, a mission school in Durban, but she pined so terribly for her family, that a social worker suggested Nellie stop writing to her because it only upset her more. Her life changed irrevocably one year later. In 1951, expecting to go home for the holidays, Bessie was instead, to her total confusion, swept off to court for a hearing to establish whether she qualified for government assistance. No-one had bothered to tell her the hearing was coming up or prepare her for the devastating information she was about to receive.

When Bessie threw a tantrum, wailing that she would die if she didn't go home to her mother, the principal snapped that her mother was *not* Nellie Heathcote. Apparently unaware of the cruel shock of her words, the principal told Bessie that her mother was a white woman who had been insane and her father was a 'native'. In court, the magistrate confirmed it and when Bessie saw her again, Nellie confessed the truth in tears.

Bessie, quite illogically, blamed the principal and Christianity in general and never set foot in a church again, although she did request a Catholic priest for her funeral. She found solace in the broad philosophies of Hinduism instead and started to break ties with Nellie and the limitations of her close-minded poverty, claiming later that pursuing a 'life with books' over family was 'the blind choice for survival'.

Bessie went on to qualify for the inferior teaching degree available to coloured people at the time, but quickly discovered that she was terrible, especially when it came to maintaining order in the classroom. Just before her 21st birthday, *gatvol* of trying to get through to her class, Bessie marched up to her favourite teacher, Margaret Cadmore, and told her she was packing it in and moving to Cape Town. When Margaret questioned her on such a rash decision, without money or anywhere to go, Bessie burst into hysterical tears and ran away. But she had made up her mind. She was going to be a reporter. It was just like Bessie to be such a bolshy drama queen.

In 1958 she moved to Cape Town and promptly landed a job with the *Golden City Post*, sister paper to the already legendary *Drum*. The editor assigned her a freelance piece more out of pity for the clearly intelligent but quiveringly nervous girl than any real hope she would deliver, but deliver she did and she was soon writing regular human interest stories. What she really longed for, though, was 'a good murder', such as those covered by *Drum* writers Can Themba, Dennis Brutus and Lewis Nkosi.

She didn't always make ends meet and with a letter to Margaret Cadmore, started a long history of reluctantly borrowing money from friends. It's interesting that she seems to have puffed up her CV slightly, writing to Margaret that she was doing a series of 'dream come true' stories, taking crippled children up Table Mountain in the cable car, for example, when there's no evidence she ever did.

Bessie had been desperately hoping that, in Cape Town, she would fit in. She was troubled by racism from white and black alike. Apart from the humiliation of living under apartheid, when she was sent to interview Miriam Makeba, for example, the chanteuse refused to even look at her because of her reputed dislike of coloureds.

Like the painter, Irma Stern, Bessie thought she would find peace among brown people, but even in the coloured community, she was depressed by class division and despondent because people judged her on her darker skin and her plummy Natal boarding school accent. Despite everything, she was determined to live her individuality and she gave teens the same advice when she moved to Johannesburg and took on a job with *Home Post* writing two regular columns called 'Dear Gang' and 'Hiya Teenagers'.

Bessie was never overly political, but she lived in a state of raw anger about all kinds of things, from the way coloured people blindly accepted the inferior education they were doled out, which locked them into a cycle of poverty and alcoholism, to the racist propaganda spewed by the apartheid government. She loved a good argument and would often cause a brouhaha at Labour Party get-togethers. She wrote, 'I never joined fund-raising campaigns, because I can't ask for money. I never paid at fund-raising parties because I was always broke and yet drank as much wine as I could and talked as loud as I could and quarrelled with the whites who were there.'

Bessie was present when Robert Sobukwe, the leader of the Pan African Congress was arrested, but she didn't join in the protest. Instead, she wrote a somewhat mawkish column for 'Hiya Teenagers' called 'It Takes Guts To Be A Rebel' that was more about hairdos than hair-raising political protest. Unfortunately, Bessie couldn't live up to her advice and in 1960 when she was caught with a rather pedestrian letter that tied her to the PAC and a minor fund-raising campaign she'd been involved in, she turned state witness. To anyone who knew Bessie, it wouldn't have been a surprise. Despite her beer-chugging, chain-smoking, hell-raising persona, she was shy and vulnerable. She was terrified of the dark and even making phone calls, let alone facing the tortures of the Special Branch. But she was so ashamed of her admittedly very minor betrayal that she tried to commit suicide by swallowing 50 sleeping pills. She admitted later that the pain of being 'pulled back to life with pumps and drips' was so horrific she was never tempted to try it again.

Bessie was a dreamer and a romantic and longed for a man who would be her equal, but she never had much luck with the opposite sex. In fact, her first sexual encounter was so traumatic she never spoke about it. While she was always a bit prudish, how much this first encounter warped her sense of her sexuality only became evident when she wrote *A Question of Power*, where the devilish tempter Dan, taunts the protagonist, Elizabeth, about sex and his coterie of 'nice time girls' with evocative names such as Madame Squelch-Squelch, Madame Loose-Bottom and Miss Sewing Machine.

It's even more remarkable then that when she met a sharp young journalist, Harold Head, she felt brave enough to remove her clothes, stripping off unexpectedly in the sultry darkness of the community centre one night when they were alone – although maybe it's more shocking that he told her to get dressed again, waiting to make love to her later that night. They married a few weeks later, but like so many of Bessie's joys, the marriage was fleeting.

For a time, they were happy eking out a living as freelance writers and living in a crowded tenement on William Street, in the high-spirited slum that was District Six, with its packs of barefoot children that tumbled down the cobbled walks and stairways, the air heavy with the mingled scent of garbage and masala curry. Harold seemed well equipped to handle Bessie's temperamental mood swings with a casual grace, and when she fell pregnant they were both delighted.

Bessie found an outlet for her ferocious anger in writing for a new magazine, *The New African*, edited by Randolph Vigne and penned her first novel, *The Cardinals*, about race relations, although she wasn't able to get it published.

There was a growing sense of unease in the country. The government crackdowns escalated and when 69 peaceful protestors were killed in the Sharpeville Massacre, many took it as a sign to leave. Bessie loudly lamented the loss of so many of her friends, but she was also struggling financially, she felt her life was a failure and she intimated that Harold had been unfaithful. She took the baby and moved in with her mother-in-law in Atteridgeville, a township outside Pretoria.

By February 1964, she was in dire straits, broke and desperate to leave the country where she felt so oppressed, but the government wouldn't issue her with a passport. She contacted her friend, the poet Patrick Cullinan, imploring him for a job on his farm, but as Patrick explains, Bessie would never have coped with the hard labour. He suggested they find a way to get her out. They met at the Pretoria Zoo, so as not to attract too much attention from the Special Branch, but were unable to sit down because the benches were segregated, marked either 'whites only' or 'coloureds only'. Patrick arranged an exit permit through a civil rights lawyer friend and Bessie fled to a bustling village in Bechuanaland (soon to become Botswana) to take up a teaching post.

She would later paint Serowe as a parochial place compared to Cape Town, but the 'village' was actually a sprawling community accommodating some 30 000 people. There was no shortage of intellectuals as it was the base of operations for the Botswana Democratic Party, headed up by the dedicated young politician Seretse Khama, who was destined both to become president and to be terribly maligned by Bessie in one of her blackest moments.

Bessie saw Serowe as a chance to start over, despite her status as a stateless person. She was still young, only 26, but while she desperately wanted to fit in, she was too abrasive, too modern, too ready to speak her mind – and as a coloured woman, she was regarded as a half-caste 'bushman dog' and inferior. It didn't help that she never bothered to learn Setswana.

She had trouble particularly from the men who aggressively tried to bed this dynamo of a woman. She made it worse by initiating playful tussles, which men interpreted as a come-on, and made the mistake of entering into a tormented and tumultous affair with a high profile villager she both admired and feared.

The constant sexual harassment eventually cost her her teaching post when the principal manhandled her in front of her class. She bit his hand to escape and fled, sobbing hysterically. She was dismissed from her job for dereliction of duty, circumstances notwithstanding. Worse, the school committee wanted to send her for tests to prove her sanity, a prospect Bessie found absolutely terrifying, but was able to evade.

After she lost her job, Bessie scraped by. It wasn't only the pinched children in her former class who were starving. She was so poor that she often didn't have money to buy food for herself and her son, Howard, let alone candles to write by at night. In her typically engaging and persuasive letters, she appealed to her friends for help and people such as Randolph Vigne, Patrick Cullinan and Patrick van Rensburg came to her aid with money. She also received a refugee grant, made a pittance working on an experimental farm and finally, triumphantly, started earning an income from her writing.

However, her neighbours saw only that she didn't have a job and accused her of being a prostitute. Other, more vicious rumours circulated that she'd had a baby by her high-profile mystery lover and had thrown the infant down a long drop toilet. Bessie was mortified and could barely go out to face the constant sneering and whispers that she believed trailed in her wake.

She had a few close friends, including Bosele Sianana, who worked tirelessly in her garden with her, the ex-diplomat, Patrick van Rensburg and a young American draft resister, Tom Holzinger who had a bit of a thing for Bessie, which she defused by calling him 'my son'. Even Harold reappeared, passing through Serowe briefly on his way to exile in Canada, but while he said he'd send for her, as far as Bessie was concerned the marriage was over.

In 1965, she sold a story, 'Woman from America', to the highly reputed British paper, the *New Statesmen*, for £30. It was two months salary for her, but more importantly, it was to generate a flood of interest in her work and a steady stream of commissions. Jean Highland, an editor at Simon & Schuster, picked up the story and wrote to her to ask if she'd consider doing a novel. Bessie started work on *When Rainclouds Gather* immediately, although Jean had to send her a ream of paper together with the £80 advance.

By 1967 she'd rattled off an entire novel, about a disillusioned South African exile who is healed of his cynicism and hatred in Botswana. Because it was so closely autobiographical, Bessie worried that some of her acquaintances might sue, but her publishers reassured her.

She followed that up with the fairytale of *Maru*, intended to be an African *Catcher in the Rye* about two young Botswana chieftains fighting over the love of a strangely passive outsider 'bushman' woman and for a brighter Africa. Both books were snapped up and received acclaim overseas.

Bessie was beginning to receive fan mail from influential people such as American author Alice Walker, who became a lifelong admirer, even after Bessie broke ties with her through the furious invective of one of her infamous letters years later. She had already flamed one of her friends who made a tactless tactical blunder when she advised Bessie, 'You really must not write with your heart on fire. It's not literature. I really mean it.' Bessie cut her off cold and refused to hear her apologies. It was to become a pattern.

In her 30s, her life and her writing turned darker. Her loneliness and isolation had started to snarl her circuits. She wrote long letters talking about her unequivocal belief in reincarnation, that she believed she was the new embodiment of the Bible's King David as well as Mary Queen of Scots and her true father was Shaka. She claimed she had been born in Africa at this time to play a great role in the order of the universe. At the same time, she laughed it off with a little admonition to 'B. Head' as she often referred to herself in her letters, that after three months in the wilderness she was starting to see things.

She became increasingly paranoid and claimed that she was being persecuted. Her thoughts became muddled and bleak and were accompanied by a hissing sound, like the needle clicking on a gramophone. Whereas once she'd hated white people, now she learned to despise black people. She wrote, 'I sometimes can't look at the face of a black man or woman without thinking that they are the epitome of all that is grasping, greedy, cruel, back stabbing and a betrayal of all that is good in mankind.'

Her first breakdown came in March 1969. She suddenly snapped in a little shop when she bought a transistor radio and shouted at the three black men attending her, 'You bloody bastards,' while Howard watched wide-eyed. She then started to scream so hysterically that passers-by rushed in, convinced there was a murder in progress. Bessie was bustled into an ambulance and off to hospital where she spent 15 hours sleeping, tanked up to the eyeballs on tranquillisers. When she woke up, she seemed to be fully recovered and discharged herself. She claimed the outburst had purged her hatred, saying, 'It gets lost when you spit it out.'

Bizarrely, her breakdown meant that she actually gained status in the village. While suspected whores were to be vilified, mad people were happily tolerated.

The delusions worsened. She wrote about weird visitors, including a monk that stood by her bedside and various evil demons, who tortured her mind with sexual corruption and racist slurs. She became convinced that Seretse Khama was evil incarnate and that he had murdered his prime minister, Dr Masire. She could not be dissuaded, even when her old friend Randolph Vigne reported seeing the man in the flesh and when he appeared on the news or in the papers. She obstinately maintained it was a grand conspiracy. Apart from the Seretse debacle, Bessie seemed able to distinguish between levels of reality, but she was still ticked off when her correspondents, who were becoming more and more worried by her letters, didn't get it. And then she really lost it.

She had been badly depressed for weeks and when a kindly old lady neighbour popped in to see how she was doing, Bessie chased her out with expletives and later barged into her house, punched her in the head and started screaming hysterically before she fled home and locked herself in. The next morning she set off to the post office and stuck up a slanderous notice on the wall that was often used for ads and community news (not unlike the one that landed Dr James Barry in hot water, 145 years prior). Her notice claimed that President Seretse had not only assassinated Dr Masire, but that he had also committed incest with his daughter.

It was a serious offence. The police arrived at her house shortly after and hauled her off to jail, sobbing and wailing. In court, she seemed so confused and made the most outrageous accusations that no-one in their right mind could doubt that she had lost her's. Seretse was remarkably understanding about the whole thing and Bessie was sent to the only psychiatric ward in the country.

In the hospital, Bessie was alternately abusive and apathetic and deranged, and then quite suddenly, she was better. She was released on condition that she not mention a certain person's name ever again, particularly in connection with incest or murder or any of other diabolical crime she could imagine.

Bessie turned the experience into a book, *A Question of Power*, her most notable work for its unflinching, but admittedly terribly confusing account of her descent into madness with a protagonist clearly named for her – Elizabeth. The book proved too gruesomely candid for her agent or her previous publishers who politely rejected it as incomprehensible.

Bessie torched several bridges with the spitting mad and deeply offensive letters she wrote in response. After eight months, her new agent finally secured a publisher and in 1974 *A Question of Power* was nominated for the Booker prize, although it didn't make the shortlist.

By August 1972, Bessie was broke again and writing morbid letters that skirted around the idea of her death. She was offered residency in Norway, which seemed like the miracle she'd been hoping for to escape the hellhole of Serowe, but at the last minute she backed out, claiming she wasn't going to live longer than five more years anyway, so what was the point?

Bessie was in desperate need of money and a distraction from the tangles in her head. Her friend Ken McKenzie, the Cape Town editor of *Drum*, came to the rescue when he suggested she make a return to journalism and write a history of Serowe. The book buoyed her spirits and with her mind focused on the task, she didn't have time to obsess about her demons. It brought sanity for a time, until it came to getting the thing published.

Bessie's tax situation was a mess and when her agent Giles Gordon and her old friend Patrick Cullinan tried to negotiate some way around it, she became convinced they were conspiring against her. It was a complicated business, but Bessie didn't see that they were trying to help and sent them both vile letters accusing them of cheating her and stealing her money. They were shocked and hurt, but when Patrick came to Serowe and gently tried to point out that she was having another breakdown, she flatly denied it, even in light of a bizarre letter she'd penned to Seretse Khama himself that started off sanely enough about how ludicrous it was that a refugee should pay taxes and then lapsed into a ramble about Satan. Her friends stuck by her and the book finally came out, thanks to the tireless campaigning of Patrick Cullinan, although Bessie continued to write terrible things about him behind his back.

Her life stabilised somewhat when she finally gained citizenship in 1979 and she was enjoying some international success, travelling to Ohio, Australia, Nigeria and Denmark to attend conferences and give speeches. However, Bessie couldn't shake her sense of persecution. When she met Alice Walker in 1977 as a guest of the University of Ohio, she left the meeting convinced that the negativity with which the American wrote about obese people was a personal attack on Bessie and she cut contact.

Similarly, she'd always enjoyed the intellectual stimulation of visiting scholars, but now she saw that they were profiting off her, receiving grants and accolades while she lived on the brink of starvation. She cut off the universities altogether and shouted at one poor German girl who rocked up at her door, even though she'd invited her to visit 'anytime' when she met her at a conference in Denmark.

In the meantime, Bessie had produced another history, *A Bewitched Crossroad*, which was the first to explore the Mfecane or dispersal of Shaka's time from a black perspective, but she admitted that she was holding out for the not-so-secret dream of winning the Nobel Prize for Literature. When she submitted her taxes, she even included a cheeky p.s. asking how much she could expect to be taxed if she won.

Despite her successes, Bessie still had worries and she remained mostly terminally broke. Howard weighed on her greatly; he'd become spoilt and lived off her income, but rather than bump him off the way Daisy de Melker had with her ingrate son, she sent him to Harold in Canada in 1982, hopefully to find better prospects.

She was also drinking. A lot. Bessie had always been fond of her beer and had a remarkable tolerance for alcohol. She could down six in a row and still be just chipper, but when everything she'd hoped for suddenly landed in her lap, Bessie couldn't handle it – or being forced to confront her past.

In 1984, she was commissioned to write her autobiography. Bessie agreed readily, but said she'd rather skirt over her painful childhood and start with her adult life. The publishers retorted that they weren't interested unless the book specifically tackled her early years and Bessie reluctantly agreed. They paid her a huge advance, which yanked her out of her financial insecurity but she seemed unable to make a start. She meticulously sorted her papers and mucked around in her garden and took to drinking a bottle of gin or whisky or vodka a day, literally pissing away the money – anything to avoid writing

In 1986 she was diagnosed with chronic hepatitis, but still she didn't stop drinking. It seemed her past was too much for her to bear, or perhaps she'd already fallen so far into the clutches of alcohol dependency that there was no way back.

She was hospitalised and on 17 April, at the still tender age of 49, she slipped into unconsciousness from which she never emerged. After the desperately tragic, torrid torments of her life, Bessie died peacefully. She was buried in the Botolaote cemetery, leaving behind her tortured life and an extraordinary collection of writings.

The Magnificent Ma-Brrr

Brenda Fassie

In May 2004, in Johannesburg's exclusive Sunninghill Clinic, South Africa's most effervescent and notorious pop star lay dying to the mournful backbeat of the life support machines, the high hat susurrus of the ventilator.

For a time, it seemed that the 'queen of African pop', the 'Madonna of the townships', the irrepressible Ma-Brrr might pull through for one last comeback. She'd done it before. Over the next 13 days, the nation held its breath. Fans wept or prayed or raged, writing impassioned tributes on her website, phoning the premium-rate cell phone hotline her record label set up to leave a message or update themselves on her condition. CD sales doubled.

A shifting vigil thronged her bedside or paced the halls; of friends and family, CCP/EMI record label execs, and luminaries including Nelson Mandela, Thabo Mbeki, Miriam Makeba and her mentor-mother, Winnie Madikizela-Mandela, who held her hand and prayed to God to 'save the child'. Tabloid reporters, suddenly sympathetic after years of vilifying her, hung around in the corridor outside, clamouring for headlines. Allegedly among the visitors was the dealer who sold her the crack that killed her.

Initial reports claimed it was an asthma attack; Brenda was known to be a sufferer. She kept an oxygen tank at her Buccleuch home and once, when drowning for air, had asked her 27-year old girlfriend, Gloria Chaka, to cut open her chest with a knife so she could breathe. But the post mortem revealed that asthma was only a complication. Like Marilyn Monroe, Kurt Cobain, Tupac Shakur and Billie Holiday; her life had played out that tired formula of fame and fortune with the certainty of cliché. Sex and drugs and rocking disco-soul equals a life too fast. A death too soon.

Like 'Mama Afrika' Miriam Makeba, Brenda had received the ancestor's call to become a sangoma. And like Miriam, she chose to stay with music rather than begin the rites of *thwasa* (or initiate), although some saw songs like 1990s 'Black President' as prophetic. Perhaps she had received a different kind of call from the other world. Or perhaps she felt it in her guts that her trajectory had taken a sharp downwards spike.

Whatever it was, Brenda knew she wasn't going to be around for an encore. A week before her collapse, she phoned producer Teny Maribatsi to make urgent arrangements for her to lay down the track 'Malibongwe', a praise piece to God and the power of love for her album *Gimme Some Volume* while she still had the chance. She'd already recorded a song that warned a friend, possibly Gloria, that she had to learn independence and asked what would happen when she was gone.

Much has been made of her six hour-long sojourn at His Church Kingdom Ministries in Atholl, praying and singing on the day before her collapse. Brenda confessed before the congregation that she had done all the wrong things there were to be done and vowed to change her life, to destroy all the 'things' she had been using. They absolved her. And God did too. Pastor Linda Godobo told the *Sunday Times*, 'On the one day she had, she made it right.'

Gloria revealed the details of Brenda's last day in fits and starts to the newspapers. That evening, Gloria says, they had a quiet dinner of spaghetti and chicken and she braided her hair – she often sang to Brenda or played with her to help her sleep. From eight until midnight, Brenda freebased cocaine. By that stage, Gloria said, Brenda was spending R3 000 a day on her habit and had degenerated to searching the carpet for leftover rocks and trying to smoke balls of wax. She had lost so much weight, she had dropped from a size 32 to a size 26 – although there were other rumours on that score, that Brenda was HIV positive.

The tragic irony was that her career was booming. She was lined up to play Australia, Germany, America, Uganda, Mali and Sierra Leone. If only she had been able to avoid returning to that tired chorus of her life: 'I'll change. I'll be back.' – never quite succeeding.

When she awoke on Monday, 26 April, she came up gasping for air, struggling to breathe, let alone speak. To attract attention, she rushed through to the kitchen and started stamping frantically on the floor. While Gloria went for the oxygen tank, Brenda's brother Themba wrapped his arms around her as she shook hysterically. She raised her right fist and hurled her crack pipe away. But it was too late. The vicious blend of crack and anti-depressants she was on seized her heart and her lungs.

She was rushed to the hospital, but by the time she was admitted at 10:34, she was already clinically dead. She had no pulse, no blood pressure, no breath to stir the lungs that had stirred stadiums to rapturous mayhem. The medical staff succeeded in resuscitating her after 12 minutes, but not before she had sustained brain damage from the lack of oxygen.

Brenda's prolonged death was as controversial as her life. There was a flutter of conspiracy theories during those days as she languished in hospital and in the weeks thereafter, rumours that her drugs had been spiked with rat poison, some claimed deliberately. Others said that the break-in at her house a few months prior had been no random crime, but a follow-up on a 1999 raid when her dealers claimed clothes and possessions in lieu of the payment owed to them.

A chilling video filmed by her long-time on-again off-again producer, Sello 'Chicco' Twala, in 2003, and released after she died, revealed a

Brenda morbidly preoccupied with her own death, begging him to get her out of town before the drug dealers killed her over the money she owed them.

While the newspapers gleefully seized on every scrap of information and screaming headlines guessed pre-emptively at death or, spurred by her hand twitching, a miraculous recovery, Brenda's friends and family had to come to terms with the inevitability that she wasn't going to bounce back from this, especially after she contracted a lung infection from the ventilator. On 9 May, on the doctor's recommendation, the family permitted her life support to be terminated. Brenda Fassie passed away quietly in her sleep at the age of 39. The golden voice was stilled forever.

Actually, to call that lush, resonant tenor merely 'golden' is an injustice. Brenda's voice was pure platinum. In the lingo of the music industry, going platinum in South Africa means topping 50 000 album sales. Brenda, always one for excess, went triple platinum in her early 20s and multi-platinum on many of her releases thereafter. Her best-loved album, *Memeza*, sold 50 000 copies in four hours and after her death, at the 2004 South African Music Awards (SAMAs), it was declared Best-Selling Album of the Decade, moving more units than any other South African artist. Ever.

Brenda started singing almost as soon as she could speak. She was born in Cape Town's oldest township, Langa, in 1964 as the youngest of nine. Her family, like many families living in the townships in that time, were poor and their precarious finances were further upset when her father died two years later.

For money, the family would head down to the harbour to entertain the tourists with a little song and dance routine, although Brenda, as the baby, had to be told off for scrabbling to pick up the coins tossed their way in the middle of the performance.

By four, the little girl named for US country singer and child prodigy Brenda Lee, was singing with a neighbourhood group, the Tiny Tots, accompanied by her mother, Sarah on piano. At 12, she was headlining a teenage group called Cosmos from Elsiesriver.

In 1979, having heard the buzz about this township girl with the voice from several musician friends, Johannesburg producer Koloi Lebona made a point of going to Langa to find her. He had no problems hunting her down; she was already legendary in the community and his enquiries quickly lead directly to Sarah's modest house at 26 Makana Square. While Sarah played the piano, the teenager demonstrated her vocal range. Koloi knew immediately that he had heard 'the voice of the future'. Brenda sussed out his awed reaction and sassily chirped, 'So, when are we going to Jo'burg?'

In a 1997 *New York Times* interview, Brenda claimed that she ran away from home at 14 and hitched to Jozi in petrol trucks, sleeping in bus shelters until she found theatre doyen Gibson Kente in Soweto. Her official biography is less dramatic. Sarah gave permission for Koloi to take Brenda to Jozi to launch her career, on condition her daughter stayed with his family in their home in White City, Soweto, and that she complete her schooling.

Brenda enrolled at Phefini High to continue her standard eight and started gigging, while learning showmanship at Bra Gibson's music and drama school. She was a born crowd pleaser who craved the limelight and could be found at all hours in the streets entertaining the neighbourhood kids or breaking into song at parties. It was to be a habit she fostered for the rest of her life. While her peers maintained an aloof distance from the public who made them, Brenda would join in the *jol* with the ordinary people in the streets or shebeens at the slightest prompting, even after she hit the big time.

And hit it she did. She didn't wait long for her break. In 1980, Afro-pop trio Joy were dominating the airwaves with their soulful number, 'Paradise Road'. The band, which included Anneline Malebo (who became a committed AIDS activist before her death in 2002), Thoko Dlozi and Felicia Marion, was sculpted in the mode of black American groups such as the Supremes, with big hair and svelte sequinned dresses, and a soul sound that won over black and white audiences alike. When Anneline became pregnant and went on maternity leave, Brenda was handpicked to replace her. She bunked school, and for three years rocked the charts with Joy. But she was becoming too big to play third fiddle and she moved on and up, headlining solo with the male disco revue, Papa And Blondie, on their roadshow.

A breakaway group formed out of Papa And Blondie, called Brenda And The Big Dudes with a line-up that included Brenda, naturally, Dumisani Ngobeni (who would father her son, Bongani), bassist Sammy Klaasen and drummer David Mabaso. Their first disco single 'Weekend Special', about a mistress who only sees her man on the weekends, blasted the band – and Brenda – to overnight stardom. The 12-inch maxi brought out by the CCP Record Company became the fastest-selling record of 1983 and the single inspired a horde of remixes and covers, including one by Van Gibbs, which topped the US charts for eight weeks. Brenda's original hit the prestigious Billboard Hot Black Single charts in 1986 and consequently opened the world. She promptly embarked on tours to America, Europe, Australia and Brazil, and through Africa.

Her success re-ignited a fizzling homegrown scene in South Africa burned by the political and social oppression of the townships. Brenda was the pioneer, breaking ground for her lifelong friend and rival Yvonne Chaka Chaka, among others, to claim their place as icons of the new genre of bubblegum pop and later kwaito.

By the late '80s, Brenda was a solo artist, with a little help from hit-maker musician-turned producer Chicco Twala, dubbed the 'Quincy Jones of South Africa' by *Time* magazine. Their collaboration cemented her superstar status on the back of a string of number ones such as 'No No No Senor', the daringly political, 'Black President', which was banned in 1990 (prompting Brenda to declare she would only sing in Xhosa, Zulu and Sotho from then on), and the monster album *Too Late for Mama*. Was it any wonder she was developing a monster ego?

She could be petty and petulant, throwing tantrums or bursting into tears with little provocation. She was highly emotional and craved acknowledgement. All it needed was for a fan to say 'I love you', to set her weeping. She worked to a relentless schedule, sometimes playing several gigs, miles apart in one day, but by the mid-90s she had a reputation for being late or not showing up at all.

In 1992, she was fined R2 000 for assaulting *The Sowetan* photographer, Mbuzeni Zulu, and smashing his camera when he snapped her brawling with her brother, Themba, and another woman. When testifying, Brenda broke into an impromptu unplugged rendition of 'I'm Not A Bad Girl', causing a ripple of laughter and applause. *'They don't understand me / I'm not a bad girl / no-oh / I'm nobody else / just an ordinary girl / don't push me too far / because I'm on the edge.'* How could anyone know how prophetic her words would be?

More than one music critic deconstructed her as a 'child-woman' who was desperately insecure and didn't know where to draw the boundaries, giving too freely of herself – and her stuff. Brenda was known for paying the way of everyone in her entourage. If someone said they liked what she was wearing, she would take it off and give it to them. Her money went the same way, spent in sprees or siphoned off by hangers-on or given away to a good cause. For instance, she donated R58 000 to the survivors of the Boipatong Massacre (when 50 ANC supporters were killed by Inkatha Freedom Party members) despite not being able to pay her son Bongani's school fees. For all her excesses and high living, she was a socially minded pop star.

She was also far too generous with her privacy. Her reputation as the 'Madonna of the townships', was a reference to a trait she shared with America's material girl – her blatant sexuality, as well as her outrageous outfits. Brenda didn't like being compared with anyone but the moniker stuck to the extent that local music mag, *e'Vibe* tried to get away with lifting a *Newsweek* interview with the American star in 1991 and reprinting it verbatim as a chat with Brenda, changing only the 'yeahs' to 'yebos'.

Time magazine picked up on the name tag and used it in a 2001 article that also described how Brenda popped out of her top during a three-hour-long performance in Washington DC, only to grab her boob and brandish it at the audience. 'This is Africa!' she shouted, much to the Americans' horror and the embarrassment of the South African contingent. Brenda wasn't concerned, brushing it off with a riposte that she was too hot for America to handle.

However, as the *New York Times* was to point out, the comparison was facile. Madonna's every move then (as now) was carefully choreographed to manipulate the media machine to her advantage. Brenda was too impulsive, too ingenuous to be the local equivalent, blurting outrageous statements to the press that they printed verbatim. She said, 'I'm a shocker. I like to create controversy. It's my trademark.' But she didn't always like the result. As journalist Charl Blignaut wrote, you didn't interview Brenda, you 'experienced her'.

She gradually grew to distrust the media, although she loved the attention too much to deny them an audience completely. (Agatha Christie was among her favourite authors, not least for a comment the mystery writer once made, 'I hate journalists and I always kill them badly in my books.')

Ironically, while the material girl rode her contrived erotic adventurousness to the peaks of fame in America, Brenda's candidness about her sexuality estranged conservative black South Africa. Fans were willing to overlook her lateness and no-shows, and even the drug binges she was beginning to indulge, but not her promiscuous proclivities, especially with women. As she so evocatively put it, 'I wipe the toilet paper on both sides.'

Her taste in men was bad enough. She claimed she made men cry in bed because she sang for them while they made love. In return, they assaulted her and, she said, tried to steal her money.

In 1985, Brenda gave birth to a son, Bongani, sired by Big Dude Dumisani Ngobeni, who reportedly beat her. In 1989, she married Durban playboy Nhlanhla Mbambo. The wedding was a massive public spectacle that saw the couple mobbed by 30 000 adoring fans in the Magogo stadium at KwaMashu in KwaZulu-Natal, forcing them to flee the scene.

In a *City Press* interview, Nhlanhla quite openly declared that he sometimes had to 'give her a slap or two' to show her who was boss. It should have come as no surprise then when he knocked out two of her teeth in Swaziland in 1990 after a jealous spat over a radio personality who was 'showing her too much attention'.

While she always pursued the idea of a 'lifetime special', she clearly wasn't designed for marriage and after 22 months, she lived out the lyrics of her hit, 'Wedding Song' – *'till divorce do us part'*. She dismissed Nhlanhla as a leech, a lecher and a wife-beater in the press, even going so far as to set up a R2.20 a minute 087 info-line to provide the public with all the gory details of how he only loved her stage persona, hit on her cousin and conned her label into paying his bill of R15 000 for a month's stay in a luxury hotel. He was later charged with assaulting someone else and sentenced to ten years in prison.

Next up was a long-running and tempestuous hot-cold affair with Ludwe Maki, a backing vocalist that she brought into her band and then her bed before outing him in public, she said, as a *'moffie'*. (She would later accuse a journalist who wrote an unflattering article of the same thing). At 35, she moved on to her 20-year old manager, Landile Shembe Ka Gcinga. He proposed to her at her 36th birthday bash, but it was over five days later. Brenda claimed her teenage son Bongani had warned her that Landile was a conman in love with her bank account.

Her relationships with men were as stormy and thrilling as her vibrato – and these are just the highlights – but it was her affairs with women that really caught the headlines. Brenda was the first South African celebrity, black or white, to be so forthright about her sexual experimentation. In a 1987 *Drum* magazine cover feature, she claimed she was just curious, just trying it on; she had all these girls lusting after her and it was 'a good experience'. 'I am lesbian. I'm bisexual, but I prefer men, of course.' It was a taboo subject, especially in the more traditional black communities and her frankness cost her dearly.

She may well have been oblivious to the horrified gasps. While she never forgot her roots, it may have been convenient to forget how conservative her upbringing had been, especially when her apartment at the Century Plaza in Hillbrow in the early '90s, was the epicentre of black bohemia. When the area was abandoned as an exclusive upmarket white playground, it became decidedly more edgy. Middle class black families, fashionistas, artists, intellectuals and gay people flocked to fill the deserted residential blocks in the inner city and Century Plaza was the most rocking of them all, a debauched hub of musicians, gay pride and extravagance fuelled by wine and gender-bending orgies and, for some, drugs. Brenda was the loudest and most stylish at the nucleus of everything.

Brenda felt little *skaam* about her sexual exploits, which were openly endorsed by her wild intimate circle. She had no qualms about outing her lovers in print, even playing off married couples against each other, by sleeping with both of them behind each other's backs.

Unfortunately, her relationships with women were as damaged and damaging as those she indulged in with men, only in her female liaisons, Brenda was the one who raised her fists against her partners. She shocked journalists by describing in graphic detail how she forced girls to go down on her, but refused to reciprocate.

On Valentine's Day 1999, her lover, Karen Baker, told the papers that Brenda used her and took her belongings, including her cell phone, TV and radio. Brenda shrugged it off, retorting in a radio interview that Karen was simply a vengeful woman scorned and trying to win her back. And besides, they'd sold those things together, Brenda said, 'we wanted to buy drugs'.

In December 2002, she 'married' her lesbian lover, Sindisiwe Khambule in a media extravaganza in Yeoville, but the relationship turned sour, some dark rumours claim on the basis that Sindi tried to lure Brenda's teenage son, Bongani, into a sex and drugs orgy. Even Gloria Chaka, who was with her at the end, was not an ideal match. Quite apart from the drugs, Gloria went public with claims that Brenda treated her and other girls as sex slaves in the early days of their relationship, but later retracted her statement. The Fassie family dismissed her as a gold-digger.

Her most tragic and scarring relationship was in the mid-90s. Brenda met her 'other half', Victoria 'Poppy' Sihlahla, at a music festival. The diva was captivated by the schoolgirl beauty, who in turn adored her, following her around between shady Hillbrow hotels until they both ended up at the Quirinale in Kotze Street, run by Brenda's then-manager, Spiros Vovos. According to journo Bongani Madondo, the hotel was not only the scene of degenerate clubbing, but also a meeting spot for operatives of the notorious undercover security police unit, the CCB (Civil Cooperation Bureau), which went hand-in-hand with prostitution and hard drugs.

The story goes that Brenda was introduced to crack by a Nigerian bodyguard, but while her gay friends were happy to smoke *zol*, crack was considered too hectic and her habit alienated her from many of the people close to her. Poppy and cocaine became her crutch. In a bleak foreshadowing of Brenda's death a decade later, Poppy died of an 'asthma attack' in 1995, while Brenda lay sleeping beside her.

Brenda was destroyed. She took to crawling into bed with Poppy's favourite stuffed toy panda and dolls so she wouldn't have to sleep alone, and watching endless TV. In 1996, in her loneliness and grief, she tried to commit suicide by throwing herself under an oncoming truck. The driver swerved to avoid her, but she lay in the street until another motorist beat her with a sjambok to get her to move. She later denied the incident.

She eventually came clean about the cause of Poppy's death and confessed that she'd dropped over R100 000 on crack by that stage of her life. She wrote a song for Poppy, 'Kutheni', one of many autobiographical numbers in her catalogue including 'My Baby Bongani', which achingly claims, *'When I'm up, when I'm down/ When I'm spinning all alone / He's there to please me / He'll never leave me,'* and the too hopeful 'A Person Does Change'.

She checked herself into rehab, with the encouragement of her friends and family, including Yvonne Chaka Chaka and Tokyo Sexwale who eloquently (and self-aggrandizingly) described her as a 'diamond withering away' and called on 'the spirit of Masakhane' (working together) to 'build up what has been destroyed'. During therapy, her counsellor reported admiringly that she would burst into song, weaving their conversation into the lyrics.

The '90s were a tough time for her. It seemed this might be the end of the line. In 1990, she was sued for fraud together with her then-husband Nhlanhla and a former boyfriend, Eric Mbeko. Her marriage dissolved the following year, then came the assault case, and a public disclosure from one of her lovers about how hellish his life with her had been. In 1993 her mother died, her producer, Chicco walked away from her and she lost her upmarket house in Fleurhof as well as her apartment in Lonehill. Bongani was thrown out of school for non-payment of his fees, and she just couldn't stay off the drugs, preemptively checking herself out of rehab as quickly as she checked in.

Her career also suffered. Fans were turning against her for her no-shows and consistent lateness, which had resulted in several riots and at least one death. A Namibian promoter sued her for R90 000 after she failed to arrive for three concerts and others simply gave up on booking her.

She barely made it through the recording of her 1994 release, *Abantu Bayakhuluma*, rocking up at the studio already wired to the eyeballs on coke. Working on her 1996 album, *Now Is The Time*, she was so high she couldn't remember laying down the most memorable tracks, two exceptional duets with Congolese rhumba legend, Papa Wemba. The 1997 follow-up, *Paparazzi*, which riffed off her scandal-ridden life playing out in the headlines was mediocre at best. She still drew the crowds, but it seemed they came not to hear her sing, but to ogle at the spectacle of a fallen icon, this lesbian junkie has-been.

It was Chicco who pulled her out of her pathetic morass and took control. When he found her on a pavement in Hillbrow, sobbing, he told the *Sunday Times* she confided, 'Chicco, I know that I can make a big comeback. Let's go to the studio. All these people who have turned their backs on me, let's go and make a song that will let everyone know who Brenda Fassie is.'

That song was 'Vul'indlela' (Make Way), the album *Memeza* (Shout), for all the screaming and shouting she did when no-one heard her. It went on to be the biggest-selling album in the country and Brenda said it recharged her 'like a cell phone'. 'Tell everyone Brenda's back,' she said.

The Queen Bee was back and rocking the hive. The album drew critical and popular acclaim and in 1999, the ANC used the lavish African gospel beauty of 'Vul'indlela' as the party's theme song for the general election. International music industry paper, *The Tip Sheet*, called the single 'extraordinary', 'Instantly jaw-dropping and impossible to switch off, like Eva Cassidy. Effortlessly credible like an African Unfinished Symphony'. In 1999, it scooped the Kora award for Brenda as best female artist and in 2004, it was awarded Song of the Decade. Chicco allegedly took control of her finances, dishing out cash for her to live on and she started building her mansion in Buccleuch.

She had other triumphs too. She'd been a long-term friend of Mandela, and he often popped in to see her, but her winning over of another African statesman made the headlines. She was touring the world again and in Burkina-Faso in 2001, she had an exclusive audience with Libyan president Moamar Gaddafi when he sent armed soldiers to fetch her in the middle of the night after a concert. When they met, she threw herself into his arms sobbing and he responded by inviting her to Libya and presented her with a Liberace of a ring – gold encrusted with diamonds.

But Brenda couldn't maintain. While her next three albums claimed best-seller status at the SAMAs over the next three years, some critics felt that her voice sounded strained, that her rich timbre was cracked and irrecoverable.

Certainly, she showed evidence of cracking. Despite her struggle to beat her habit, drugs resurfaced in her life like a looped sample. Over the years, she committed herself to rehab clinics at least six times, swearing to the press and her fans, that this time it would be different. Recovering addict and jazz giant Hugh Masekela refused to have her at the rehabilitation centre he'd started for artists and musicians, saying she'd made a mockery of the word. Chicco supported her through all this, although he wasn't averse to putting a spin on it either, once inviting photographers along to witness him carrying a weeping Brenda through the clinic doors.

At the 2001 SAMAs, she caused a scene by grabbing the microphone away from kwaito star Mandoza who had won Song of the Year, screaming, 'Fuck you! This is my night.' Later that evening, she threatened to kill

Sunday Times reporter Lesley Mofokeng and his family for the scathing stories he'd written about her messy love affairs. On another occasion, she arrived hours late and completely trashed for a fashion show gig at Hyde Park shopping centre. Yvonne Chaka Chaka had to be called in to replace her and her record label had to refund the R4 000 advance.

Her outrageous behaviour was most likely the reason she was sidelined from the Gift to the Nation concert to celebrate Nelson Mandela's 80th birthday and musician Mzwakhe Mbuli's release from Leeuwkop Prison in 2003. She was so distraught at being excluded, she smashed her phone against the ground.

In the last eight years of her career, Brenda apparently earned an estimated R6 million in royalties, but it all vanished. There may have been some foundation to her fears that dealers were after her, but when she died, she left many questions unresolved.

The aftermath of her death was as chaotic as her life. Chicco was implicated in a sordid scandal surrounding the actual ownership of her house and car, and just where all her money had gone. Always a controversial figure in Brenda's life, Chicco was instrumental in the making of her, but was also rumoured to beat her. When he divulged her HIV positive status to the tabloids in 2005, most dismissed it as a crass attempt to divert attention away from himself and his shady dealings with her estate.

Brenda's family weren't exempt from trying to cash in either, although at least it was to commemorate her memory. They demanded that the Provincial Government of the Western Cape spend R2 million to bury her in style, including shelling out on designer clothes for them to wear to the wake and keeping her body at Newlands Stadium for three days for fans to pay their last respects. The province demurred at the price tag, but the funeral was still one befitting a monarch of music.

The event was held at Langa Stadium, packed with 20 000 fans, musicians, celebrities and statesmen, come together to say *lala kahle* to Ma-Brrr in an emotional event that would have left Brenda snuffling with joy. Unfortunately, it was a little too highly charged and in a re-run of her wedding, it erupted into mayhem when a crush of fans broke through the barricades to reach the gold and glass coffin displayed in the centre. Nine were injured and it took Thabo Mbeki's intervention to restore peace.

Her remains were buried beside those of her parents in old Langa cemetery, although according to recent reports, the grave has fallen to ruin. Bongani has gone on to release his first album at the age of 20, a mellow jazz number, *Makana Square* named for the house in which Brenda grew up. He refuses to talk to the press about his mother.

While Brenda suffered addictions to drugs and doomed love, the high she craved more than anything was the one she found in the spotlight and for 25 years, 15 albums and 150 songs, she had it. For all her failings, she was vibrant, generous and talented and she earned her stratospheric success. As Thabo Mbeki said, 'her voice made souls rise up in bliss wherever it was heard.'

But perhaps we should leave the last word to Brenda. When she was still simplistically being compared to Madonna, she once hit back with, 'Madonna is only big within white pop. I am beyond pop. I am life. I am Brenda Fassie.'

Select Bibliography

BOOKS

Abrahams, Cecil. 1990. *The Tragic Life: Bessie Head and Literature in Southern Africa*. Africa World Press, Inc.

Arnold, Marion. 1995. *A Feast for the Eye, Irma Stern*. Fernwood Press.

Berman, Mona. 2003. *Remembering Irma*. Double Storey Books.

Bennett, Benjamin, 1959. *Genius for the Defence*. Howard Timmins.

Bennett, Benjamin, 1951. *Murder is My Business*. Howard Timmins.

Beyers, C.J. Ed. 1981. *Dictionary of South African Biography, Vol. I, II, IV*. For: The Human Sciences Research Council.

Brown, Coreen. 2003. *The Creative Vision of Bessie Head*. Rosemont Publishing and Printing Corp.

Buchanan-Gould, Vera. 1948. *Not Without Honour: The Life and Writings of Olive Schreiner*. Hutchinson & Co (Publishers) Limited.

Coetzee, Carli. 1997. *Krotoa, the uncanny mother*. University of the Western Cape.

Cronwright-Schreiner, S.C. Ed. *The Letters of Olive Schreiner: 1876–1920*. T. Fisher Unwin Ltd. London: Adelphi Terrace.

Davenport, Rodney and Saunders, Christopher. 2000. *South Africa: A Modern History*. 5th ed. Macmillan Press, Great Britain.

Daymond, M.J.; Driver, Dorothy; Meintjies, Sheila; Molema, Leloba; Musengezi, Chiedza; Orford, Margie and Rasebotsa, Nobantu. Eds. 2003. *Women Writing Africa*. Witwatersrand University Press.

Deacon, Harriet. 1996. *The Island*. Mayibuye Books UWC and David Philip, a division of New Africa Books.

Draznin, Yaffa Claire. 1992. *My Other Self: The Letters of Olive Schreiner and Havelock Ellis, 1884-1920*. Peter Lang.

Dubow, Neville. Ed. 1991. *Paradise, The Journal and Letters (1917–1933) of Irma Stern*. Chameleon Press.

Eilersen, Gillian Stead. 1995. *Bessie Head: Thunder Behind Her Ears*. David Philip.

First, Ruth and Scott, Ann. 1980. *Olive Schreiner: A Biography*. Rutgers University Press: New Brunswick.

Frankel, Glenn. 1999. *Rivonia's Children*. Farrar, Straus and Giroux.

Frederikse, Julie. 1995. *They Fought for Freedom: Helen Joseph*. Maskew Miller Longman.

Gentili, Anna Marie. 1992. *Ruth First: teaching through research*. University of the Western Cape.

Green, Lawerence G. 1950. *At Daybreak for the Isles*. Howard Timmins.

Gregg, Lyndall. 1957. *Memories of Olive Schreiner*. W&R Chambers Ltd.

Hanekom, Leandre. and Wessels Elria, E. 2000. *Woman, Thy Name is Valour*. The Anglo Boer War Museum.

Hanlon, Joseph. 1982. *Why South Africa had to kill Ruth First*. New Statesman.

Head, Bessie. 1990. *A Woman Alone, Autobiographical Writings*. Heinemann.

Hobman, D.L. 1955. *Olive Schreiner: Her Friends and Times*. Watt & Co.

Hopkins, Pat. 2003. "Letting It All Hang Out". In *Cringe the Beloved Country*. Zebra Press.

Human and Rousseau. 1999. *They Shaped Our Century: The Most Influential South Africans of the Twentieth Century.*

Joseph, Helen. 1993. *Side by Side: The Autobiography of Helen Joseph.* Ad. Donker Publishers, Johannesburg. [Originally published by Zed Books, Great Britain, 1986].

Kahn, Ellison. 2003. *Bloody Hand – Wills and Crime.* Siber Ink.

Klarer, Elizabeth. 1980. *Beyond the Light Barrier.* Howard Timmins (Pty) Ltd.

MacKenzie, Craig. 1999. *Bessie Head.* Twayne Publishers, New York.

Makeba, Miriam and Mwamuka, Nomsa. 2004. *Makeba, The Miriam Makeba Story.* STE Publishers.

Malherbe, V.C. 1990. *Krotoa, called 'Eva': A women between.* The Centre for African Studies, University of Cape Town.

Marsh, Rob. 2003. *South Africa Weird and Wonderful.* Tafelberg Publishers.

McKinnon, June. 2004. *The Tapestry of Our Lives.* Kwela Books.

Meintjes, Johannes. 1965. *Olive Schreiner: Portrait of a South African Woman.* Hugh Keartland (Publishers) (Pty) Ltd.

Metelerkamp, Petrovna. 2003. *Ingrid Jonker: beeld van a digterslewe.* Hemel & See, Vermont.

Millin, Sarah Gertrude Liebson. 1934. *Three Men Die.* London: Chatto & Windus.

Millin, Sarah Gertrude Liebson. 1941. *The Night is Long.* London: Faber & Faber.

Miller, Penny. 1979. *Myths and Legends of Southern Africa.* T.V. Bulpin Publications (Pty) Ltd.

Mills, Gwen M. 1952. *First Ladies of the Cape*. Maskew Miller Limited.

Molefe, Z.B. 1997. *A Common Hunger to Sing*. Kwela Books.

Peires, J.B. 1989. *The Dead Will Arise*. Indiana University Press.

Pinnock, Don. 1995. *They Fought for Freedom: Ruth First*. Maskew Miller Longman (Pty) Ltd, Cape Town.

Pinnock, Don. 1997. *Voices of Liberation, Volume 2: Ruth First*. HSRC Publishers, Pretoria.

Pistorius, Micki. 2004. *Fatal Femmes*. Penguin Books.

Press, Karen. 1990. *Bird Heart Stoning the Sea*. Buchu Books.

Press, Karen. 1990. *Krotoa*. Centaur Publications.

Press, Karen. 1990. *Nongqawuse's Prophecy*. Centaur Publications.

Raal, Sarah. 2000. *The Lady Who Fought*. Stormberg Publishers.

Racster, Olga and Grove, Jessica. *The Journal of Dr James Barry*. Howard B. Timmins.

Rae, Isobel. 1958. *The Strange Story of Dr James Barry*. Longmans, Green and Co.

Rive, Richard. Ed. 1987. *Letters: 1871-99*. David Philip.

Roberts, Joanna. Ed. 1990. *Radical History Review No. 46/7: History from South Africa*. MAHRO: The Radical Historians' Organisation, Inc.

[Ruth First].[S.P. : s.n]. 1983.
[Tributes to Ruth First, on the occasion of her death, August 1982]: p.1. Consulted in the African Studies Library, University of Cape Town Libraries.

Sample, Maxine. Ed. 2003. *Critical Essays on Bessie Head*. Praeger.

Schoeman, Karel. 1994. *Irma Stern: the early years, 1894-1933*. South African Library.

Schoeman, Karel. 1991. *Olive Schreiner: A woman in South Africa, 1855-1881*. Jonathan Ball Publishers.

Segal, Ronald. 1992. *Ruth First*. University of the Western Cape.

Slovo, Gillian. 1997. *Every Secret Thing: My Family, My Country*. Abacus, London.

Smith, Charlene. 1997. *Robben Island*. Smith, Cape Town.

Stein, Pippa and Jacobson, Ruth. Eds. 1986. *Sophiatown Speaks*. Junction Avenue Press.

Stern, Irma. 1943. *Congo*. J.L. Van Schaik, Ltd., Pretoria.

Stern, Irma. 1948. *Zanzibar*. J.L. Van Schaik, Limited, Pretoria.

Stewart, Dianne. 1996. *They Fought for Freedom: Lilian Ngoyi*. Maskew Miller Longman.

Thema, Derrick. 1999. *Kortboy: A Sophiatwon Legend*. Kwela Books.

Thom, H.B. 1954. *Journal of Jan Van Riebeeck, Volume II, 1656-1658*. A.A. Balkema, Cape Town, Amsterdam.

Thom, H.B. 1958. *Journal of Jan Van Riebeeck, Volume III, 1659-1662*. A.A. Balkema, Cape Town, Amsterdam.

Van Wyk, Johan. 1999. *Gesig van die Liefde: Ingrid Jonker*. AJ Van Wyk.

Vigne, Randolph. Ed. 1991. *A Gesture of Belonging: Letters from Bessie Head, 1965-1979*. Heinemann.

Webster, Roger. 2001. *At the Fireside*. Spearhead.

Webster, Roger. 2002. *At the Fireside,* Vol. 2. Spearhead.

Whaley, Andrew. 2004. *Brenda Remembered.* Spearhead.

DOCUMENTARIES & VIDEOS

Austin, Chris. 1997. *Brenda Fassie: Not a Bad Girl* [video recording]. Maverick Film Works.

Du Plessis, Chris. 1996. *Dancing with the Snakes* [video recording]. Planet Drum Productions.

Faure, William C. 1999. *Emily Hobhouse* [video recording]. Auckland Park (SA): Raymond Hancock Films for SABC.

Flascas, Penni. 1997. *A Gesture of Belonging* [video recording]. Hoya Productions.

Gerlach, Christo. 1997. *Dancing with the Ancestors* [video recording]. Chirsto Gerlach Productions.

Goldsmid, Peter. 1992. *The Road to Mecca* [video recording]. Ultimate Film Productions.

Hirsch, Lee. 2002. *Amandla: a Revolution in Four Part Harmony* [video recording]. Kwela Productions in association with Bomb Films, HBO/Cinemax Documentray Films, The Fod Foundation and the SABC.

Kentridge, William and Gibson, Angus. 1987. *Freedom Square and the Back of the Moon* [video recording]. London: Channel Four Television Company.

Kentridge, William and Gibson, Angus. 1987. *Sophiatown* [video recording]. Free Films for Channel Four: London.

Maseko, Zola. 1998. *The Life and Times of Sara Baartman* [video recording]. Johannesburg: Distributed by Film Resource Unit.

Matshikiza, John. 1999. *Saints and Sinners, Episode 3: The Day of the Two Sins* [video recording]. Phakathi Films.

Schadeberg, Jurgen. 1994 *Dolly and the Inkspots* [video recording]. Johannesburg: Schadeberg Movie Company.

ARTICLES

South African Historical Journal (40). 1999. University of South Africa.

Abrahams, Yvette. 1996. "Was Eva Raped? An Exercise in Speculative History". In *KRONOS, Journal of Cape History, No. 23.* Bellville: University of the Western Cape.

Ancer, Jonathan. "The Naked Bad Girl: Brenda Fassie". In *SA City Life.* July 2001.

Bauer, Charlotte. "Pythons and Puritans". In *The Sunday Times.* 29 September 1996

Bauer, Charlotte. "Tiny Kim makes Glenda dance for joy". In *Sunday Express.* 27 February 1983.

Bhengu, Charity. "I did not try to commit suicide". In *The Sowetan.* 6 October 1996.

Bird, Robin. "Monument to slave trade or big tourism attraction?" In *Wirral Globe.* 1 November 1989.

Birkby, Carel. "Two Spaceladies give a down-to-earth 'no'". In *The Sunday Times.* 6 September 1959.

Blignaut, Charl. "Why I'm not a rich girl". In *Mail and Guardian.* 8 August 1997.

Carey, Benedict. "Explaining Those Vivid Memories of Martian Kidnappers". In *The New York Times.* 9 August 2005.

Cavill, John. "Mrs K. goes to Venus". In *Sunday Express.* 19 April 1959.

Charney, Craig. "Ma-Ngoyi". In *The Star.* 15 October 1980.

Charter, David. "How Britain's X-Files said that UFOs were just a waste of time". In *The Times*. 04 February 2005.

Chetty, Sharon. "They can't break me, says Brenda". In *The Sowetan*. 3 October 1994.

Chikanga, Kenneth. "Our very own material girl". In *Spotlight*. 24 October 2000.

Christie, Roy. "Writhe and roll Glenda electrifying". In *The* Star. 5 April 1976.

Christie, Roy. "Our Miss Prim". In *The* Star. 2 April 1976.

De Bruyn, Pippa. "The girl in the Parisian nightgown". In *Marie Claire* October 2004.

Duff, Cilla. "Liz is in love with a harmony from space". In *The Citizen*. 18 July 1978.

Dhlomo, Herbert, I.E. "The Girl Who Killed to Save (Nongqawuse the Liberator)". In Visser, Nick and Couzens, Tim. Eds. 1985. *Collected Works H.I.E. Dhlomo*. Johannesburg: Ravan Press.

Dowling, Finuala. "Unrecognised exile from apartheid finds home in the country whose voice she still captures". In The *Sunday Times*. 31 March 1996.

Fourie, S.D. 2001. "Black Sophie". In *Gansbaai Courant*. July 2001.

Gilchrist, Angela. "The urban spaceman". In *Sunday Express*. 16 August 1981.

Govende, Sholain. "Low-key ceremony for Ma Brrr". From *The Star*. 12 May 2005.

Gray, Stephen. "Thunder of Mma-Heady". In *Weekly Mail*. 25 August 1995.

Green, Lawrence G. 1967. "Behold the Great Berg River". In *On Wings of Fire*. Cape Town: Hoard Timmins.

Grevler, Ann. "No tangible proof yet of any physical interplanetary visitors". In *The Star*. 2 June 1959.

Grevler, Ann. "Fake Spacemen behind racial flare-up?" In *Sunday Express*. 24 January 1960.

Hannerz, Ulf. 1994. "Sophiatown: The View from Afar". In *Journal of South African Studies, Vol. 20, No.2.* London: Oxford University Press.

Harris, Iain. "Brenda Fassie". In *Rootz*. November 2004.

Isaacson, Maureen. "First's friend give chilling testimony". In *The Sunday Independent*. 28 February 1999.

Jacobs, J.U. 1993. "Texts under Arrest: the Autobiographical Writings of Helen Joseph". In *Theoria: A Journal of Studies in the Arts, Humanities and Social Sciences, Numbers 81/82.*

"Jazz legend Dolly Rathebe dies". In *The Mail & Guardian* 16 September 2004.

Khumalo, Themba. "Split just a hoax to take your minds off violence, claims singer". In *City Press*. 6 January 1991.

Kieskamp, Andrea. 1997. *The Khoikhoi in Van Riebeeck's official accounts: reconstruction of a period*. Bellville: University of the Western Cape, Institute of Historical Research (paper presented at conference).

Kirby, Percival, R. 1949. *The Hottentot Venus*. In Africana notes and news 11(3). June 1949.

Kirby, Percival R. 1953. *More about the Hottentot Venus*. In Africana notes and news 10(4). September 1953.

Kotlolo, McKeed. "Row, then death". In *The Sowetan*. 26 September 1994.

Landman, Christina. Ed. 1996. *Digging Up Our Foremothers: Stories of Women in Africa*. University of South Africa.

Landman, Christine. 1996. "The Religious Krotoa". In *KRONOS, Journal of Cape History, No. 23*. Bellville: University of the Western Cape.

Leibbrandt, Hendrik Carel Vos. 1902. Precis of the Archives of the Cape of Good Hope. Journal, 1671-1674 & 1676. Cape Town: W.A. Richards: p.209.

Lelyveld, Joseph. "Feisty South African Nearly a Legend". In *The New York Times*. 4 July 1982.

Leverton, B.J. "The Story of the Alabama". In *Lantern*. June 1963.

Levin, Doreen. "Mrs Klarer's world in space". In *Sunday Times Colour Magazine*. 13 August 1972.

Louw, Reinet. "Brenda's battle to beat drugs". In *Drum*. October 1995.

Mabaso, Sibusiso. "Madame Bodyguard". In *SSA*. 2 December 1992.

Madondo, Bongani. "Bend my ear, Brenda". In *Sunday Life*. 8 November 1998.

Madondo, Bongani. "Brenda Fassie is dead. Long live the Queen." In *Marie Claire*. August 2004.

Makhaya, Elliot. "Brenda back with a bang". In *The Sowetan*. 4 February 1994.

Maposa, Sipokazi. "Has the 'Township Madonna' been forgotten?" From *Cape Argus*. 12 May 2005.

Marsh, Rob. "Crazy Daisy". In *Marie Claire*. March 2004

Mashego, Mojalefa. "Brenda's Boy". In *Drum*. 14 November 1996.

Mashego, Mojalefa. "Fassie on Fast Forward". In *The Sowetan*. 24 December 1998.

Master, Sharad. "Sarah, Sarah: More on Sarah Baartman and Her Equally Tragic Namesake". In *The Quarterly Bulletin of the National Library of South Africa, Vol. 58. No. 2.* April – June 2004. Published by Friends of the National Library of South Africa, Cape Town.

Metsoamere, Victor. "Brenda Fassie Bounces Back". In *The Sowetan*. 19 September 1994.

Metsoamere, Victor. "The Ring of Truth?". In *The Sowetan*. 20 February 1992.

Milton, Evan. "Madonna of the Townships". In *Dazed & Confused*. July 2004

Mndende, Nokuzola. 1997. *The Prophecy of Nongqawuse: a white man's lie about the Xhosa cattle killing – 1856-57*. Department of Religious Studies. University of Cape Town.

Modisane, Kenosi. "Fassie's family want inquest to go public". In *The Star*. 5 July 2004.

Modisane, Kenosi. "Fassie owned nothing, executor confirms". In *The Star*. 13 June 2005.

Modisane, Kenosi. "Tears flow as stars say goodbye to Mama Dolly". In *The Star*. 17 September 2004.

Modisane, Kenosi. "Video shows Fassie was scared of drug dealers". In *The Star*. 13 June 2005.

Mokoena, Eddie. "Hamba Kahle, Brenda". In *Drum*. 20 May 2004.

Molefe, Z.F. "Dolly Rathebe" In *Rootz*. December 2004.

Nyatsumba, Kaizer. "Fassie wedding tickets were a scam". In *The Cape Argus*. 27 January 1989.

Oliphant, Lumka. "Brenda had nothing to hide, says her son". In *The Saturday Star.* 18 June 2005.

Oliphant, Lumka. "Brenda's cursed legacy". In *The Saturday Star.* 11 June 2005.

Paxton, Hugh and Midori. 2005. "Goin' Guano, There's white gold on them thar African isles". In *The Japan Times,* January 16, 2005.

Peires, J.B. "Suicide or Genocide: Xhosa Perceptions of the Nongqawuse Catastrophe". In Bozzoli, Belinda and Delius, Peter. Eds. 1990. *History from South Africa.* New York: Radical History Review.

Philadelphia Desa. "The Madonna Of The Townships". In *Time Magazine.* 15 September 2001.

Pokwana, Vukile. "Love goes on for Mabrrr and her new man". In *City Press.* 11 July 1999.

Prendini Toffoli, Hilary. "Ingrid's Lost Legacy". In *Style.* July 2005.

Proctor, Andre. 1978. *A History of Sophiatown.* University of the Witwatersrand.

Rantsekeng, Pearl. "Much Fassie ... about politics". In *The Sowetan.* 6 May 1999.

South African Historical Journal (40). 1999. University of South Africa.

Shantall, Lauren. "Still, Life". In *Elle Decoration No. 37, Artists Issue.* Winter 2005.

Themba, Can. "Dolly and her men!" In *Drum.* January 1957.

Themba, Can. "Dolly in Films". In *Drum.* February 1957.

Themba, Can. "Dolly". In *Drum.* March 1957.

Themba, Can. "Dolly". In *Drum*. April 1957.

Themba, Can. "Dolly". In *Drum*. May 1957.

Thornycroft, Peta. "At 75, this serene old lady is still too 'dangerous' to quote". In *Sunday Express*. 8 April 1980.

Vale, Peter. "Motive behind the murder of Ruth First". In *Mail and Guardian*. 5 March 1999.

Van Schalkwyk, Angela. "The exotic woman who met a UFO". In *The Citizen*. 16 July 1979.

Wannenberg, Helmi. "Rejected manuscript became international best-seller". In *Southern Courier*. 11 August 1981

Wells, Julia. 1997. "The Story of Eva and Pieter: transcultural marriage on the road to success in Van Riebeeck's colonial outpost". In *Gender and Colonialism*. University of the Western Cape.

Williams, Gavin. 1996. "Ruth First's Contribution to African Studies". In *Journal of Contemporary African Studies, Volume 14, Number 1*. Carfax.

Woodley, Ray. "Liz's novel of love is light years from Barbara Cartland". In *Sunday Express*. 22 March 1981.

INTERNET REFERENCES

Allingham, Rob. "Dolly Rathebe" On Afropop (www.afropop.org)

"Brenda Fassie 1964 – 2004". On *News24.com*. From Music.org.za / EMI. 10 May 2004.

"Brenda Fassie: A very human hero". *BBC News: World: Africa* www.bbc.co.uk. 10 May 2004

"Brenda Fassie, Township Madonna". *BBC News: World: Africa* www.bbc.co.uk.12 May 2004.

"Entertainer Dolly Rathebe dies". In *The Washington Times* (United Press International). 17 September 2004.

Evans, Jenni. "Take a left at Miriam Makeba, you can't miss it..." 10 November 2004. www.iol.co.za

"Fassie died after using crack, inquest finds". SAPA. www.iol.co.za. 18 December 2004.

Muli, Wayua. "Queen of the night". *BBC News: World: Africa* www.bbc.co.uk. 23 May 2004

Wa Sepotokele, Themba. "Winnie, Makeba pay tribute to diva Dolly". 14 February 2001. www.iol.co.za

Credits

Images reproduced on this cover have been used with the kind permission of the following copyright holders:

Daisy de Melker portrait courtesy of *The Sunday Times*
Glenda Kemp portrait courtesy of *The Cape Argus*/Trace Images
Brenda Fassie portrait courtesy of EMI Music South Africa (Pty) Ltd
Dolly Rathebe 'mine dump' portrait and Drum cover courtesy of Jurgen Schadeberg and Bailey's African History Archive
Nguni cow beaded wire sculpture by Gerald Makubela: 083 330 9458

Text quoted in this book has been used with the kind permission of the following copyright holders:

Quotes from *Congo* by Irma Stern, 1943, published by J L Van Schaik Ltd are used with permission of Van Schaik Publishers.

Quotes from *Beyond the Light Barrier* by Elizabeth Klarer, 1980, published by Howard Timmins (Pty) Ltd, are used with permission of David Klarer.

Quotes from *Side by Side: The Autobiography of Helen Joseph* by Helen Joseph, 1993 published by AD Donker are used with permission of Jonathan Ball Publishers.

Quotes from *The Dead Will Arise* by J B Peires, 1989, published by Ravan Press Ltd Jhb, are used with permission of Prof J B Peires.

Quotes from *The Lady Who Fought* by Sarah Raal, 2000, published by Stormberg Publishers, are used with permission of Stormberg Publishers.

Quotes from *Ingrid Jonker: Beeld van 'n Digterslewer* by Petrovna Meterkamp, 2003, published by Hemel & See, Vermont, are used with permission of Petrovna Meterkamp.

Quotes from *Krotoa, Called Eva, A Woman Between* by VC Malherbe, 1990, published by Centre for African Studies, University of Cape Town, are used with permission of Centre for African Studies, University of Cape Town.

Quotes from *The Night is Long* by Sarah Millin, 1941, published by Faber and Faber, London, are used with permission of Faber & Faber London.

Quotes from *Paradise, The Journal and Letters (1917-1933) of Irma Stern,* by Neville Dubow, 1991, published by Chameleon Press, are used with permission of Chameleon Press.

Quotes from the documentary video The Life and Times Of Sara Baartman by Zola Maseka, are used with permission of Zola Maseko.

Quotes from the 'Dolly on Dolly' series by Can Themba, 1957, published by *Drum* magazine, are used with permission of Bailey's African History Archives.

Quotes from *Bessie Head: Thunder Behind Her Ears* by Gillian Stead Eilerson, 1995, published by David Philip Publishers, are used with permission of David Philip Publishers.

Quotes from "I'm not a Bad Girl" and "My Baby Bogani" by Brenda Fassie, published by EMI Music South Africa (Pty) Ltd, are used with permission of EMI Music South Africa (Pty) Ltd.

Author Biography

©Pieter Hugo

As a freelance journalist for the likes of *Colors, Dazed & Confused, The Hollywood Reporter and Cosmopolitan,* Lauren Beukes gets to hang out with reluctant base jumpers, trendoid swingers, township vigilantes, AIDS activists, cable thieves and live and kicking mavericks of both sexes. For the sake of a story, she's jumped out of planes and into shark-infested waters, learned how to make *mqombothi* in *mqalis* in Langa and been taught how to twist herself around a pole by an artificially-enhanced ex-stripper called Gaynor. She's written video game scripts, a screenplay called *Porno* and had several short stories published in various anthologies including Oshun's *180°.* She is currently wrapping up her novel, *Branded* and her MA in Creative Writing at UCT, where she also lectures part-time. She was born in 1976 and lives and works in Cape Town.